THE WOODS™

JAMES **TYNION IV** • MICHAEL **DIALYNAS** • JOSAN **GONZALEZ**

VOL. **4**
MOVIE NIGHT

▲

BOOM!
S T U D I O S

THE WOODS Volume Four, June 2016. Published by BOOM! Studios, a division of Boom Entertainment, Inc. The Woods is ™ & © 2016 James Tynion IV. Originally published in single magazine form as THE WOODS No. 13-16. ™ & © 2015 James Tynion IV. All rights reserved. BOOM! Studios™ and the BOOM! Studios logo are trademarks of Boom Entertainment, Inc., registered in various countries and categories. All characters, events, and institutions depicted herein are fictional. Any similarity between any of the names, characters, persons, events, and/or institutions in this publication to actual names, characters, and persons, whether living or dead, events, and/or institutions is unintended and purely coincidental. BOOM! Studios does not read or accept unsolicited submissions of ideas, stories, or artwork.

A catalog record of this book is available from OCLC and from the BOOM! Studios website, www.boom-studios.com, on the Librarians page.

BOOM! Studios, 5670 Wilshire Boulevard, Suite 450, Los Angeles, CA 90036-5679. Printed in China. First Printing.

ISBN: 978-1-60886-822-3, eISBN: 978-1-61398-493-2

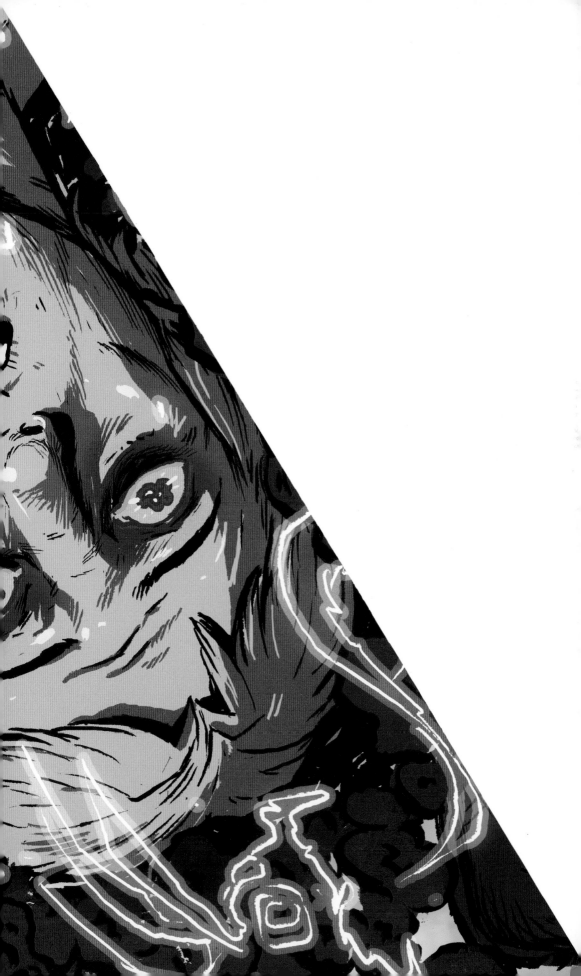

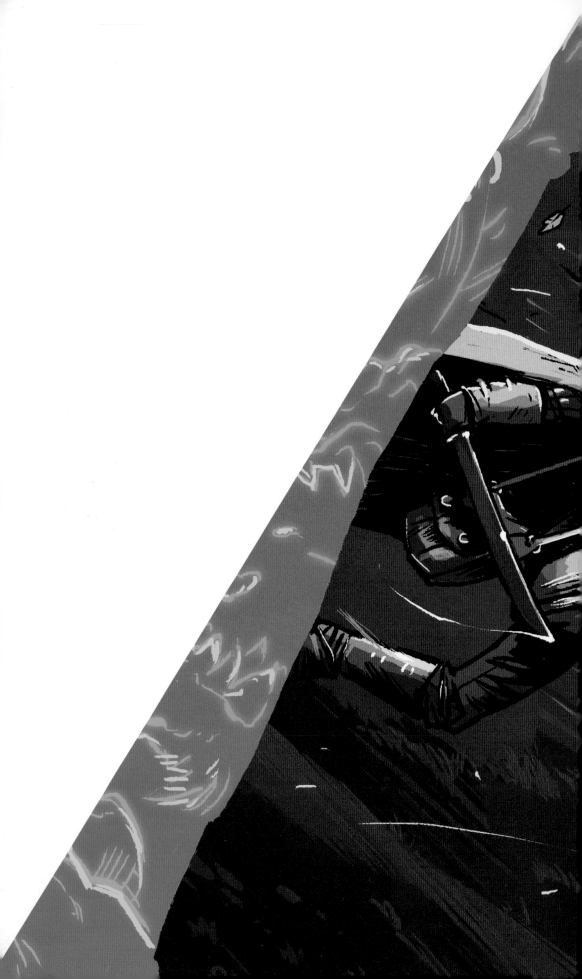

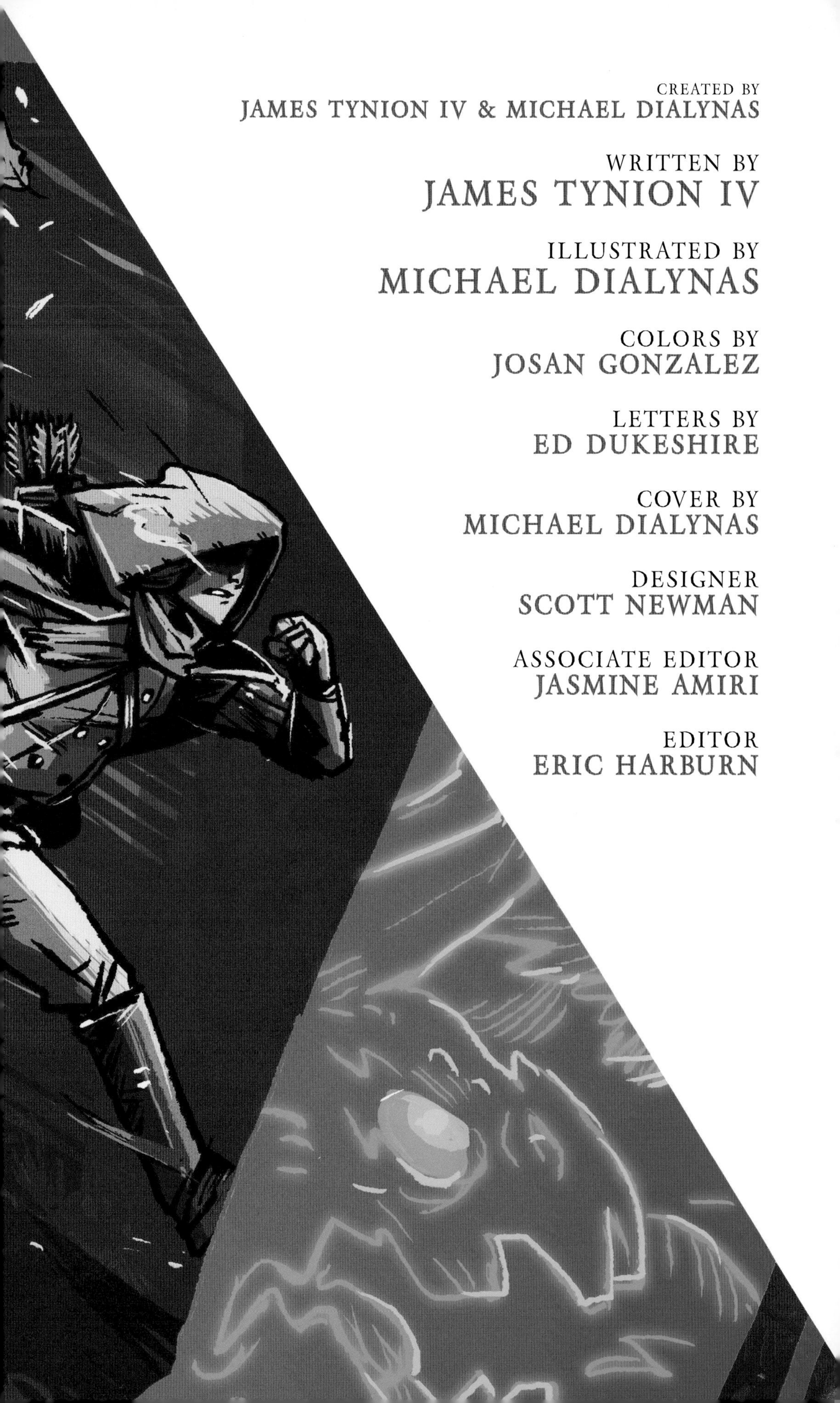

CREATED BY
JAMES TYNION IV & MICHAEL DIALYNAS

WRITTEN BY
JAMES TYNION IV

ILLUSTRATED BY
MICHAEL DIALYNAS

COLORS BY
JOSAN GONZALEZ

LETTERS BY
ED DUKESHIRE

COVER BY
MICHAEL DIALYNAS

DESIGNER
SCOTT NEWMAN

ASSOCIATE EDITOR
JASMINE AMIRI

EDITOR
ERIC HARBURN

CHAPTER THIRTEEN

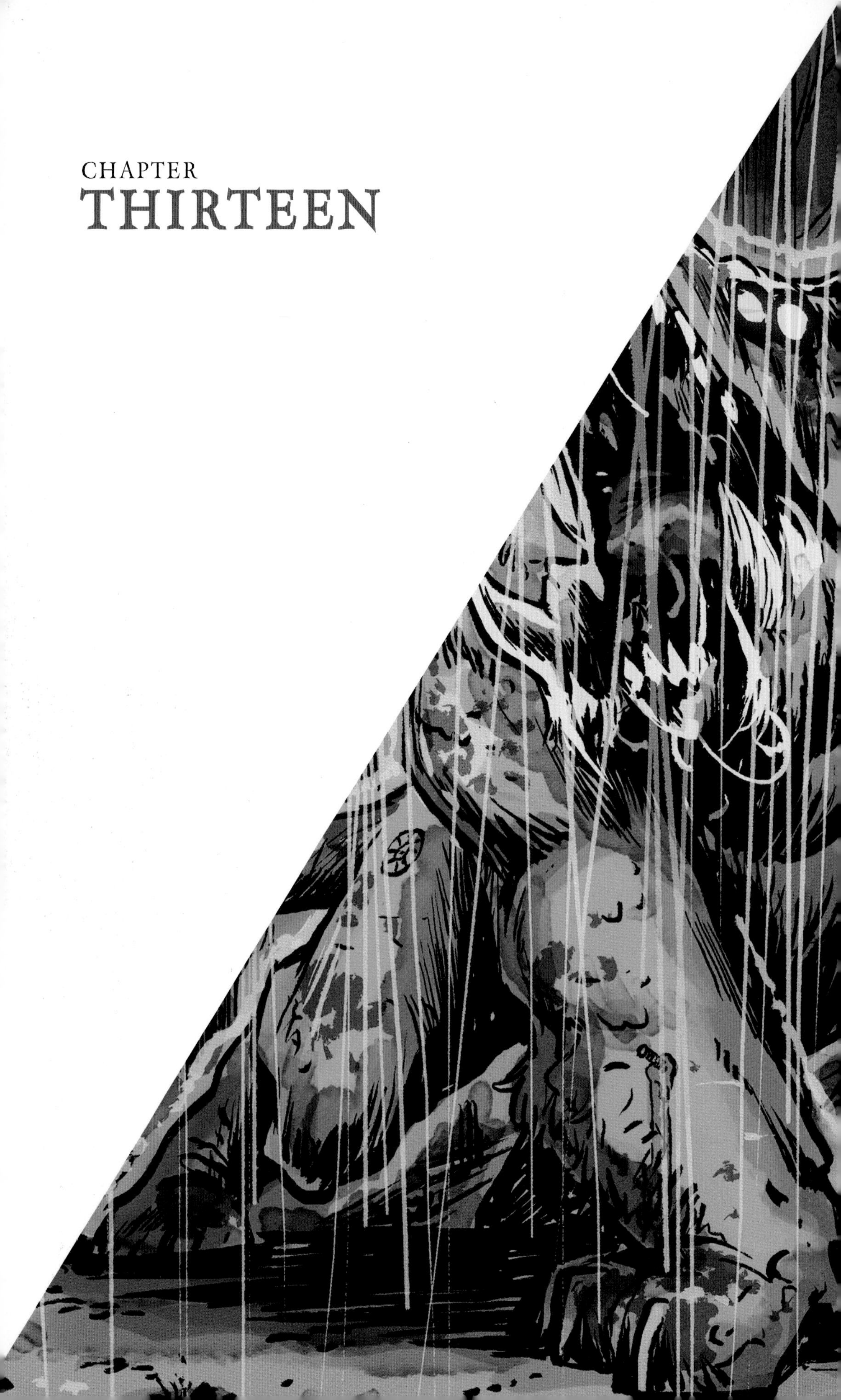

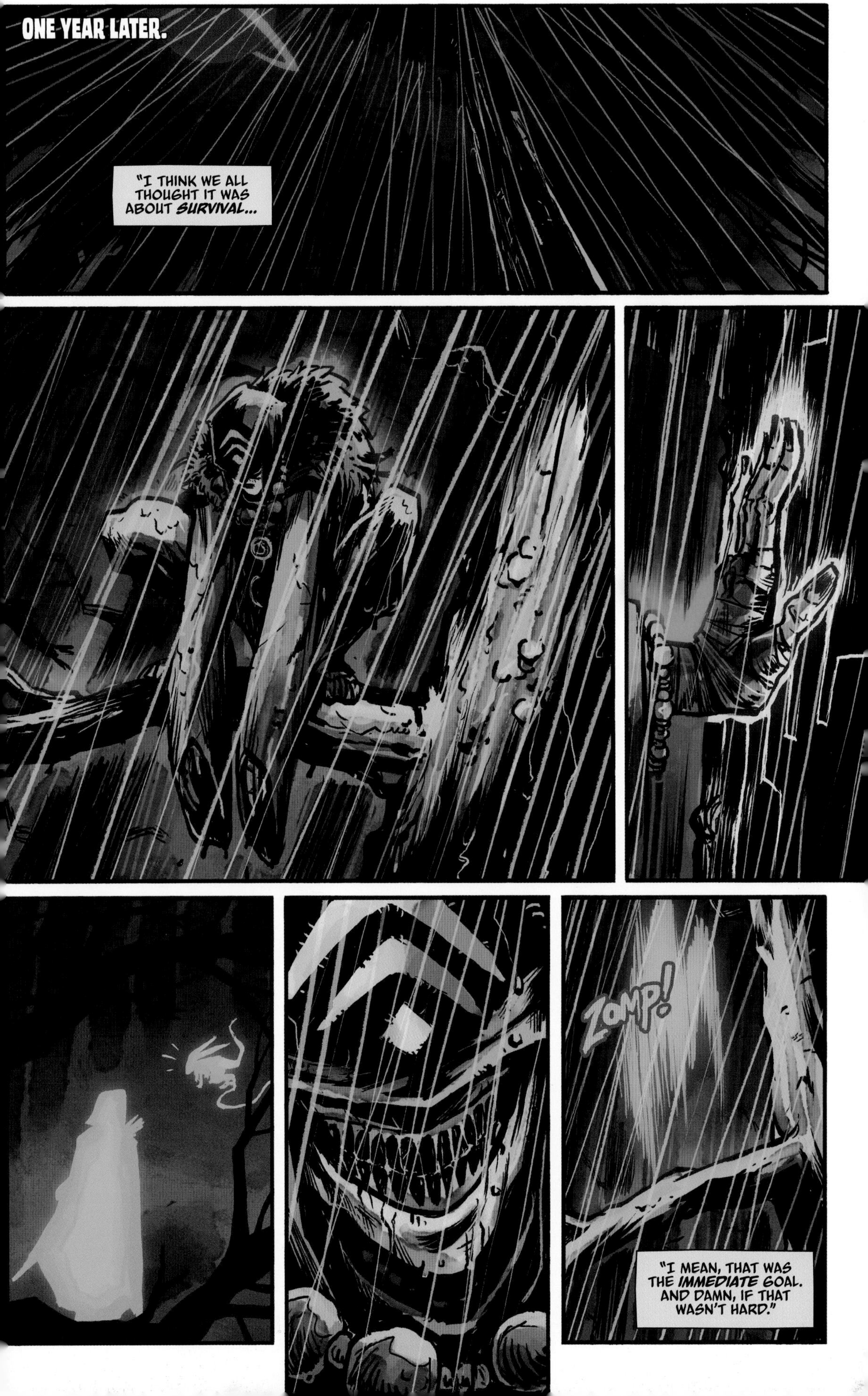
ONE YEAR LATER.
"I THINK WE ALL THOUGHT IT WAS ABOUT SURVIVAL...
ZOMP!
"I MEAN, THAT WAS THE IMMEDIATE GOAL. AND DAMN, IF THAT WASN'T HARD."

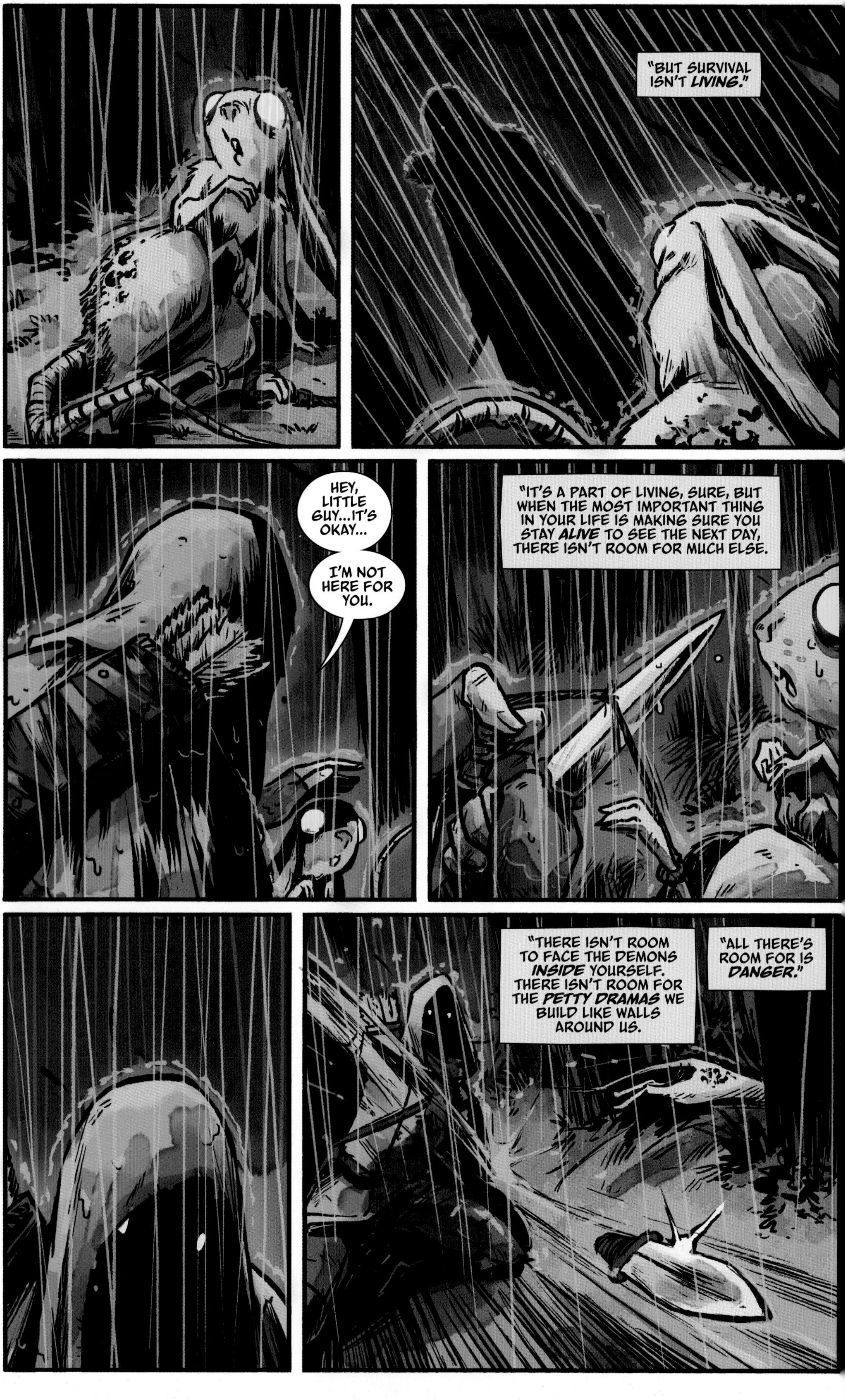
"BUT SURVIVAL ISN'T LIVING."
HEY, LITTLE GUY...IT'S OKAY...
I'M NOT HERE FOR YOU.
"IT'S A PART OF LIVING, SURE, BUT WHEN THE MOST IMPORTANT THING IN YOUR LIFE IS MAKING SURE YOU STAY ALIVE TO SEE THE NEXT DAY, THERE ISN'T ROOM FOR MUCH ELSE.
"THERE ISN'T ROOM TO FACE THE DEMONS INSIDE YOURSELF. THERE ISN'T ROOM FOR THE PETTY DRAMAS WE BUILD LIKE WALLS AROUND US.
"ALL THERE'S ROOM FOR IS DANGER."

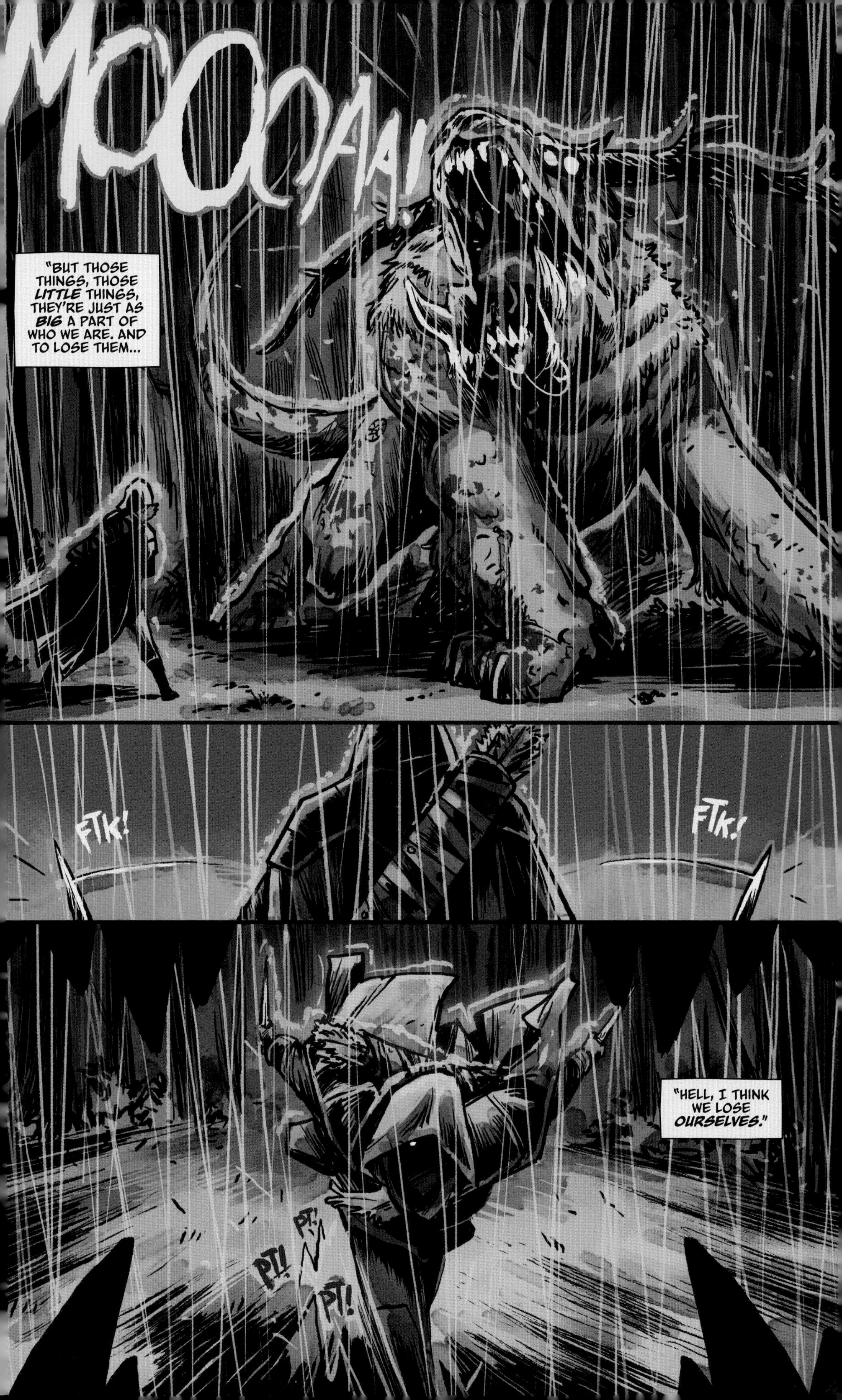
MOOOAAA!
"BUT THOSE THINGS, THOSE *LITTLE* THINGS, THEY'RE JUST AS *BIG* A PART OF WHO WE ARE. AND TO LOSE THEM...
FTK!
FTK!
"HELL, I THINK WE LOSE *OURSELVES*."
PT!
PT!
PT!

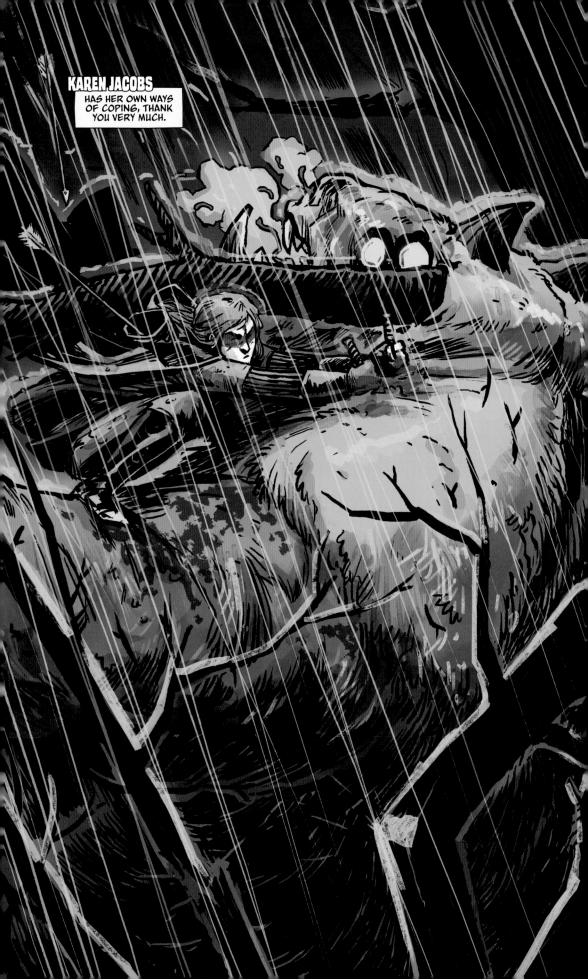

KAREN JACOBS
HAS HER OWN WAYS
OF COPING, THANK
YOU VERY MUCH.

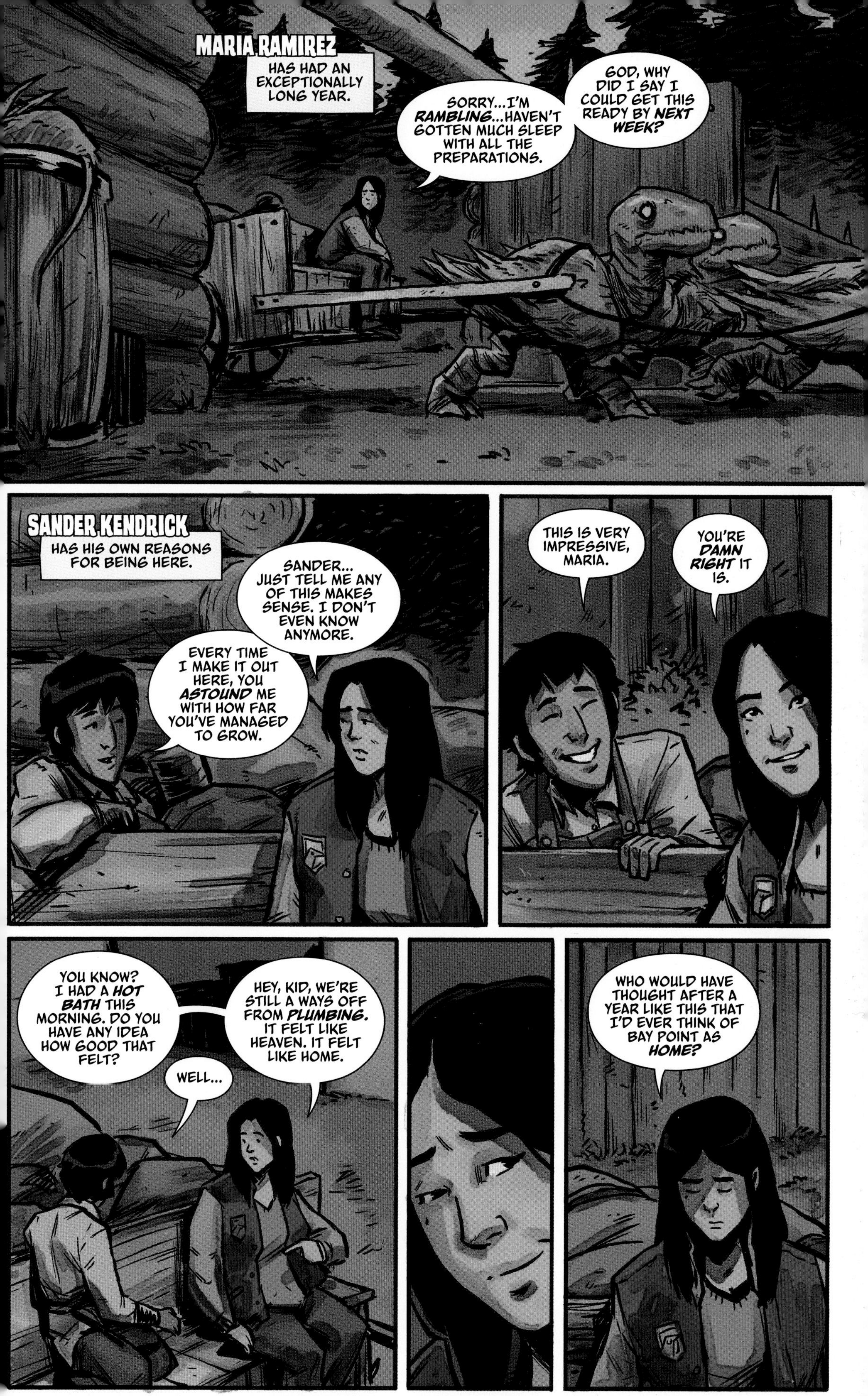
MARIA RAMIREZ
HAS HAD AN EXCEPTIONALLY LONG YEAR.
SORRY...I'M RAMBLING...HAVEN'T GOTTEN MUCH SLEEP WITH ALL THE PREPARATIONS.
GOD, WHY DID I SAY I COULD GET THIS READY BY NEXT WEEK?
SANDER KENDRICK
HAS HIS OWN REASONS FOR BEING HERE.
SANDER... JUST TELL ME ANY OF THIS MAKES SENSE. I DON'T EVEN KNOW ANYMORE.
EVERY TIME I MAKE IT OUT HERE, YOU ASTOUND ME WITH HOW FAR YOU'VE MANAGED TO GROW.
THIS IS VERY IMPRESSIVE, MARIA.
YOU'RE DAMN RIGHT IT IS.
YOU KNOW? I HAD A HOT BATH THIS MORNING. DO YOU HAVE ANY IDEA HOW GOOD THAT FELT?
HEY, KID, WE'RE STILL A WAYS OFF FROM PLUMBING. IT FELT LIKE HEAVEN. IT FELT LIKE HOME.
WELL...
WHO WOULD HAVE THOUGHT AFTER A YEAR LIKE THIS THAT I'D EVER THINK OF BAY POINT AS HOME?

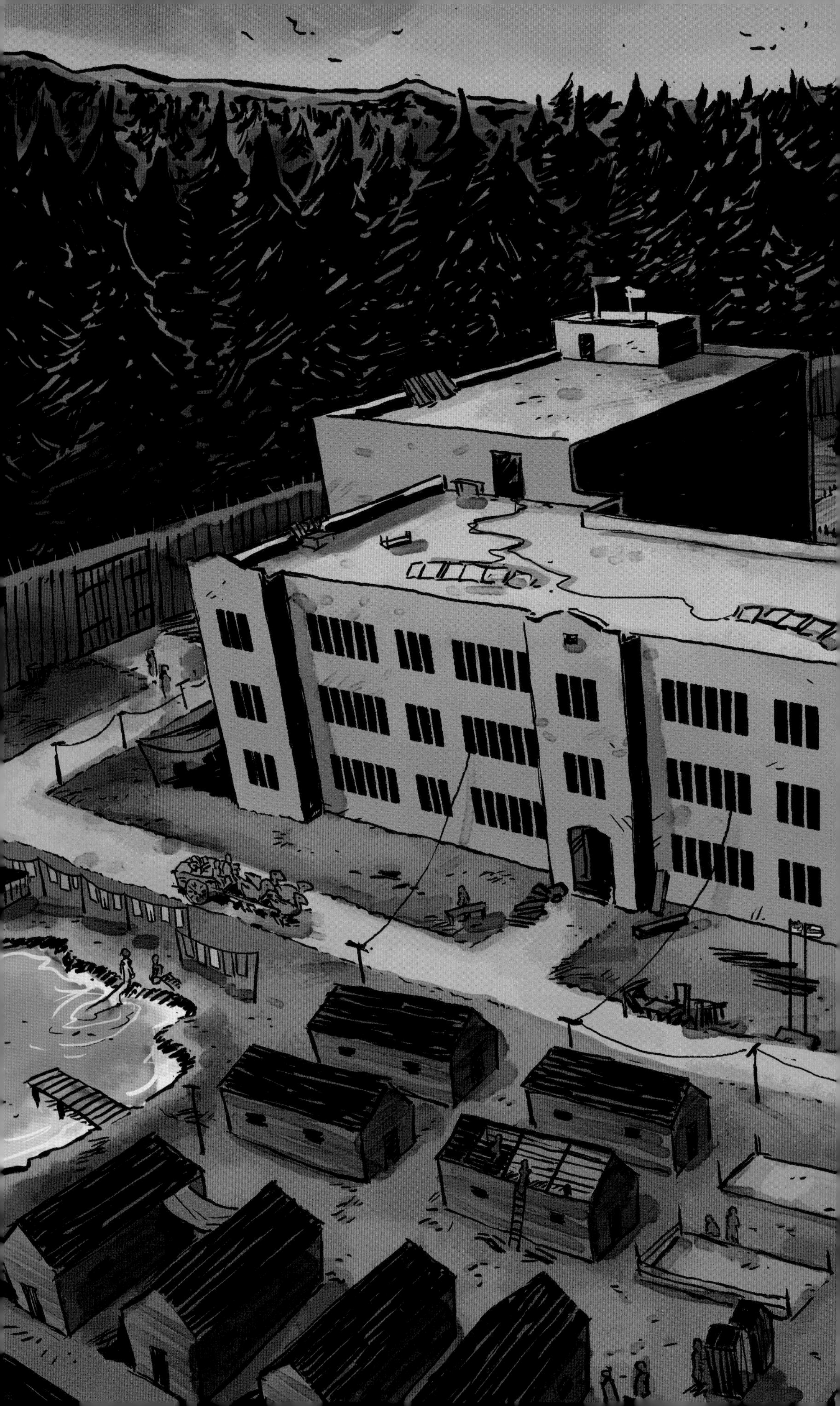

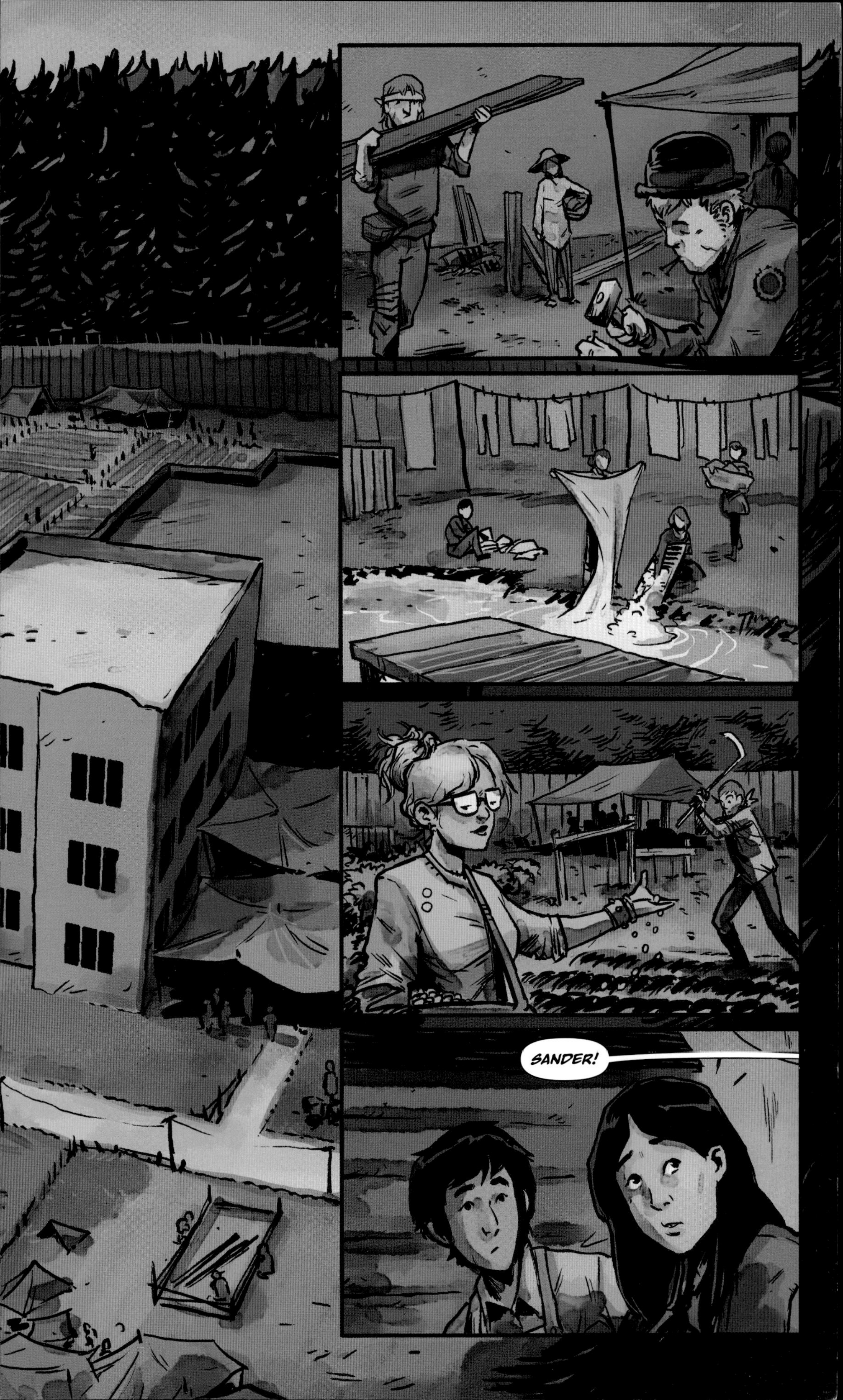
SANDER!

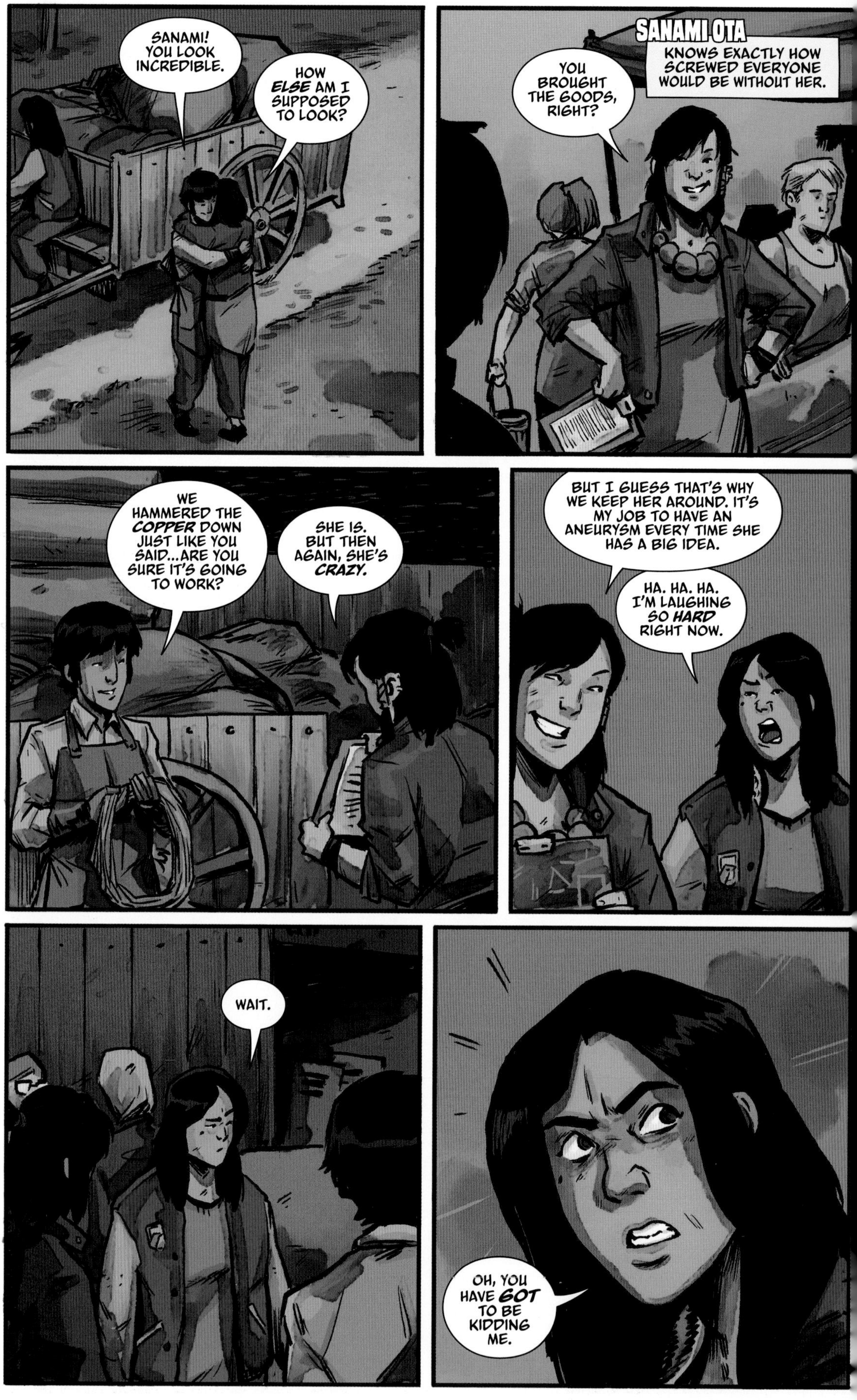
SANAMI! YOU LOOK INCREDIBLE.
HOW ELSE AM I SUPPOSED TO LOOK?
SANAMI OTA
KNOWS EXACTLY HOW SCREWED EVERYONE WOULD BE WITHOUT HER.
YOU BROUGHT THE GOODS, RIGHT?
WE HAMMERED THE COPPER DOWN JUST LIKE YOU SAID...ARE YOU SURE IT'S GOING TO WORK?
SHE IS. BUT THEN AGAIN, SHE'S CRAZY.
BUT I GUESS THAT'S WHY WE KEEP HER AROUND. IT'S MY JOB TO HAVE AN ANEURYSM EVERY TIME SHE HAS A BIG IDEA.
HA. HA. HA. I'M LAUGHING SO HARD RIGHT NOW.
WAIT.
OH, YOU HAVE GOT TO BE KIDDING ME.

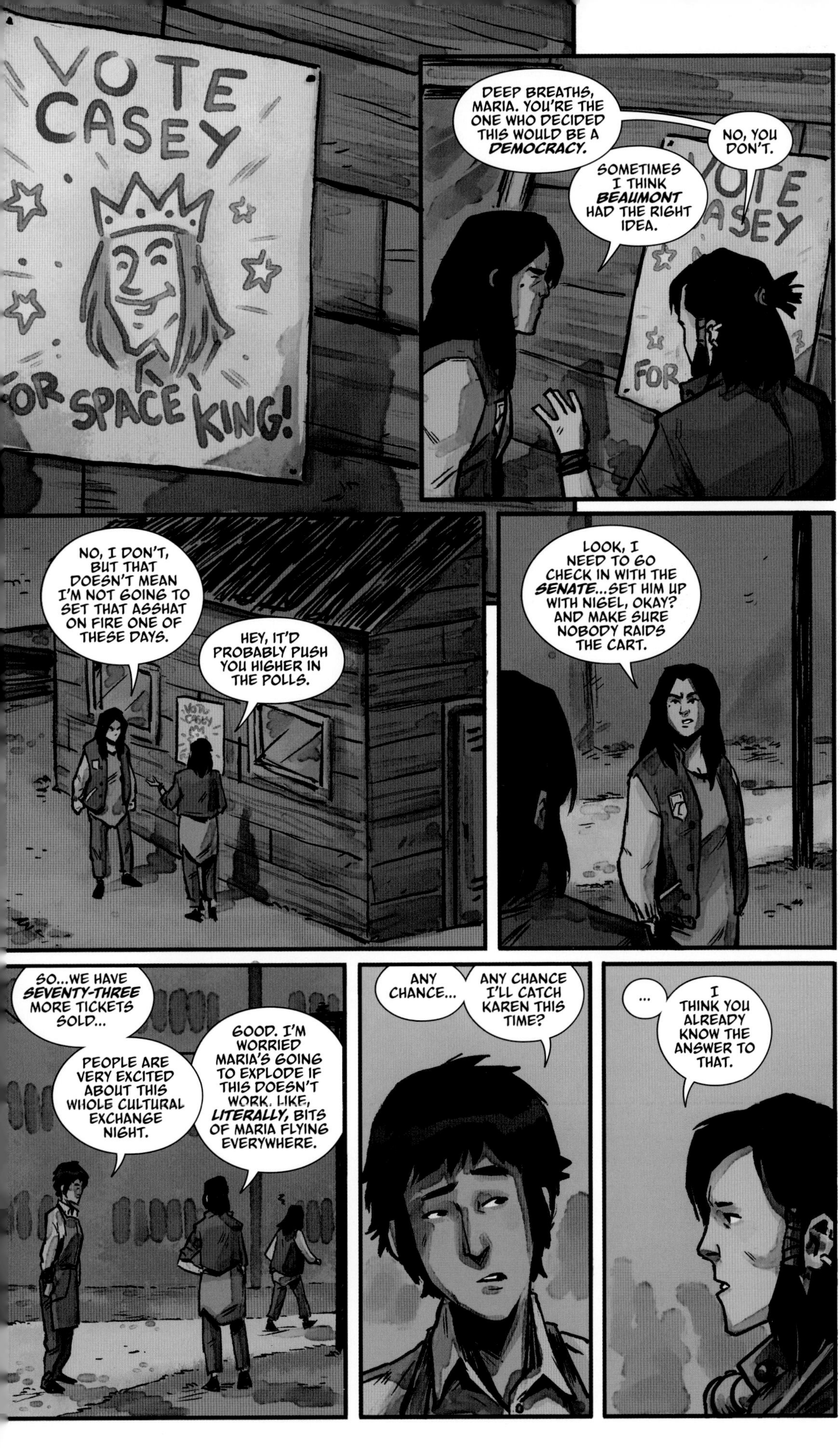
VOTE CASEY FOR SPACE KING!
DEEP BREATHS, MARIA. YOU'RE THE ONE WHO DECIDED THIS WOULD BE A DEMOCRACY.
SOMETIMES I THINK BEAUMONT HAD THE RIGHT IDEA.
NO, YOU DON'T.
VOTE CASEY FOR
NO, I DON'T, BUT THAT DOESN'T MEAN I'M NOT GOING TO SET THAT ASSHAT ON FIRE ONE OF THESE DAYS.
HEY, IT'D PROBABLY PUSH YOU HIGHER IN THE POLLS.
LOOK, I NEED TO GO CHECK IN WITH THE SENATE...SET HIM UP WITH NIGEL, OKAY? AND MAKE SURE NOBODY RAIDS THE CART.
SO...WE HAVE SEVENTY-THREE MORE TICKETS SOLD...
PEOPLE ARE VERY EXCITED ABOUT THIS WHOLE CULTURAL EXCHANGE NIGHT.
GOOD. I'M WORRIED MARIA'S GOING TO EXPLODE IF THIS DOESN'T WORK. LIKE, LITERALLY, BITS OF MARIA FLYING EVERYWHERE.
ANY CHANCE...
ANY CHANCE I'LL CATCH KAREN THIS TIME?
...
I THINK YOU ALREADY KNOW THE ANSWER TO THAT.

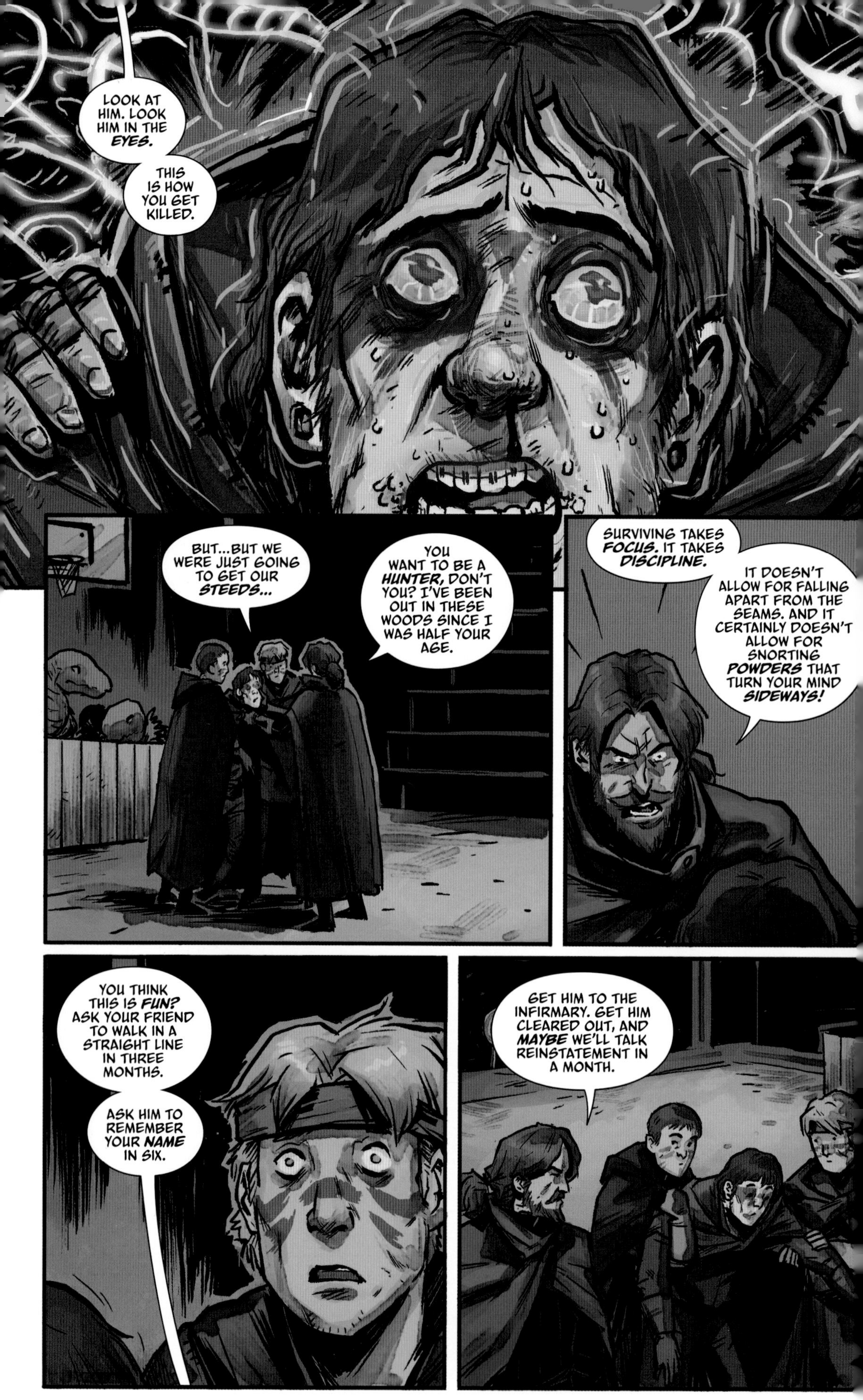
LOOK AT HIM. LOOK HIM IN THE *EYES.*
THIS IS HOW YOU GET KILLED.
BUT...BUT WE WERE JUST GOING TO GET OUR *STEEDS...*
YOU WANT TO BE A *HUNTER,* DON'T YOU? I'VE BEEN OUT IN THESE WOODS SINCE I WAS HALF YOUR AGE.
SURVIVING TAKES *FOCUS.* IT TAKES *DISCIPLINE.*
IT DOESN'T ALLOW FOR FALLING APART FROM THE SEAMS. AND IT CERTAINLY DOESN'T ALLOW FOR SNORTING *POWDERS* THAT TURN YOUR MIND *SIDEWAYS!*
YOU THINK THIS IS *FUN?* ASK YOUR FRIEND TO WALK IN A STRAIGHT LINE IN THREE MONTHS.
ASK HIM TO REMEMBER YOUR *NAME* IN SIX.
GET HIM TO THE INFIRMARY. GET HIM CLEARED OUT, AND *MAYBE* WE'LL TALK REINSTATEMENT IN A MONTH.

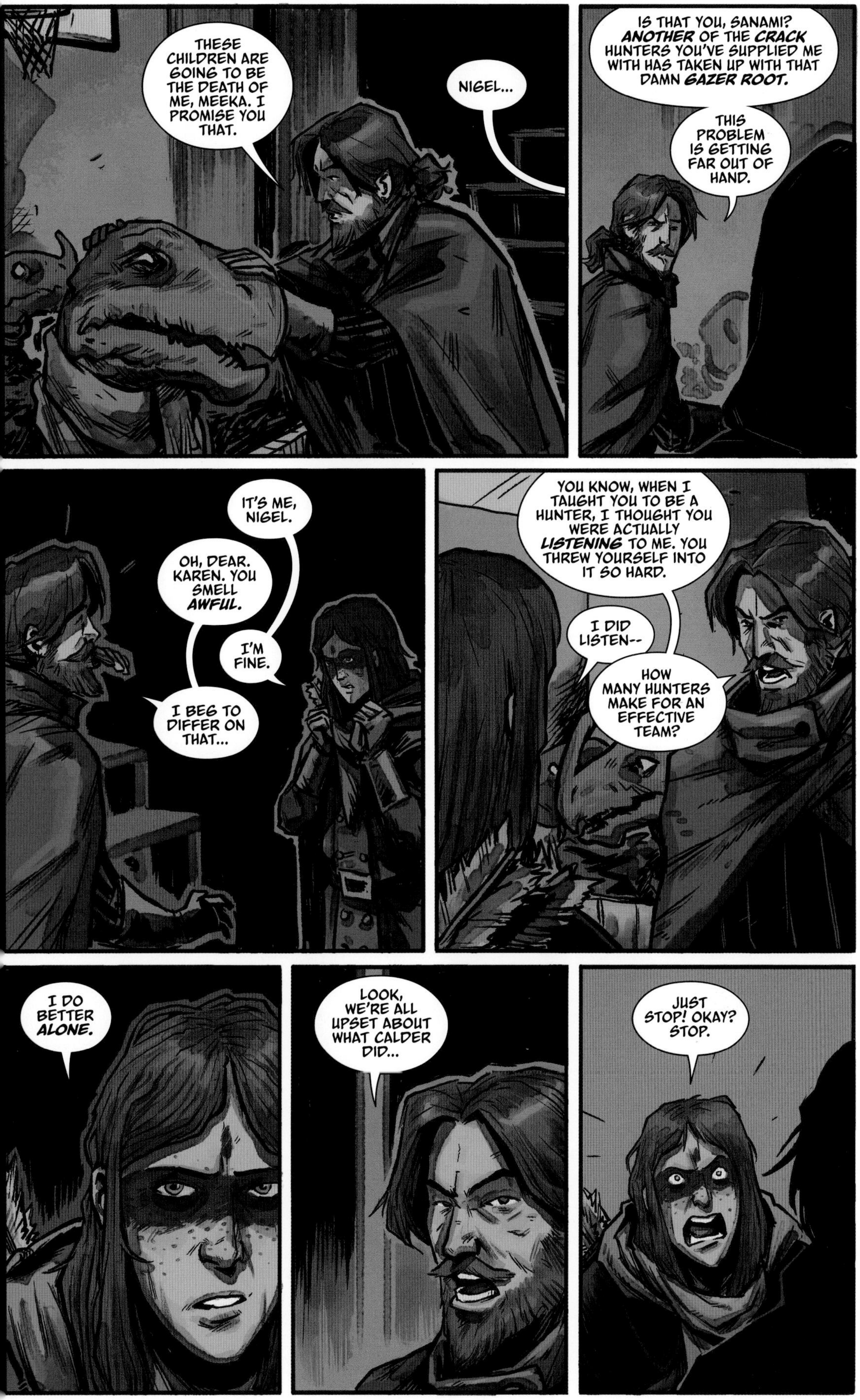

THESE CHILDREN ARE GOING TO BE THE DEATH OF ME, MEEKA. I PROMISE YOU THAT.
NIGEL...
IS THAT YOU, SANAMI? ANOTHER OF THE CRACK HUNTERS YOU'VE SUPPLIED ME WITH HAS TAKEN UP WITH THAT DAMN GAZER ROOT.
THIS PROBLEM IS GETTING FAR OUT OF HAND.
IT'S ME, NIGEL.
OH, DEAR. KAREN. YOU SMELL AWFUL.
I'M FINE.
I BEG TO DIFFER ON THAT...
YOU KNOW, WHEN I TAUGHT YOU TO BE A HUNTER, I THOUGHT YOU WERE ACTUALLY LISTENING TO ME. YOU THREW YOURSELF INTO IT SO HARD.
I DID LISTEN--
HOW MANY HUNTERS MAKE FOR AN EFFECTIVE TEAM?
I DO BETTER ALONE.
LOOK, WE'RE ALL UPSET ABOUT WHAT CALDER DID...
JUST STOP! OKAY? STOP.

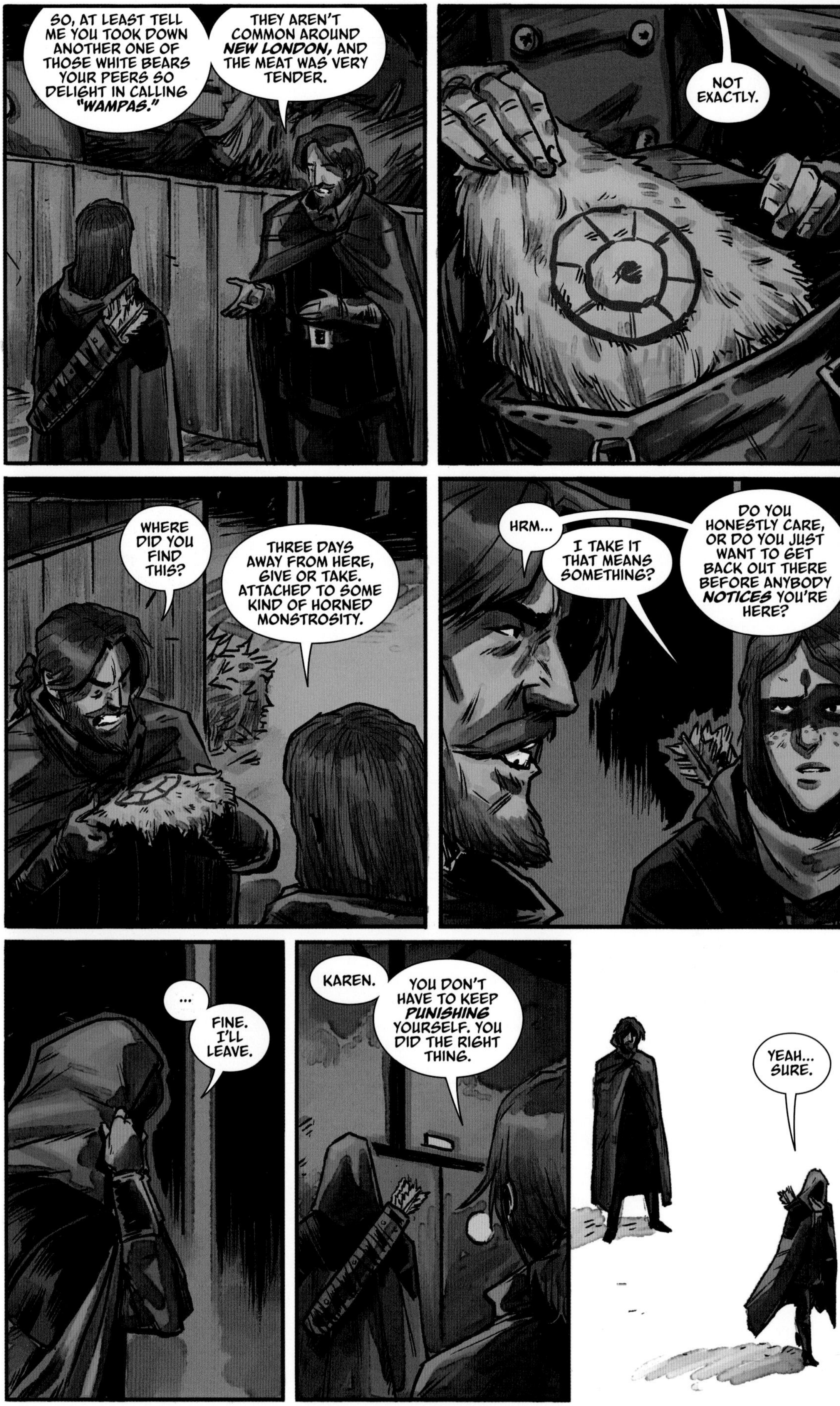
SO, AT LEAST TELL ME YOU TOOK DOWN ANOTHER ONE OF THOSE WHITE BEARS YOUR PEERS SO DELIGHT IN CALLING "WAMPAS."
THEY AREN'T COMMON AROUND NEW LONDON, AND THE MEAT WAS VERY TENDER.
NOT EXACTLY.
WHERE DID YOU FIND THIS?
THREE DAYS AWAY FROM HERE, GIVE OR TAKE. ATTACHED TO SOME KIND OF HORNED MONSTROSITY.
HRM...
I TAKE IT THAT MEANS SOMETHING?
DO YOU HONESTLY CARE, OR DO YOU JUST WANT TO GET BACK OUT THERE BEFORE ANYBODY NOTICES YOU'RE HERE?
...
FINE. I'LL LEAVE.
KAREN.
YOU DON'T HAVE TO KEEP PUNISHING YOURSELF. YOU DID THE RIGHT THING.
YEAH... SURE.

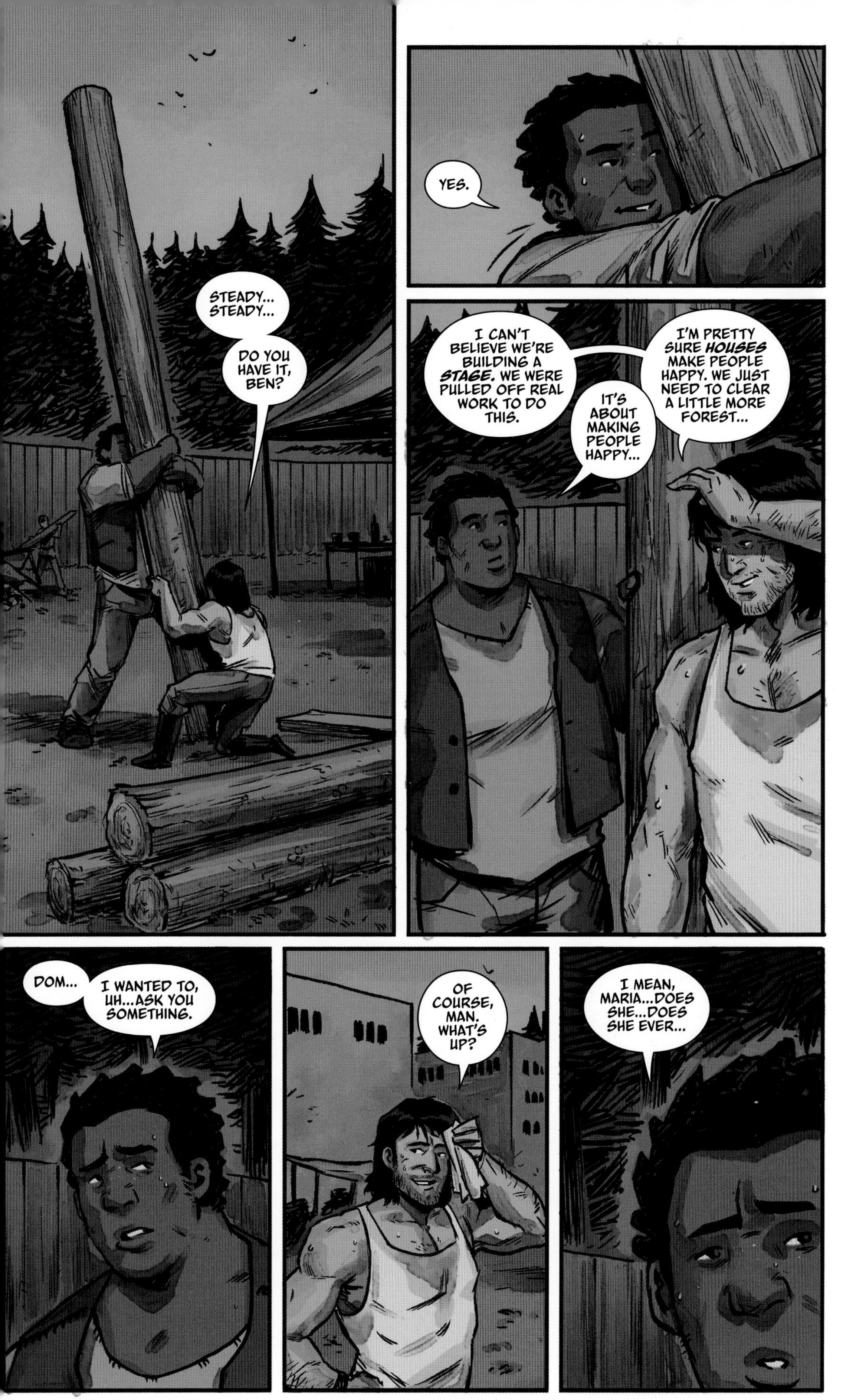
STEADY... STEADY...
DO YOU HAVE IT, BEN?
YES.
I CAN'T BELIEVE WE'RE BUILDING A STAGE. WE WERE PULLED OFF REAL WORK TO DO THIS.
IT'S ABOUT MAKING PEOPLE HAPPY...
I'M PRETTY SURE HOUSES MAKE PEOPLE HAPPY. WE JUST NEED TO CLEAR A LITTLE MORE FOREST...
DOM...
I WANTED TO, UH...ASK YOU SOMETHING.
OF COURSE, MAN. WHAT'S UP?
I MEAN, MARIA...DOES SHE...DOES SHE EVER...

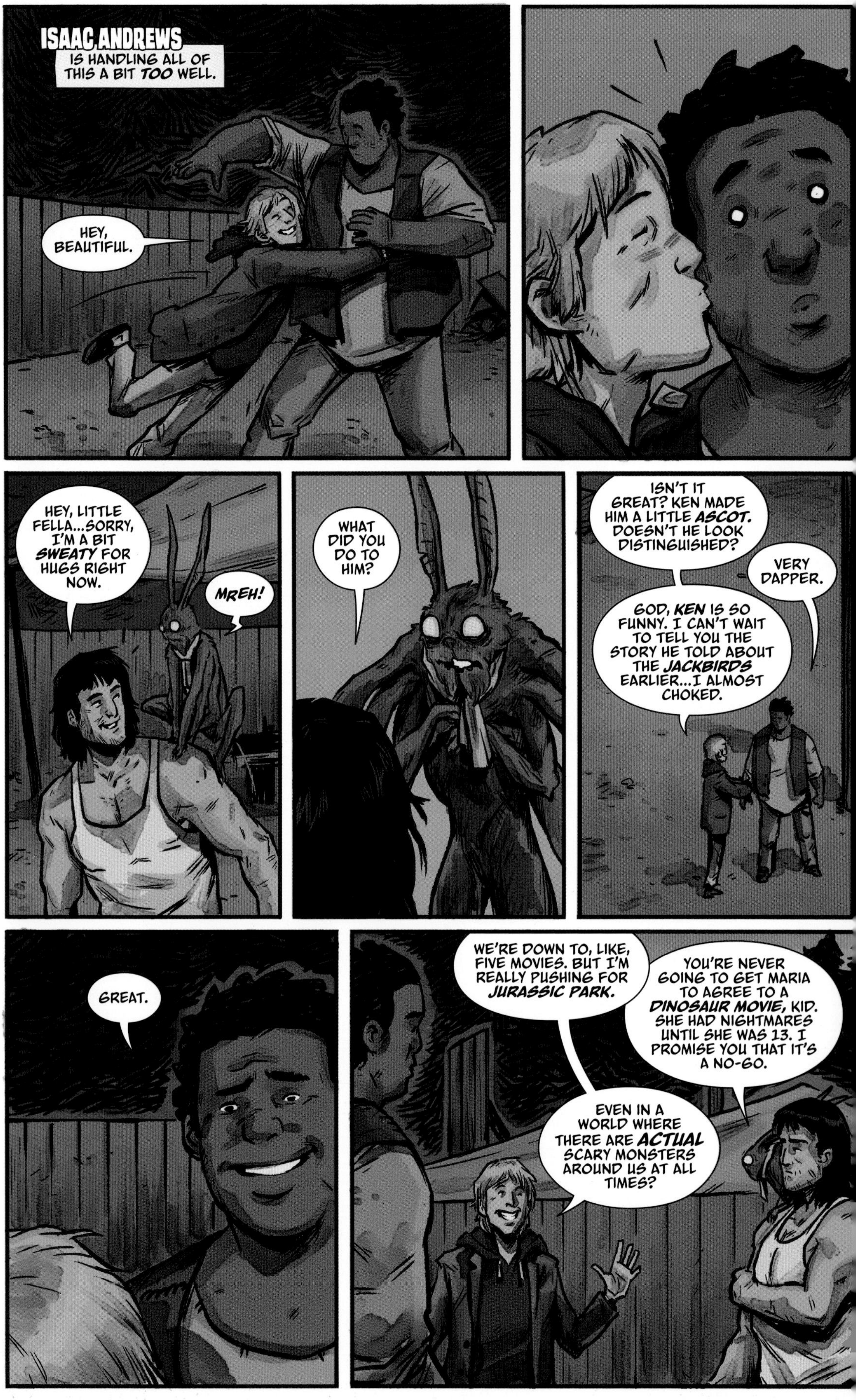
ISAAC ANDREWS
IS HANDLING ALL OF THIS A BIT TOO WELL.
HEY, BEAUTIFUL.
HEY, LITTLE FELLA...SORRY, I'M A BIT SWEATY FOR HUGS RIGHT NOW.
MREH!
WHAT DID YOU DO TO HIM?
ISN'T IT GREAT? KEN MADE HIM A LITTLE ASCOT. DOESN'T HE LOOK DISTINGUISHED?
VERY DAPPER.
GOD, KEN IS SO FUNNY. I CAN'T WAIT TO TELL YOU THE STORY HE TOLD ABOUT THE JACKBIRDS EARLIER...I ALMOST CHOKED.
GREAT.
WE'RE DOWN TO, LIKE, FIVE MOVIES. BUT I'M REALLY PUSHING FOR JURASSIC PARK.
YOU'RE NEVER GOING TO GET MARIA TO AGREE TO A DINOSAUR MOVIE, KID. SHE HAD NIGHTMARES UNTIL SHE WAS 13. I PROMISE YOU THAT IT'S A NO-GO.
EVEN IN A WORLD WHERE THERE ARE ACTUAL SCARY MONSTERS AROUND US AT ALL TIMES?

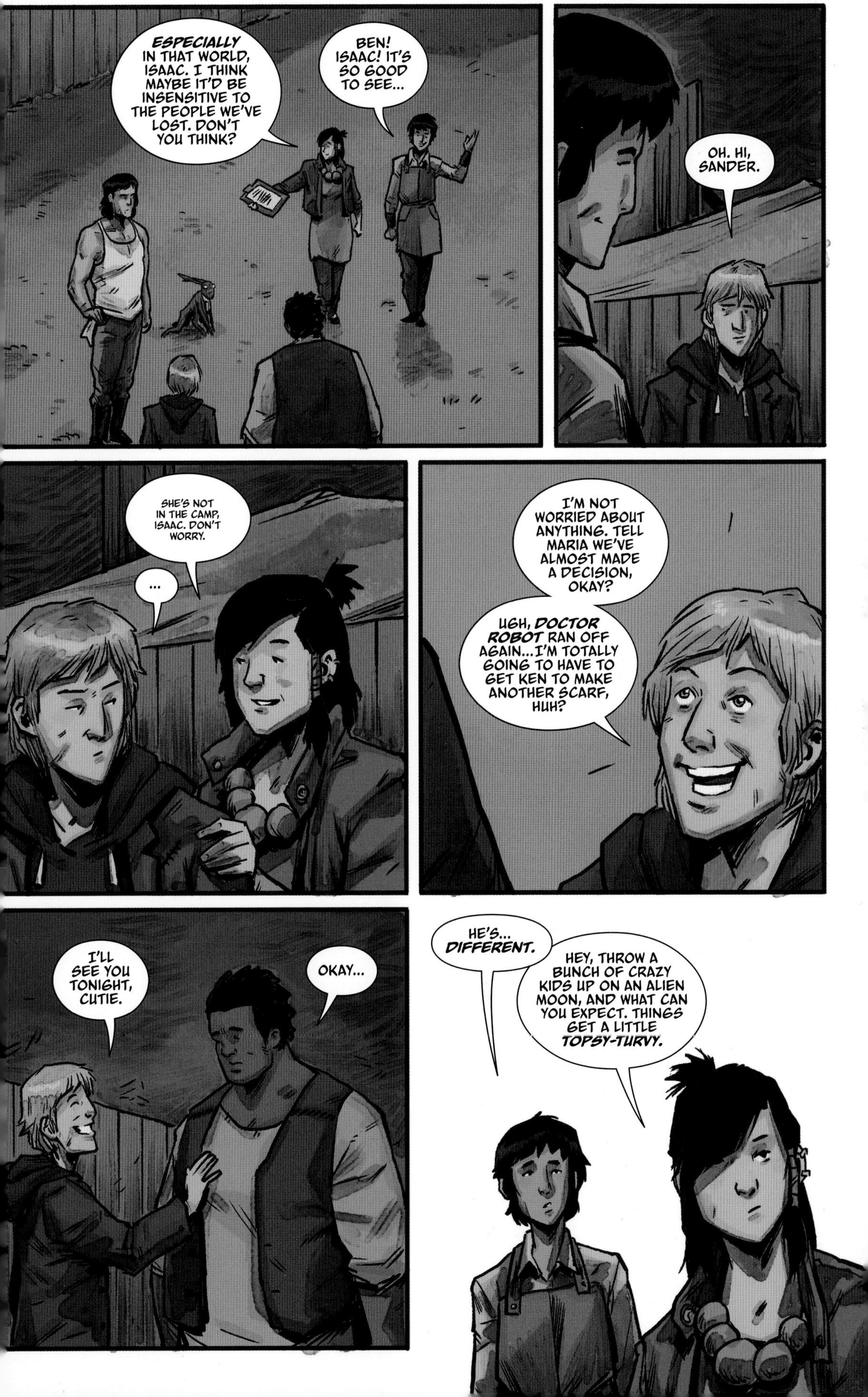
ESPECIALLY IN THAT WORLD, ISAAC. I THINK MAYBE IT'D BE INSENSITIVE TO THE PEOPLE WE'VE LOST. DON'T YOU THINK?
BEN! ISAAC! IT'S SO GOOD TO SEE...
OH. HI, SANDER.
SHE'S NOT IN THE CAMP, ISAAC. DON'T WORRY.
...
I'M NOT WORRIED ABOUT ANYTHING. TELL MARIA WE'VE ALMOST MADE A DECISION, OKAY?
UGH, DOCTOR ROBOT RAN OFF AGAIN...I'M TOTALLY GOING TO HAVE TO GET KEN TO MAKE ANOTHER SCARF, HUH?
I'LL SEE YOU TONIGHT, CUTIE.
OKAY...
HE'S... DIFFERENT.
HEY, THROW A BUNCH OF CRAZY KIDS UP ON AN ALIEN MOON, AND WHAT CAN YOU EXPECT. THINGS GET A LITTLE TOPSY-TURVY.

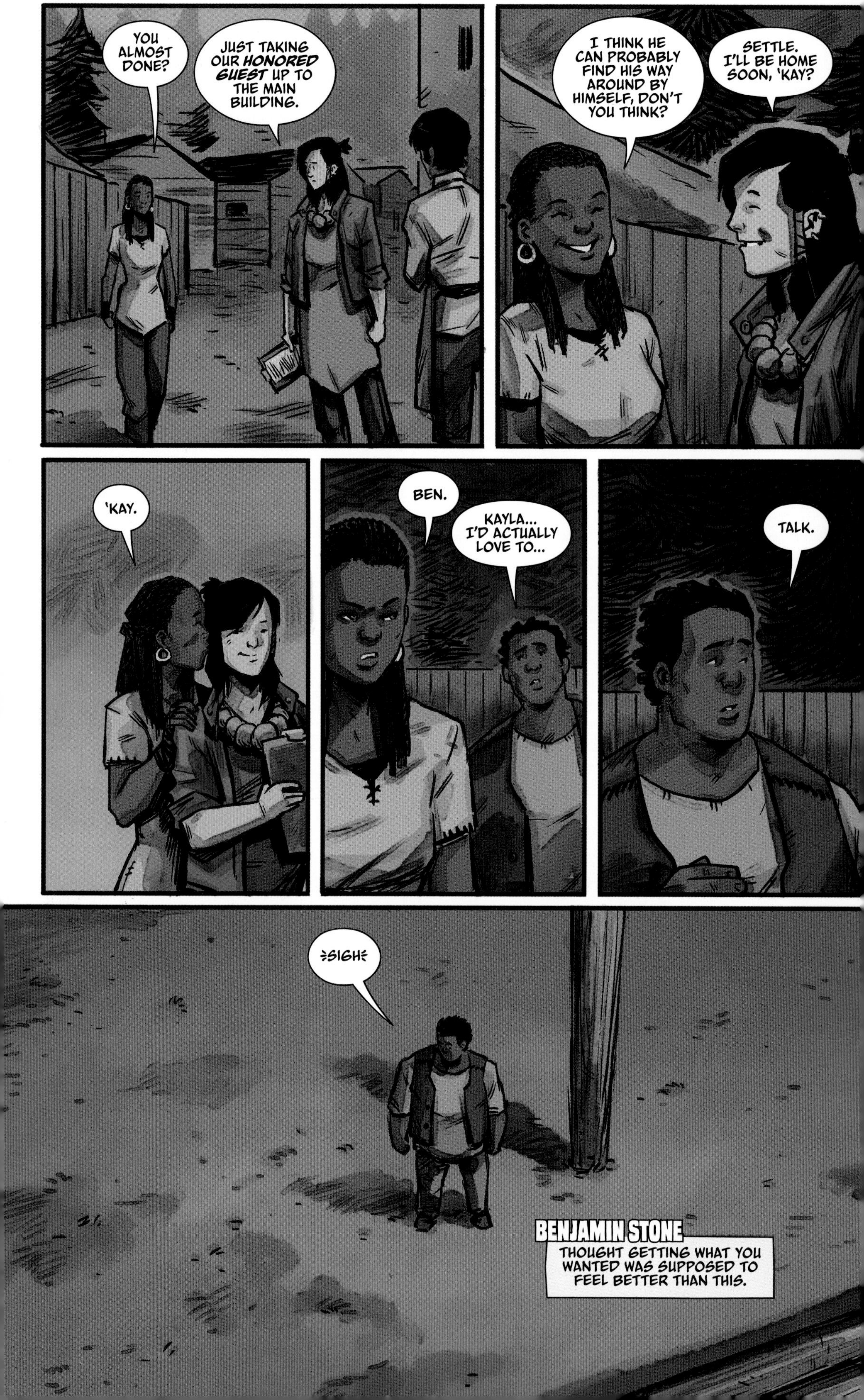

YOU ALMOST DONE?
JUST TAKING OUR HONORED GUEST UP TO THE MAIN BUILDING.
I THINK HE CAN PROBABLY FIND HIS WAY AROUND BY HIMSELF, DON'T YOU THINK?
SETTLE. I'LL BE HOME SOON, 'KAY?
'KAY.
BEN.
KAYLA... I'D ACTUALLY LOVE TO...
TALK.
SIGH
BENJAMIN STONE
THOUGHT GETTING WHAT YOU WANTED WAS SUPPOSED TO FEEL BETTER THAN THIS.

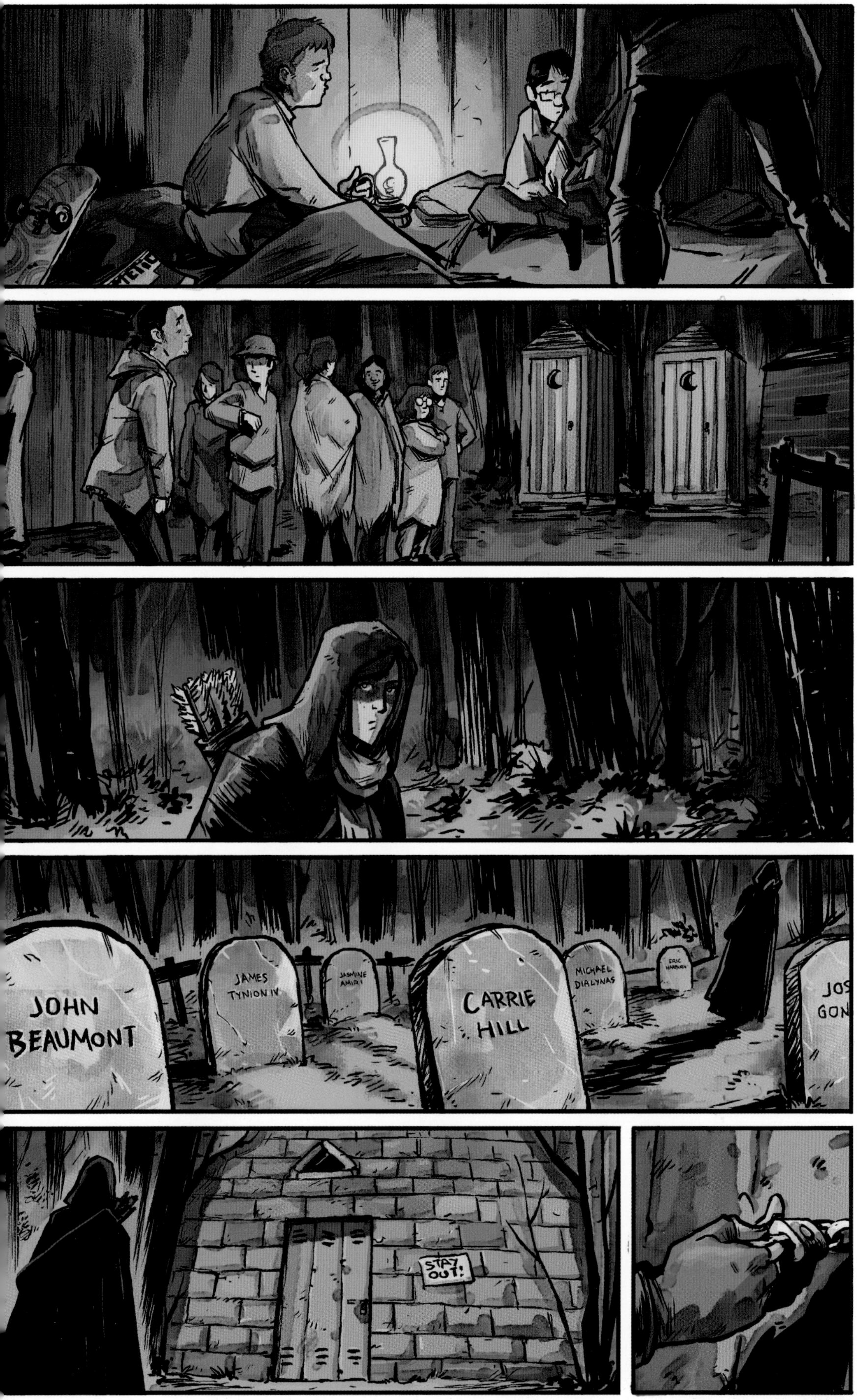

JOHN BEAUMONT
JAMES TYNION IV
JASMINE AMIRI
CARRIE HILL
MICHAEL DIALYNAS
ERIC HARBURN
STAY OUT!

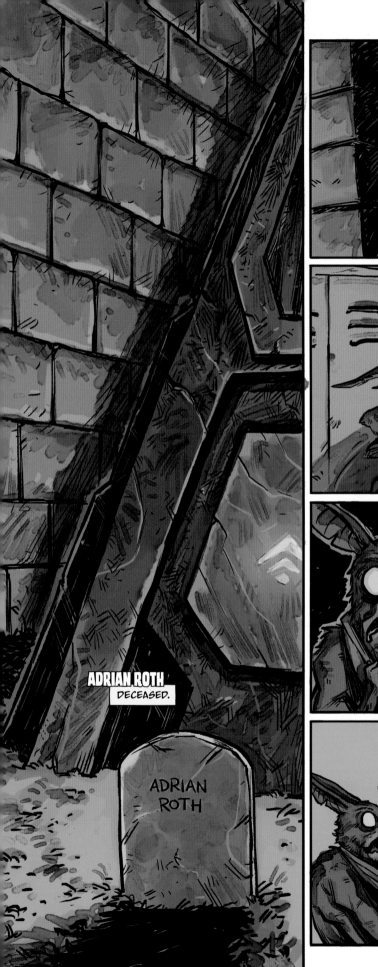

ADRIAN ROTH
DECEASED.

ADRIAN ROTH

DOCTOR ROBOT?

OH, WHAT DID YOU LET THEM DO TO YOU?

THERE, THAT'S BETTER, HUH?

MREH

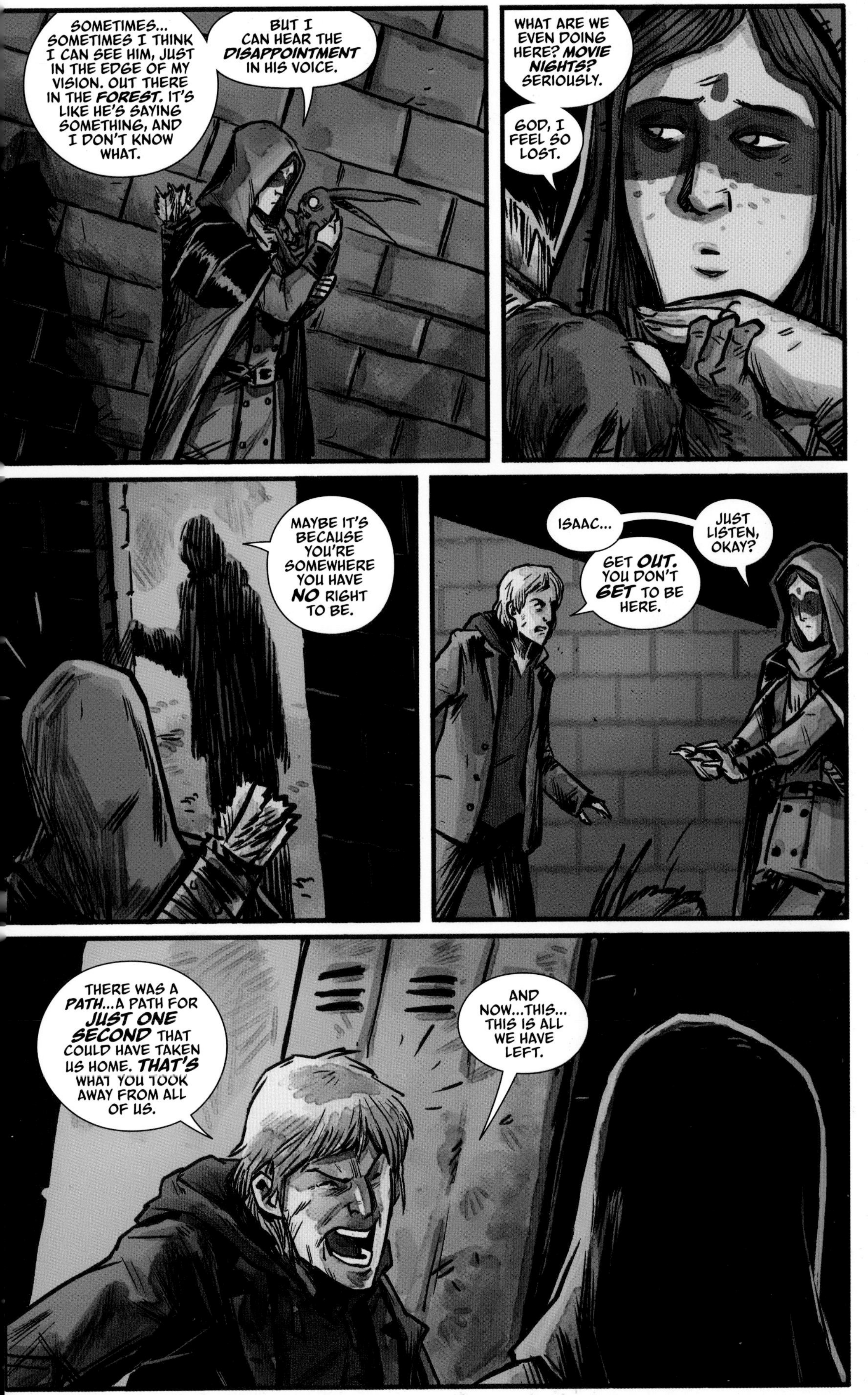
SOMETIMES... SOMETIMES I THINK I CAN SEE HIM, JUST IN THE EDGE OF MY VISION. OUT THERE IN THE FOREST. IT'S LIKE HE'S SAYING SOMETHING, AND I DON'T KNOW WHAT.
BUT I CAN HEAR THE DISAPPOINTMENT IN HIS VOICE.
WHAT ARE WE EVEN DOING HERE? MOVIE NIGHTS? SERIOUSLY.
GOD, I FEEL SO LOST.
MAYBE IT'S BECAUSE YOU'RE SOMEWHERE YOU HAVE NO RIGHT TO BE.
ISAAC...
JUST LISTEN, OKAY?
GET OUT. YOU DON'T GET TO BE HERE.
THERE WAS A PATH...A PATH FOR JUST ONE SECOND THAT COULD HAVE TAKEN US HOME. THAT'S WHAT YOU TOOK AWAY FROM ALL OF US.
AND NOW...THIS... THIS IS ALL WE HAVE LEFT.

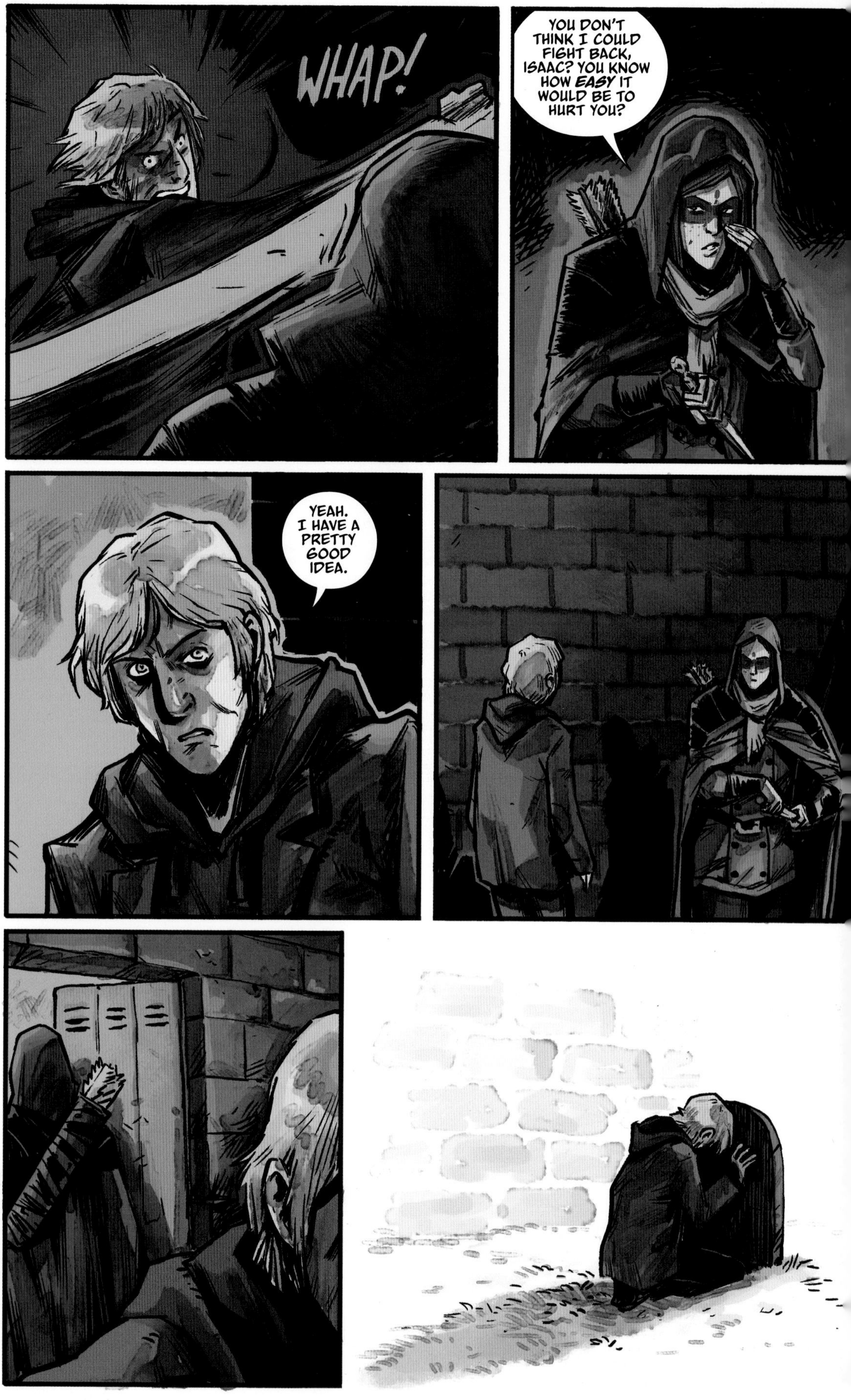
WHAP!
YOU DON'T THINK I COULD FIGHT BACK, ISAAC? YOU KNOW HOW EASY IT WOULD BE TO HURT YOU?
YEAH. I HAVE A PRETTY GOOD IDEA.

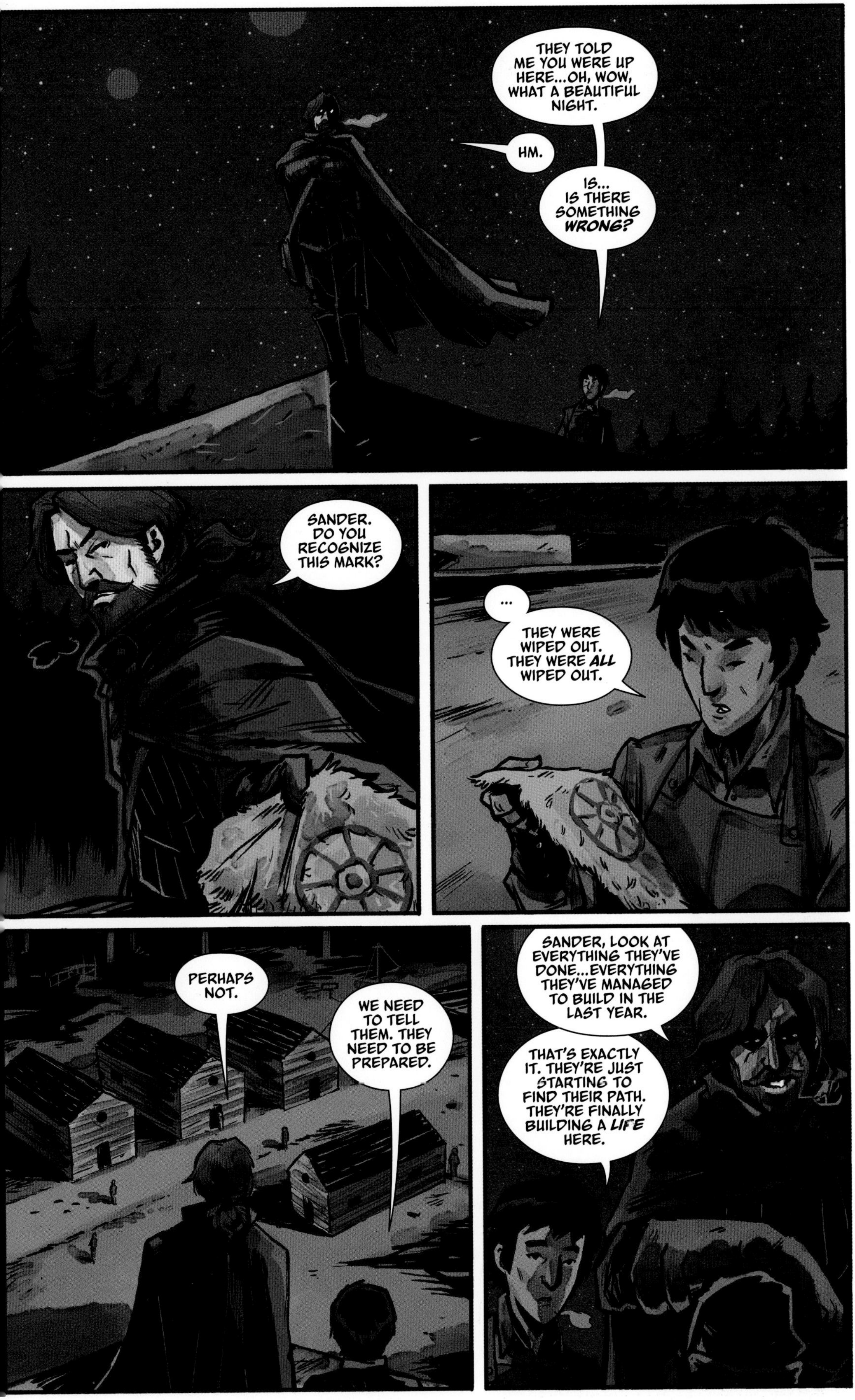
THEY TOLD ME YOU WERE UP HERE...OH, WOW, WHAT A BEAUTIFUL NIGHT.
HM.
IS... IS THERE SOMETHING WRONG?
SANDER. DO YOU RECOGNIZE THIS MARK?
...
THEY WERE WIPED OUT. THEY WERE ALL WIPED OUT.
PERHAPS NOT.
WE NEED TO TELL THEM. THEY NEED TO BE PREPARED.
SANDER, LOOK AT EVERYTHING THEY'VE DONE...EVERYTHING THEY'VE MANAGED TO BUILD IN THE LAST YEAR.
THAT'S EXACTLY IT. THEY'RE JUST STARTING TO FIND THEIR PATH. THEY'RE FINALLY BUILDING A LIFE HERE.

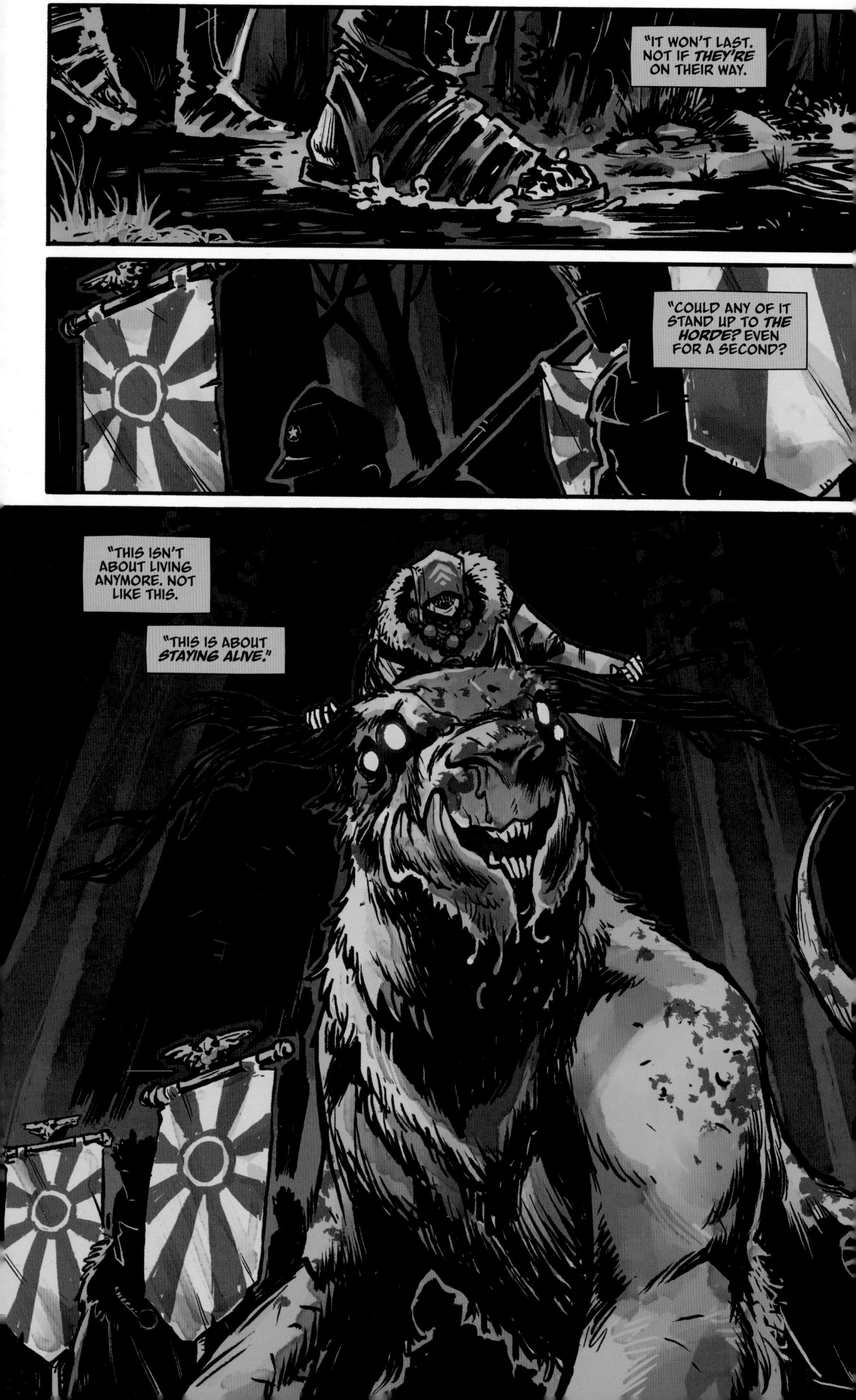
"IT WON'T LAST. NOT IF THEY'RE ON THEIR WAY.
"COULD ANY OF IT STAND UP TO THE HORDE? EVEN FOR A SECOND?
"THIS ISN'T ABOUT LIVING ANYMORE. NOT LIKE THIS.
"THIS IS ABOUT STAYING ALIVE."

CHAPTER
FOURTEEN

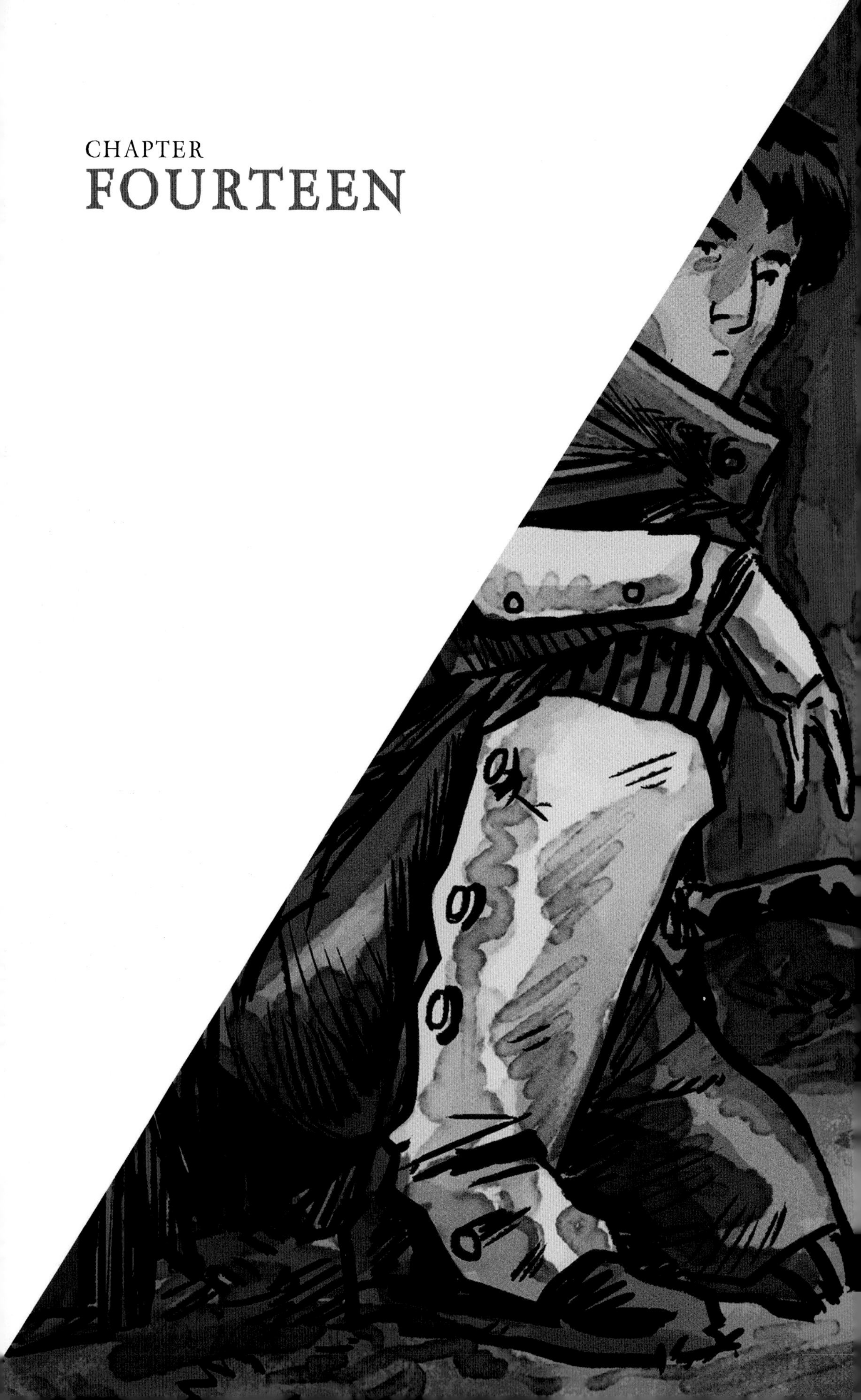

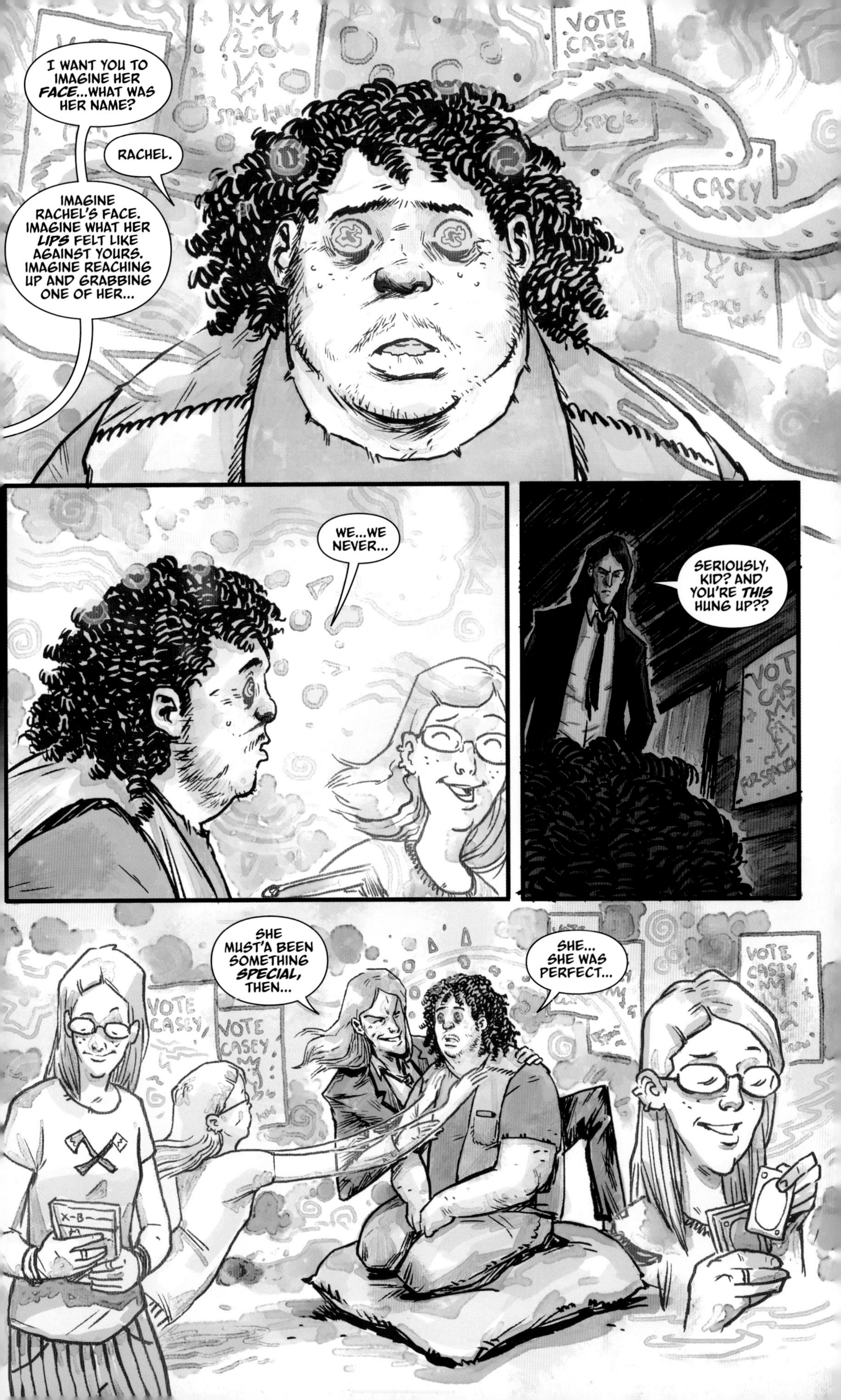
I WANT YOU TO IMAGINE HER *FACE*...WHAT WAS HER NAME?
RACHEL.
IMAGINE RACHEL'S FACE. IMAGINE WHAT HER *LIPS* FELT LIKE AGAINST YOURS. IMAGINE REACHING UP AND GRABBING ONE OF HER...
VOTE CASEY
CASEY
WE...WE NEVER...
SERIOUSLY, KID? AND YOU'RE *THIS* HUNG UP??
SHE MUST'A BEEN SOMETHING *SPECIAL*, THEN...
SHE... SHE WAS PERFECT...
VOTE CASEY
VOTE CASEY
VOTE CASEY

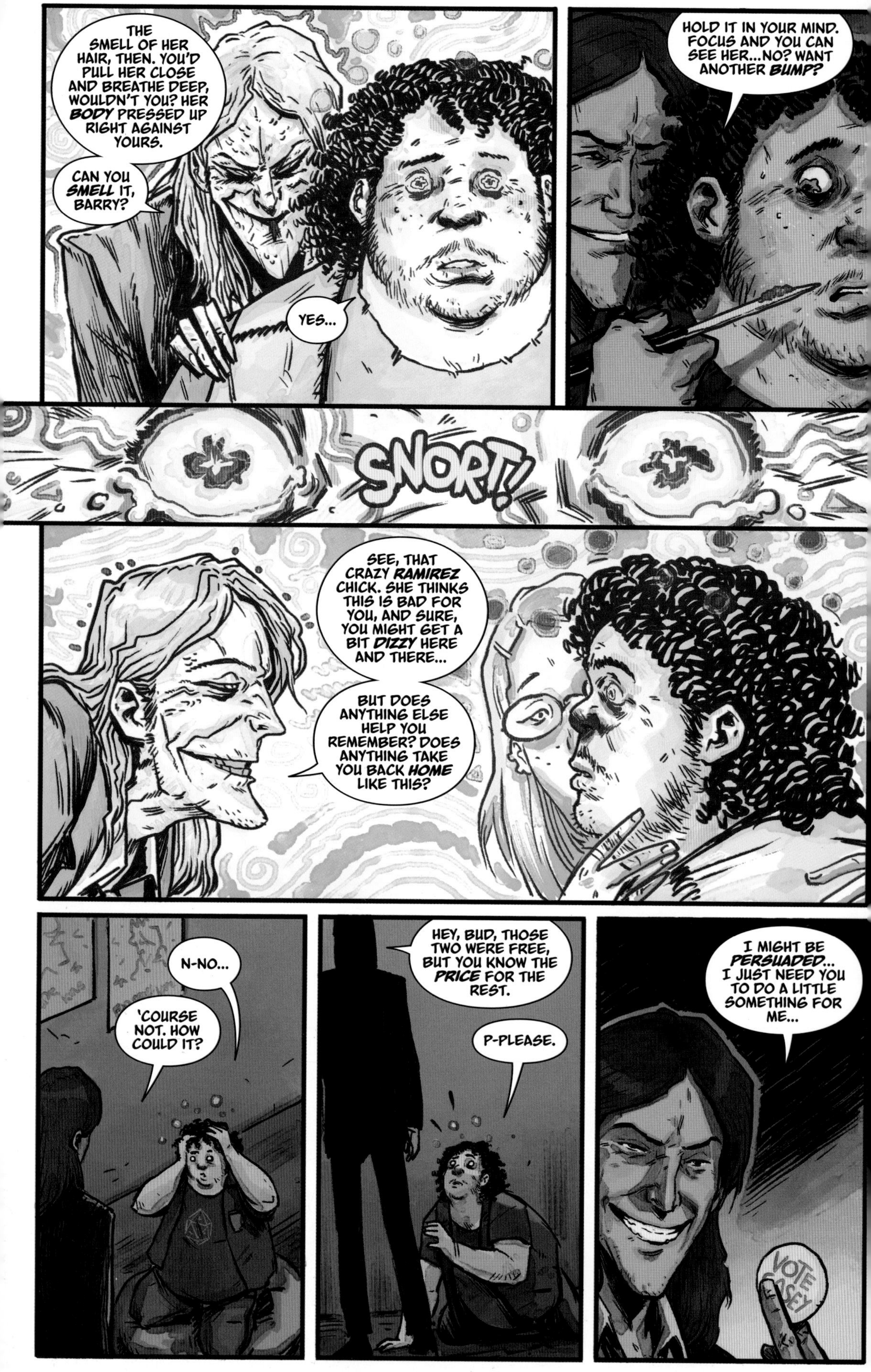
THE SMELL OF HER HAIR, THEN. YOU'D PULL HER CLOSE AND BREATHE DEEP, WOULDN'T YOU? HER BODY PRESSED UP RIGHT AGAINST YOURS.
CAN YOU SMELL IT, BARRY?
YES...
HOLD IT IN YOUR MIND. FOCUS AND YOU CAN SEE HER...NO? WANT ANOTHER BUMP?
SNORT!
SEE, THAT CRAZY RAMIREZ CHICK. SHE THINKS THIS IS BAD FOR YOU, AND SURE, YOU MIGHT GET A BIT DIZZY HERE AND THERE...
BUT DOES ANYTHING ELSE HELP YOU REMEMBER? DOES ANYTHING TAKE YOU BACK HOME LIKE THIS?
N-NO...
'COURSE NOT. HOW COULD IT?
HEY, BUD, THOSE TWO WERE FREE, BUT YOU KNOW THE PRICE FOR THE REST.
P-PLEASE.
I MIGHT BE PERSUADED... I JUST NEED YOU TO DO A LITTLE SOMETHING FOR ME...
VOTE CASEY

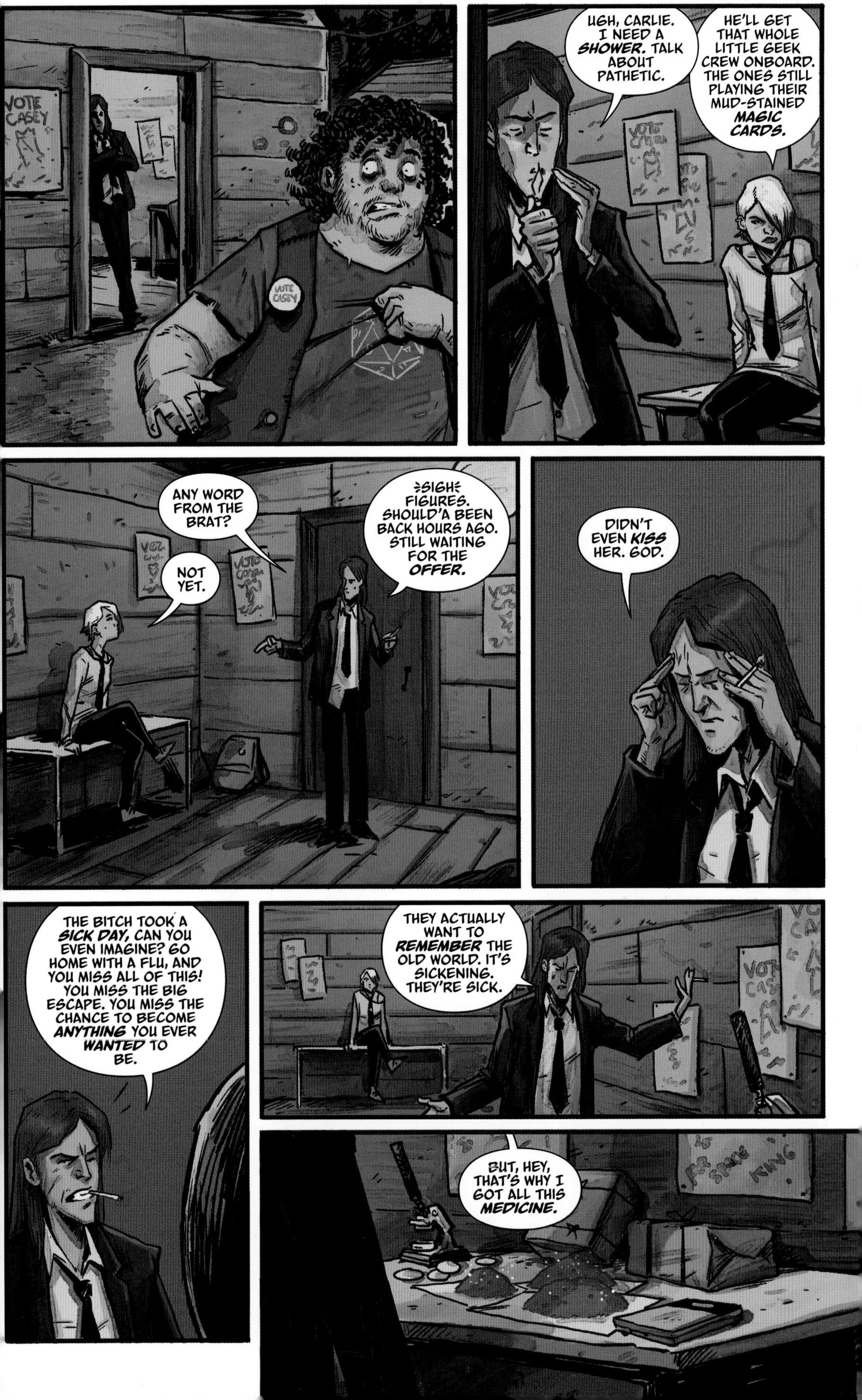
VOTE CASEY
VOTE CASEY
UGH, CARLIE. I NEED A *SHOWER.* TALK ABOUT PATHETIC.
HE'LL GET THAT WHOLE LITTLE GEEK CREW ONBOARD. THE ONES STILL PLAYING THEIR MUD-STAINED *MAGIC CARDS.*
ANY WORD FROM THE BRAT?
NOT YET.
SIGH FIGURES. SHOULD'A BEEN BACK HOURS AGO. STILL WAITING FOR THE *OFFER.*
DIDN'T EVEN *KISS* HER. GOD.
THE BITCH TOOK A *SICK DAY,* CAN YOU EVEN IMAGINE? GO HOME WITH A FLU, AND YOU MISS ALL OF THIS! YOU MISS THE BIG ESCAPE. YOU MISS THE CHANCE TO BECOME *ANYTHING* YOU EVER *WANTED* TO BE.
THEY ACTUALLY WANT TO *REMEMBER* THE OLD WORLD. IT'S SICKENING. THEY'RE SICK.
BUT, HEY, THAT'S WHY I GOT ALL THIS *MEDICINE.*

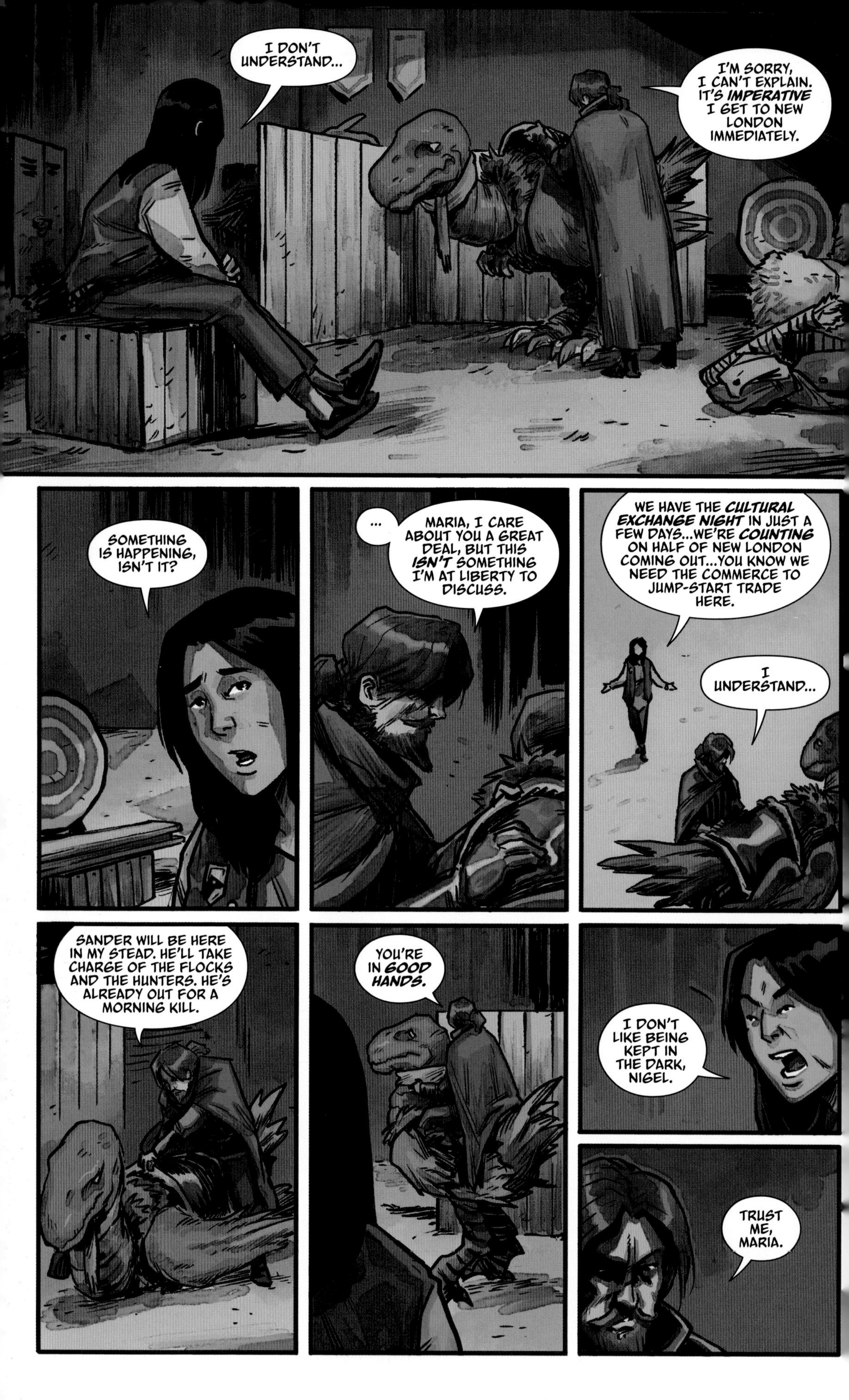

I DON'T UNDERSTAND...
I'M SORRY, I CAN'T EXPLAIN. IT'S *IMPERATIVE* I GET TO NEW LONDON IMMEDIATELY.
SOMETHING IS HAPPENING, ISN'T IT?
...
MARIA, I CARE ABOUT YOU A GREAT DEAL, BUT THIS *ISN'T* SOMETHING I'M AT LIBERTY TO DISCUSS.
WE HAVE THE *CULTURAL EXCHANGE NIGHT* IN JUST A FEW DAYS...WE'RE *COUNTING* ON HALF OF NEW LONDON COMING OUT...YOU KNOW WE NEED THE COMMERCE TO JUMP-START TRADE HERE.
I UNDERSTAND...
SANDER WILL BE HERE IN MY STEAD. HE'LL TAKE CHARGE OF THE FLOCKS AND THE HUNTERS. HE'S ALREADY OUT FOR A MORNING KILL.
YOU'RE IN *GOOD HANDS.*
I DON'T LIKE BEING KEPT IN THE DARK, NIGEL.
TRUST ME, MARIA.

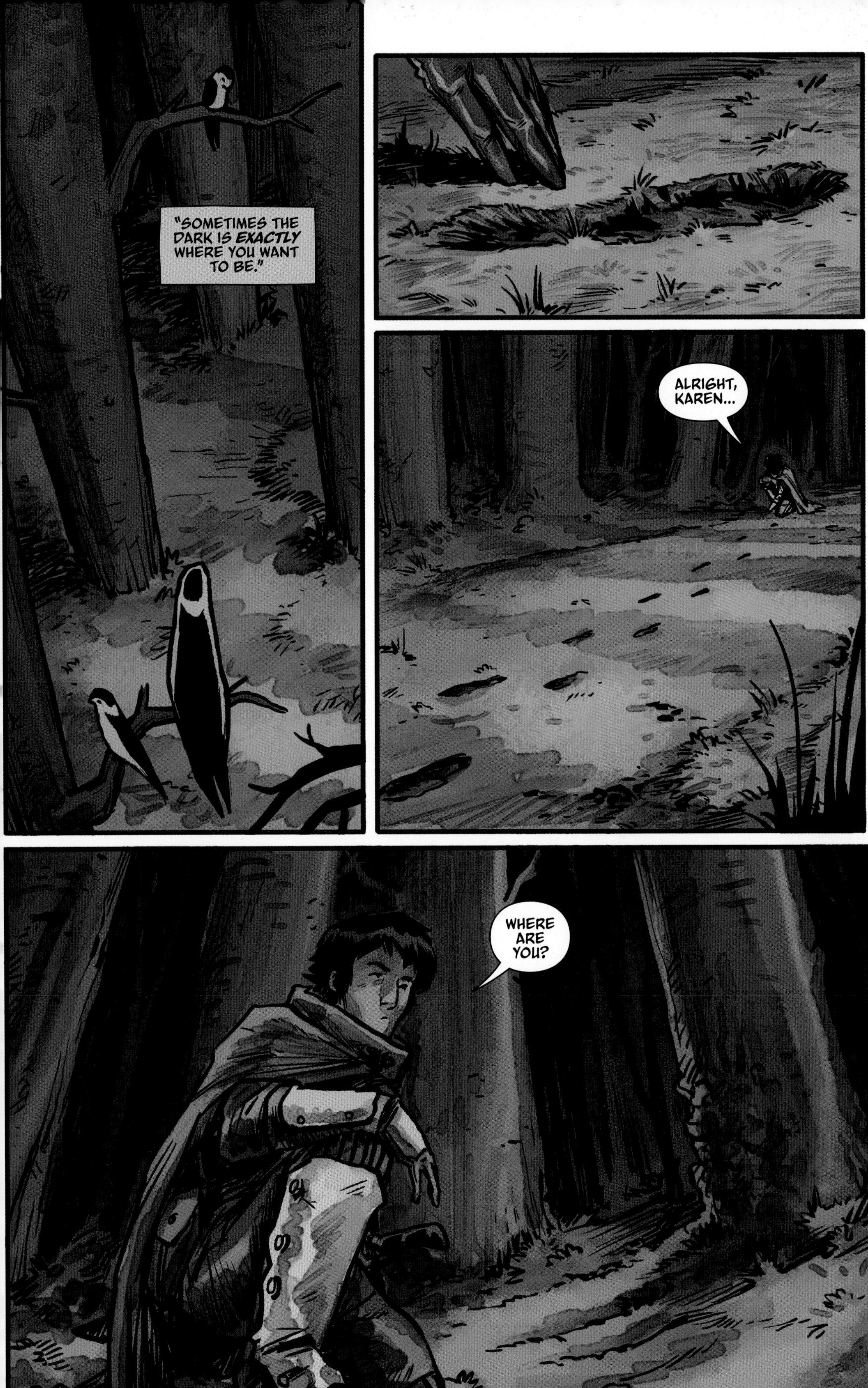
"SOMETIMES THE DARK IS *EXACTLY* WHERE YOU WANT TO BE."
ALRIGHT, KAREN...
WHERE ARE YOU?

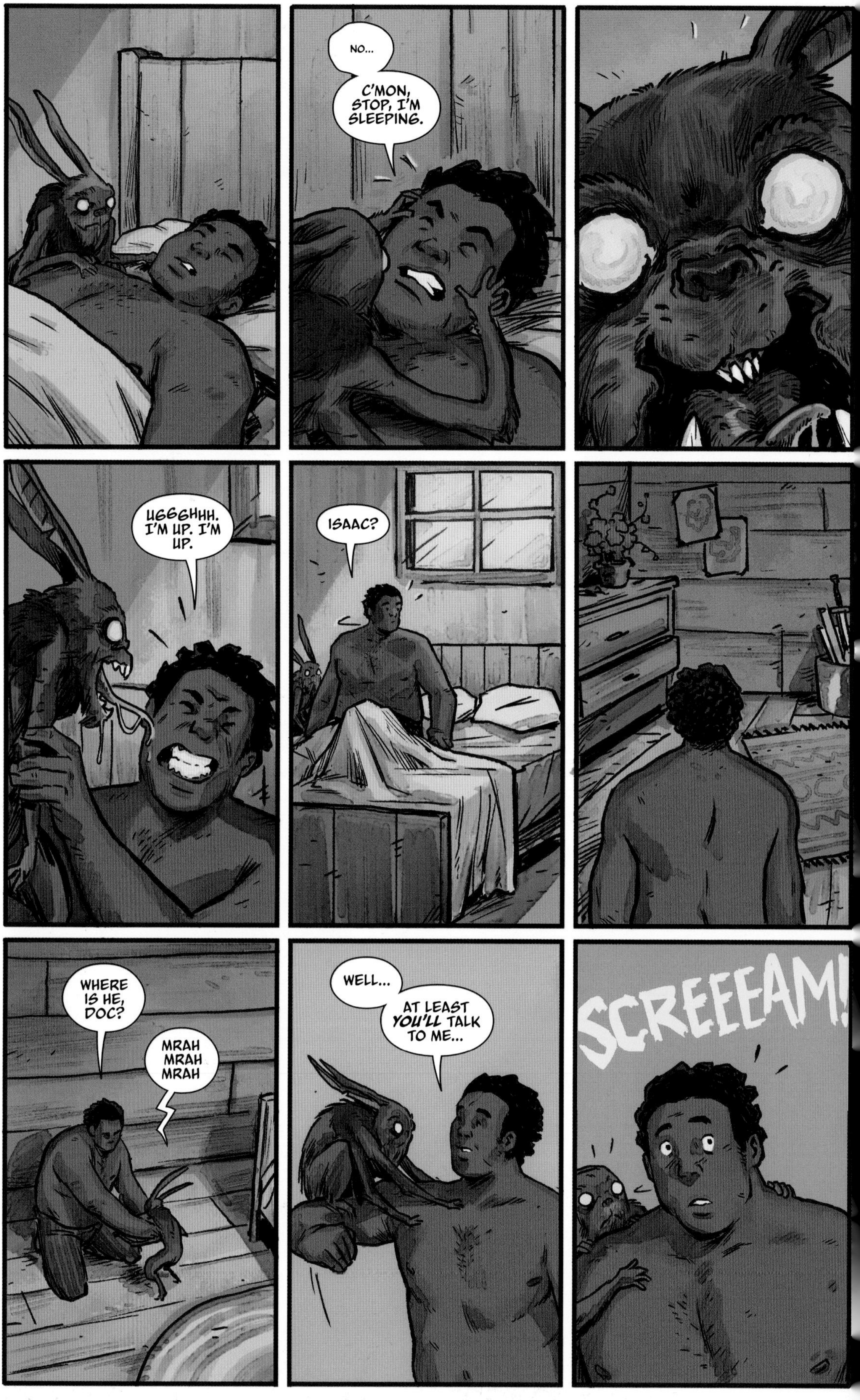
NO...
C'MON, STOP, I'M SLEEPING.
UGGGHHH. I'M UP. I'M UP.
ISAAC?
WHERE IS HE, DOC?
MRAH MRAH MRAH
WELL...
AT LEAST YOU'LL TALK TO ME...
SCREEEAM!

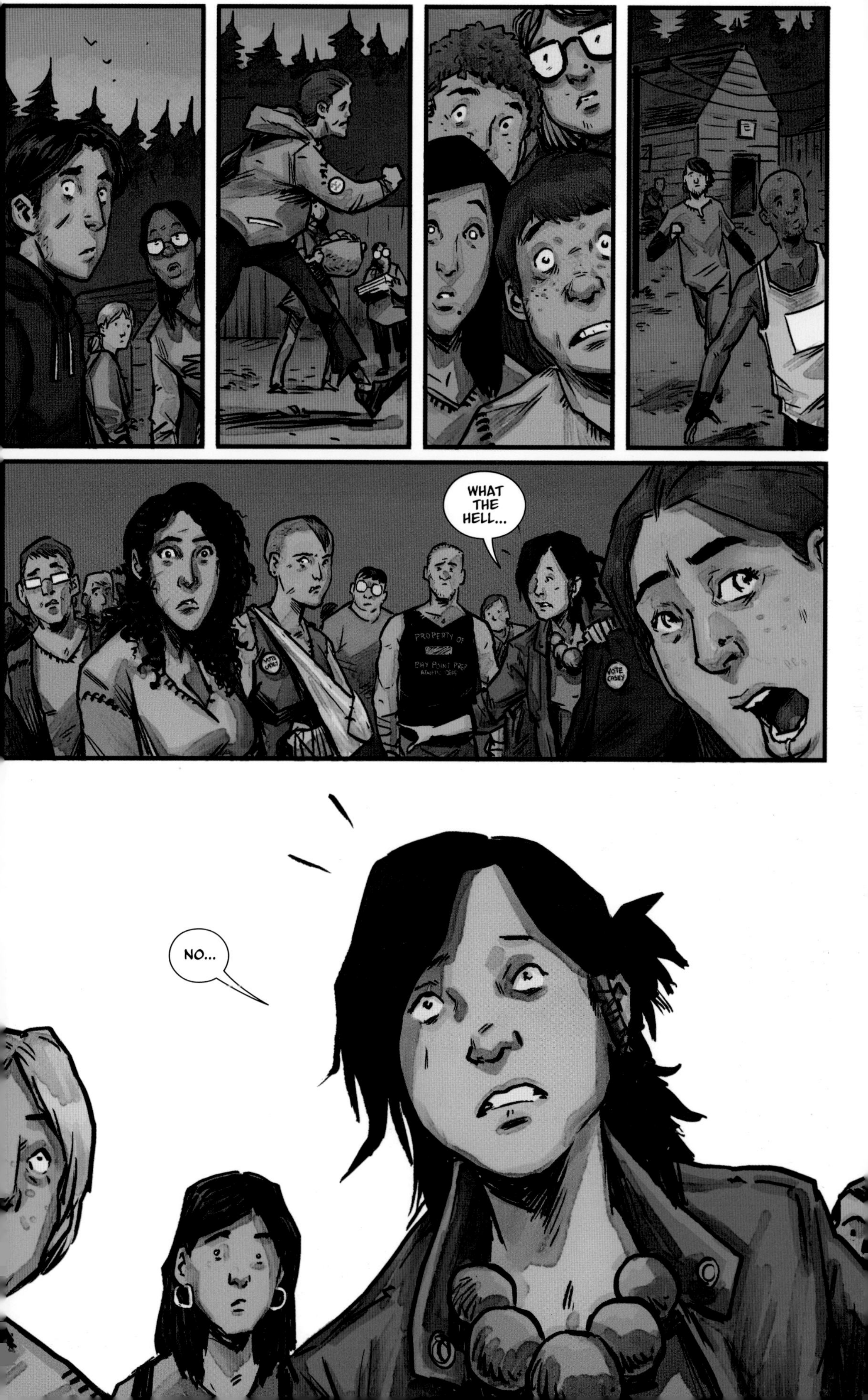
WHAT THE HELL...
NO...

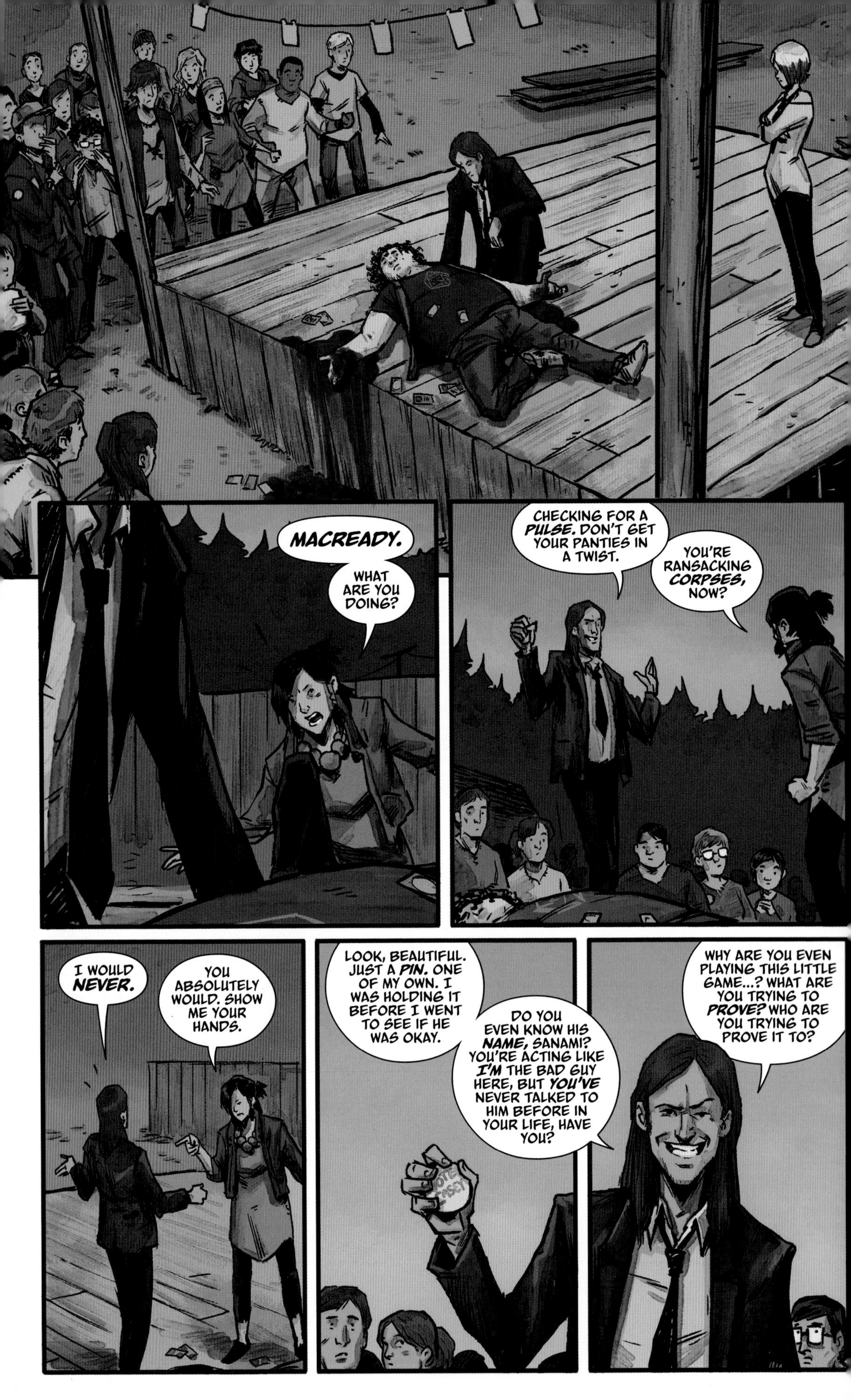
MACREADY.
WHAT ARE YOU DOING?
CHECKING FOR A PULSE. DON'T GET YOUR PANTIES IN A TWIST.
YOU'RE RANSACKING CORPSES, NOW?
I WOULD NEVER.
YOU ABSOLUTELY WOULD. SHOW ME YOUR HANDS.
LOOK, BEAUTIFUL. JUST A PIN. ONE OF MY OWN. I WAS HOLDING IT BEFORE I WENT TO SEE IF HE WAS OKAY.
DO YOU EVEN KNOW HIS NAME, SANAMI? YOU'RE ACTING LIKE I'M THE BAD GUY HERE, BUT YOU'VE NEVER TALKED TO HIM BEFORE IN YOUR LIFE, HAVE YOU?
WHY ARE YOU EVEN PLAYING THIS LITTLE GAME...? WHAT ARE YOU TRYING TO PROVE? WHO ARE YOU TRYING TO PROVE IT TO?

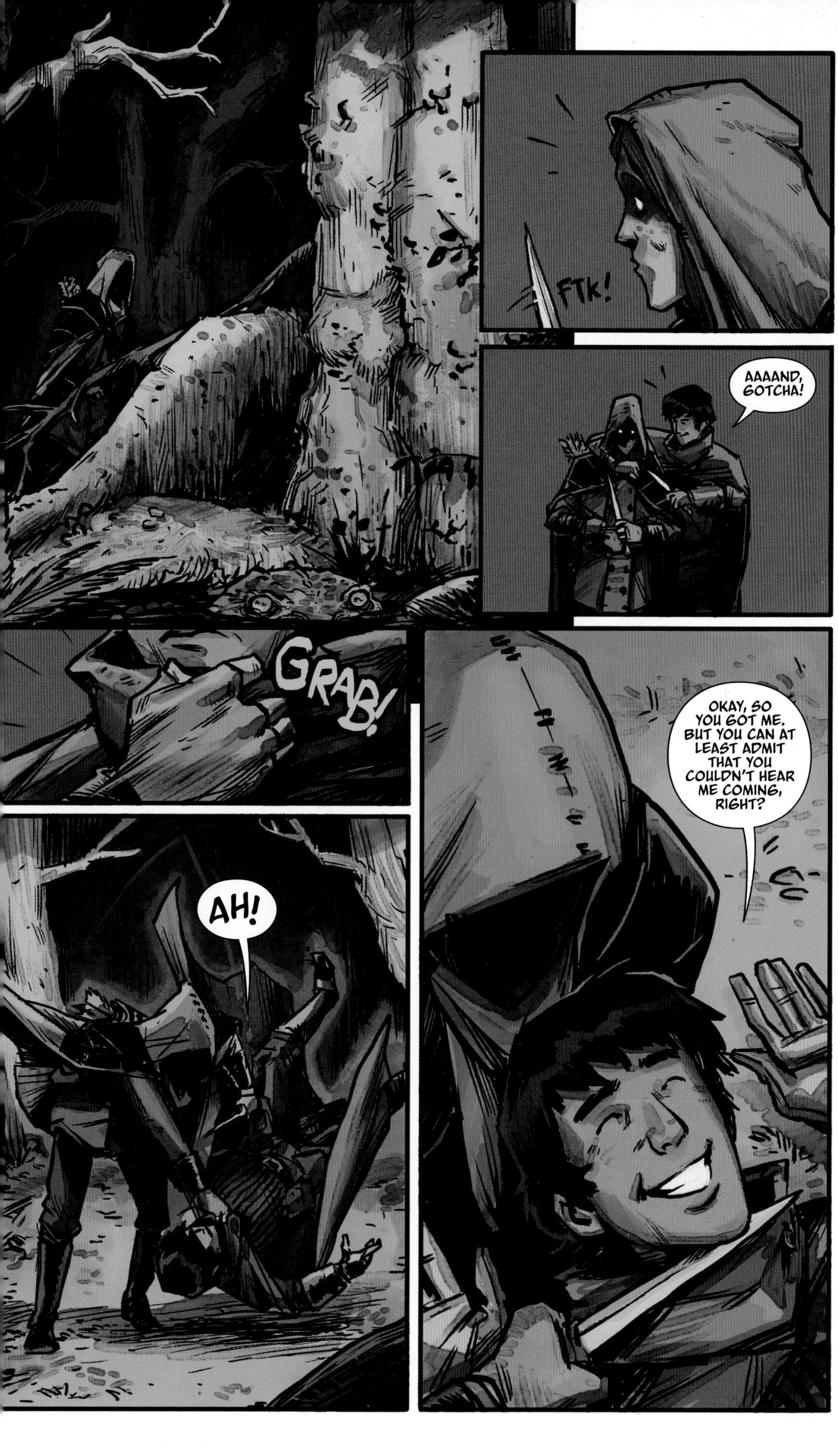
FTK!
AAAAND, GOTCHA!
GRAB!
OKAY, SO YOU GOT ME. BUT YOU CAN AT LEAST ADMIT THAT YOU COULDN'T HEAR ME COMING, RIGHT?
AH!

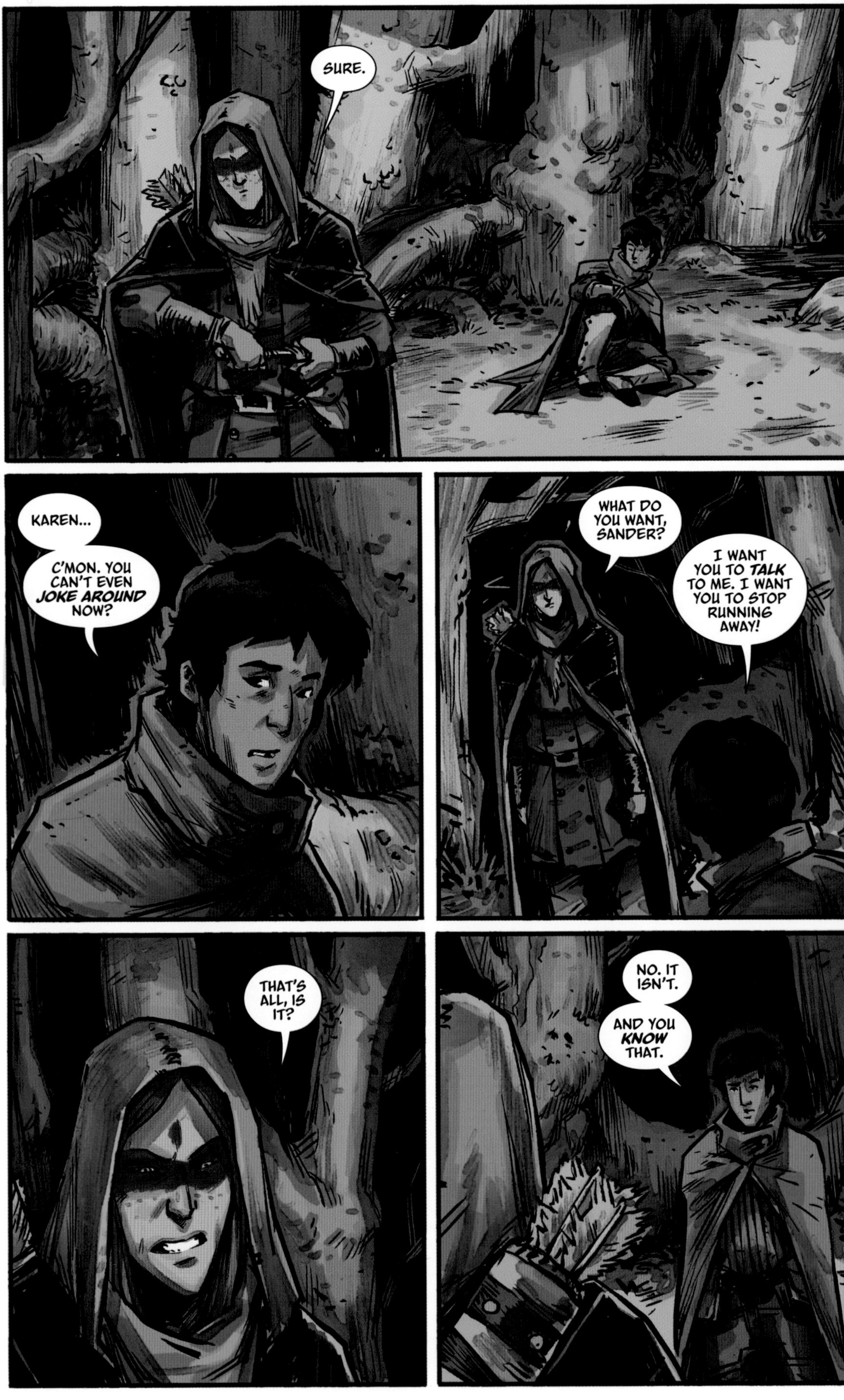
SURE.
KAREN...
C'MON. YOU CAN'T EVEN JOKE AROUND NOW?
WHAT DO YOU WANT, SANDER?
I WANT YOU TO TALK TO ME. I WANT YOU TO STOP RUNNING AWAY!
THAT'S ALL, IS IT?
NO. IT ISN'T.
AND YOU KNOW THAT.

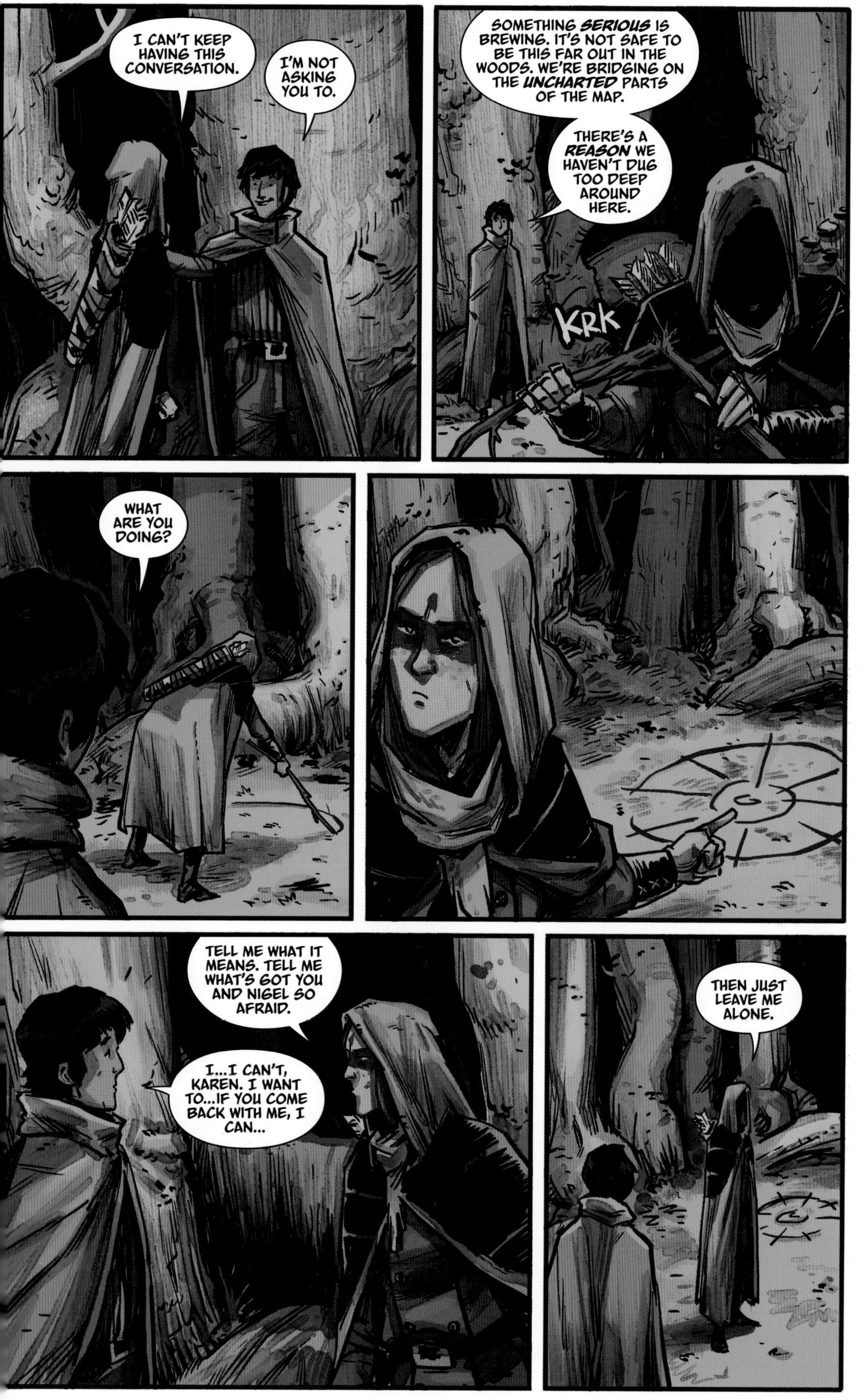
I CAN'T KEEP HAVING THIS CONVERSATION.
I'M NOT ASKING YOU TO.
SOMETHING SERIOUS IS BREWING. IT'S NOT SAFE TO BE THIS FAR OUT IN THE WOODS. WE'RE BRIDGING ON THE UNCHARTED PARTS OF THE MAP.
THERE'S A REASON WE HAVEN'T DUG TOO DEEP AROUND HERE.
KRK
WHAT ARE YOU DOING?
TELL ME WHAT IT MEANS. TELL ME WHAT'S GOT YOU AND NIGEL SO AFRAID.
I...I CAN'T, KAREN. I WANT TO...IF YOU COME BACK WITH ME, I CAN...
THEN JUST LEAVE ME ALONE.

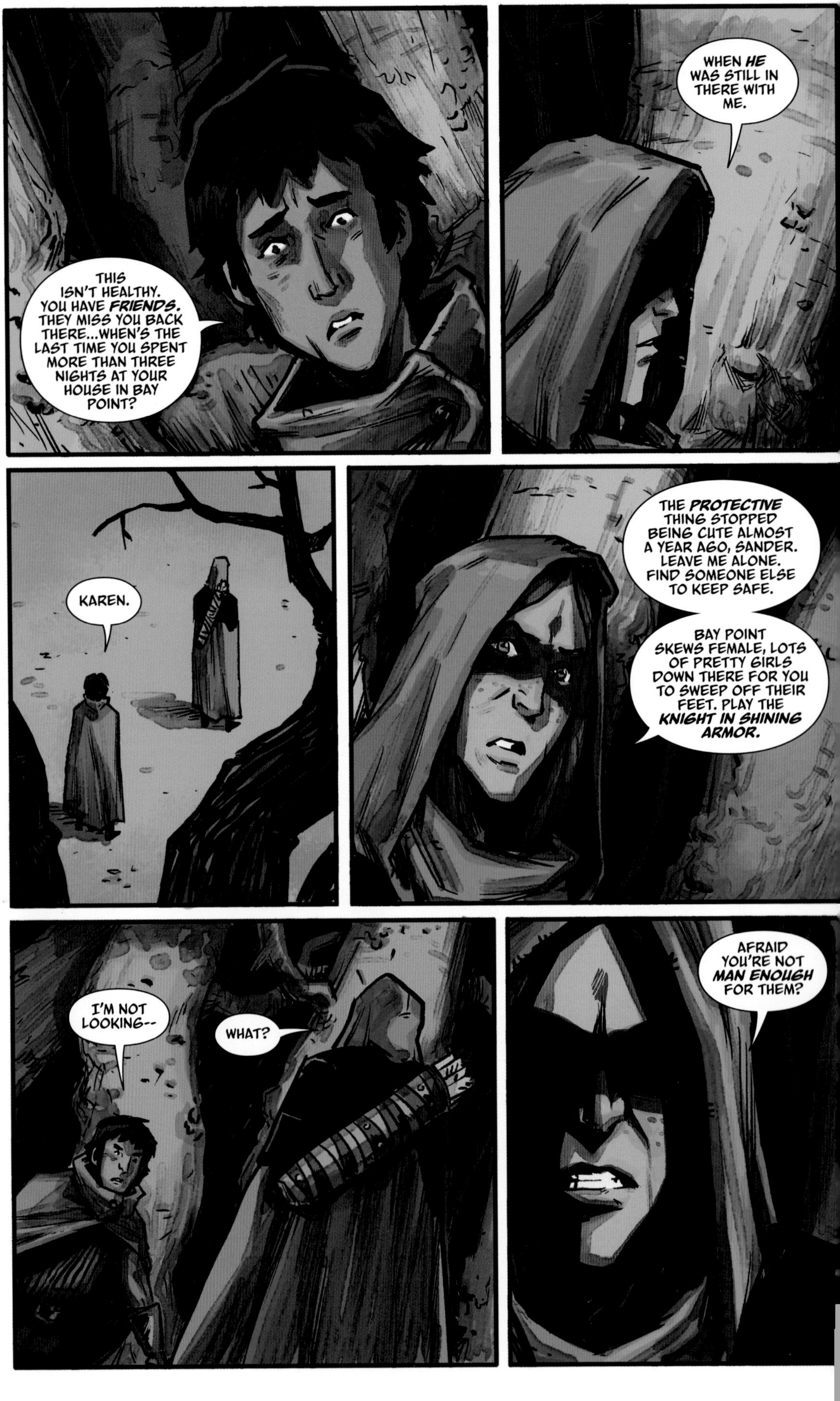
THIS ISN'T HEALTHY. YOU HAVE *FRIENDS.* THEY MISS YOU BACK THERE...WHEN'S THE LAST TIME YOU SPENT MORE THAN THREE NIGHTS AT YOUR HOUSE IN BAY POINT?
WHEN *HE* WAS STILL IN THERE WITH ME.
KAREN.
THE *PROTECTIVE* THING STOPPED BEING CUTE ALMOST A YEAR AGO, SANDER. LEAVE ME ALONE. FIND SOMEONE ELSE TO KEEP SAFE.
BAY POINT SKEWS FEMALE, LOTS OF PRETTY GIRLS DOWN THERE FOR YOU TO SWEEP OFF THEIR FEET. PLAY THE *KNIGHT IN SHINING ARMOR.*
I'M NOT LOOKING--
WHAT?
AFRAID YOU'RE NOT *MAN ENOUGH* FOR THEM?

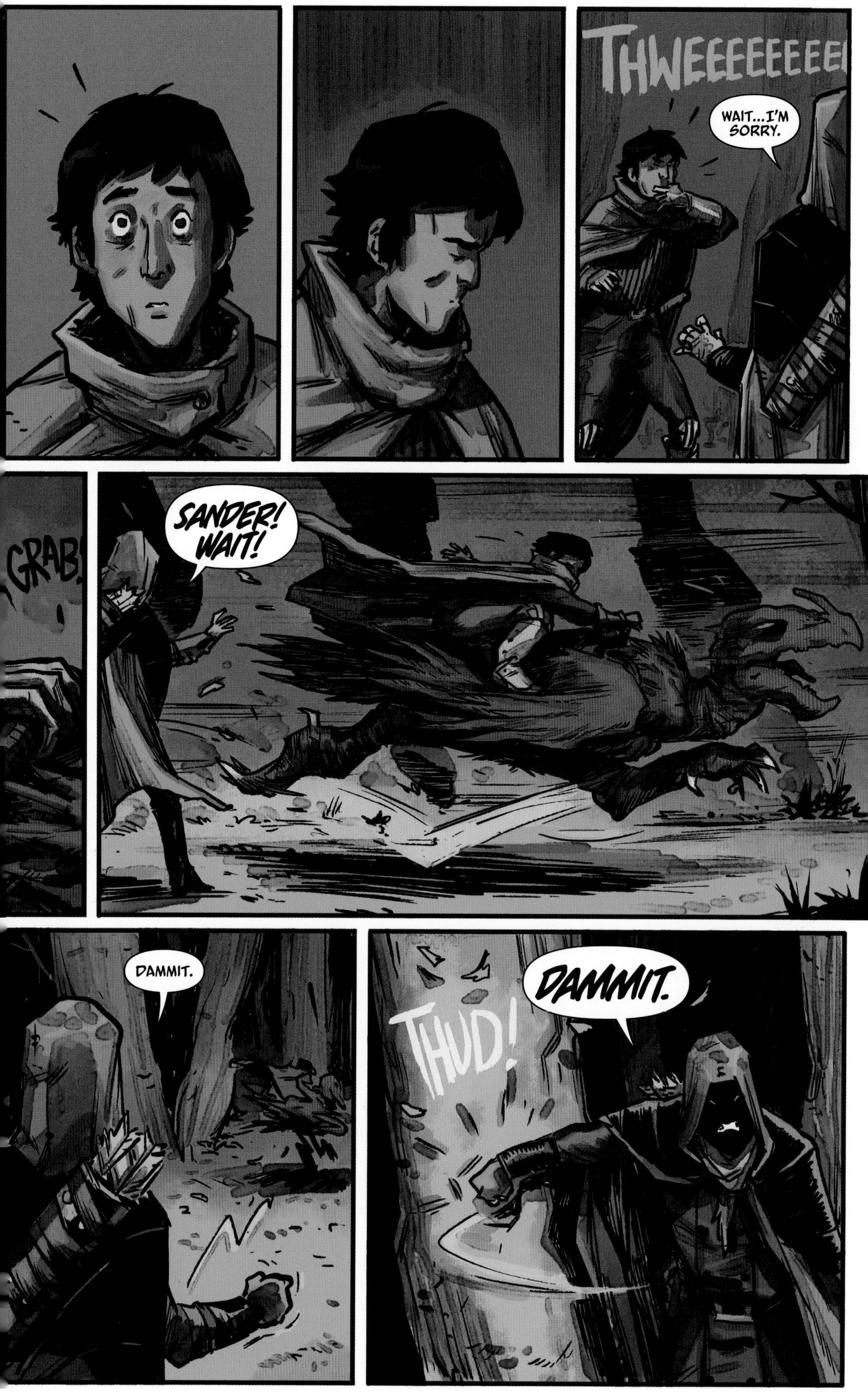
THWEEEEEEEE
WAIT...I'M SORRY.
GRAB
SANDER! WAIT!
DAMMIT.
THUD!
DAMMIT.

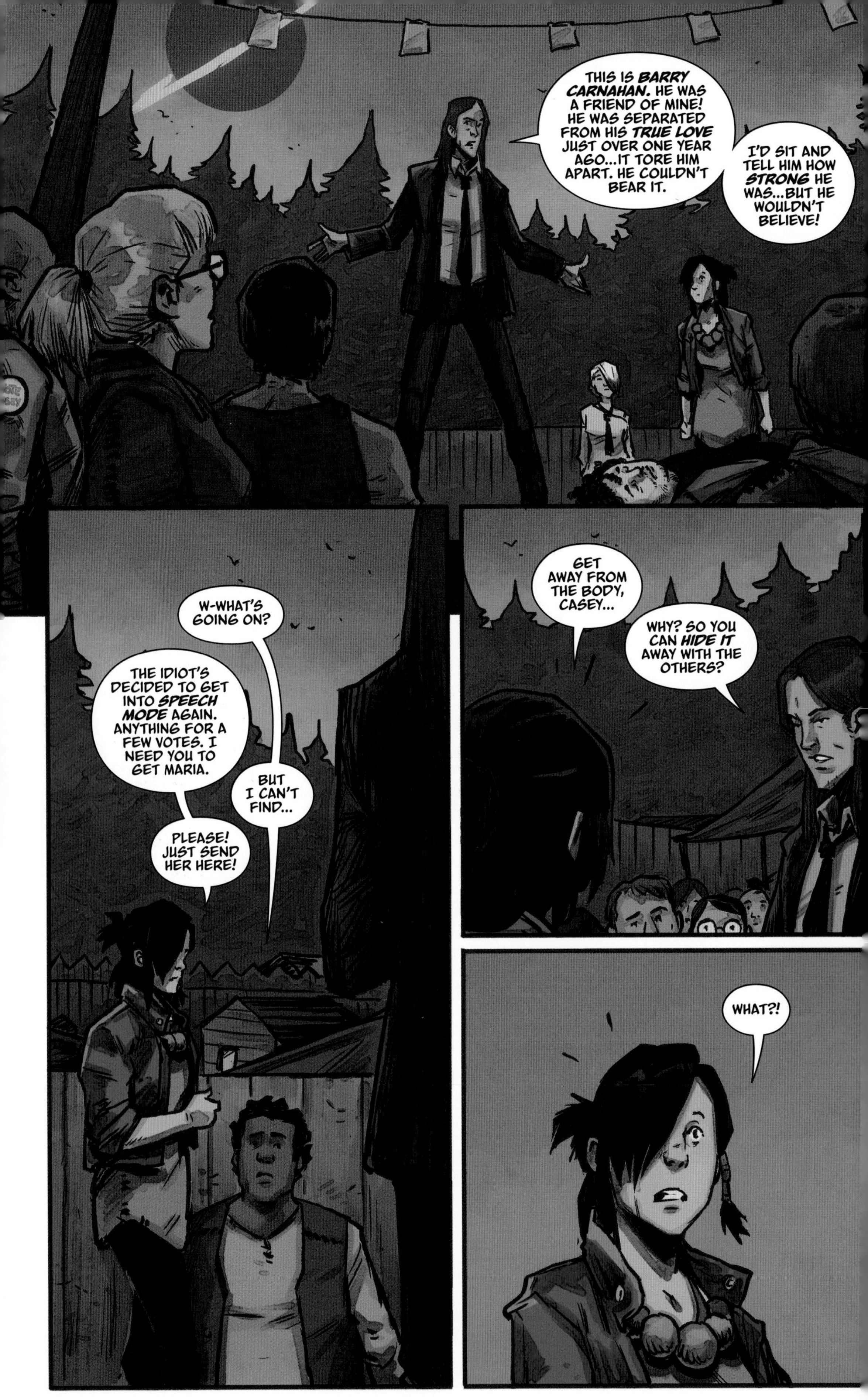
THIS IS BARRY CARNAHAN. HE WAS A FRIEND OF MINE! HE WAS SEPARATED FROM HIS TRUE LOVE JUST OVER ONE YEAR AGO...IT TORE HIM APART. HE COULDN'T BEAR IT.
I'D SIT AND TELL HIM HOW STRONG HE WAS...BUT HE WOULDN'T BELIEVE!
W-WHAT'S GOING ON?
THE IDIOT'S DECIDED TO GET INTO SPEECH MODE AGAIN. ANYTHING FOR A FEW VOTES. I NEED YOU TO GET MARIA.
BUT I CAN'T FIND...
PLEASE! JUST SEND HER HERE!
GET AWAY FROM THE BODY, CASEY...
WHY? SO YOU CAN HIDE IT AWAY WITH THE OTHERS?
WHAT?!

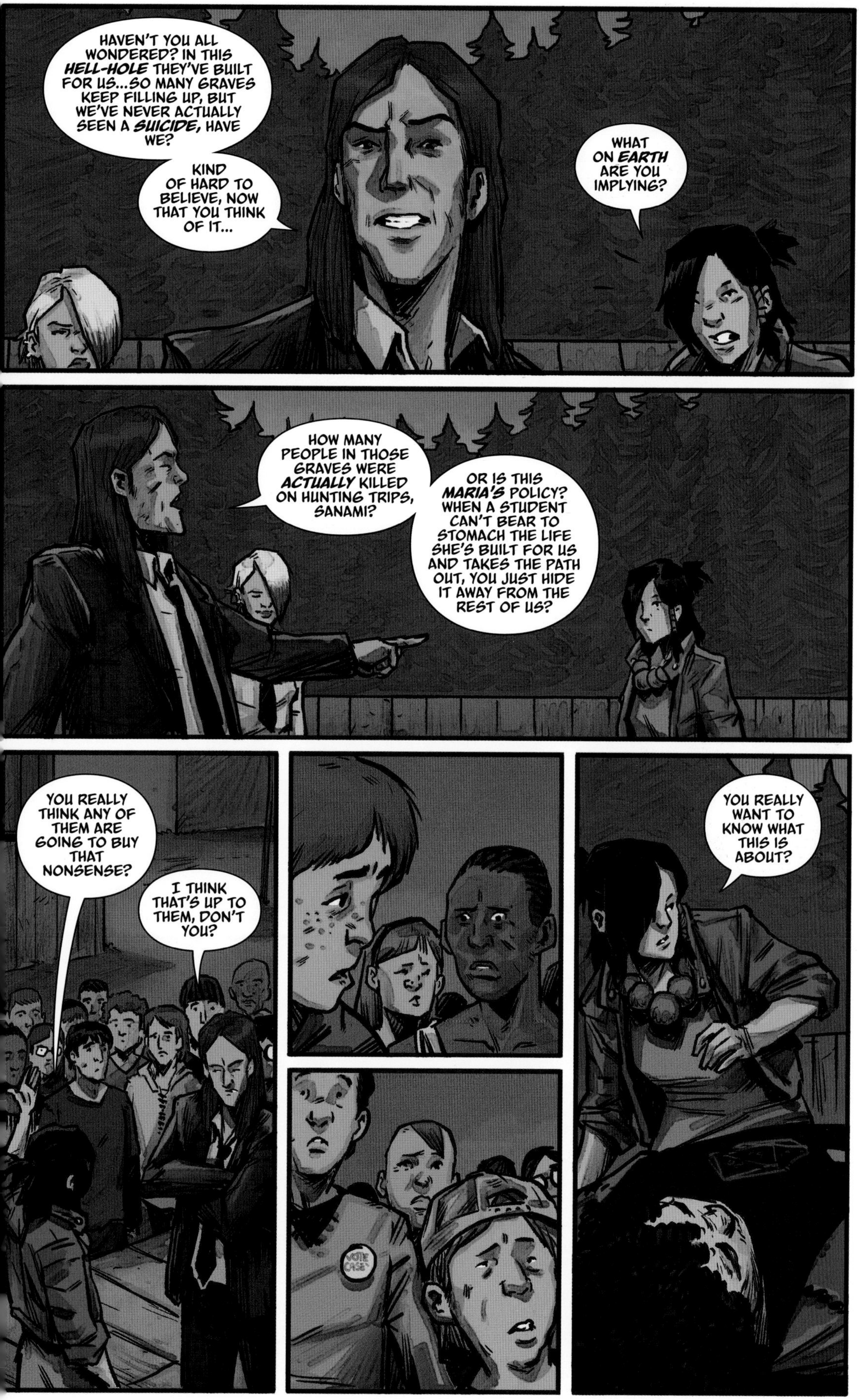
HAVEN'T YOU ALL WONDERED? IN THIS HELL-HOLE THEY'VE BUILT FOR US...SO MANY GRAVES KEEP FILLING UP, BUT WE'VE NEVER ACTUALLY SEEN A SUICIDE, HAVE WE?
KIND OF HARD TO BELIEVE, NOW THAT YOU THINK OF IT...
WHAT ON EARTH ARE YOU IMPLYING?
HOW MANY PEOPLE IN THOSE GRAVES WERE ACTUALLY KILLED ON HUNTING TRIPS, SANAMI?
OR IS THIS MARIA'S POLICY? WHEN A STUDENT CAN'T BEAR TO STOMACH THE LIFE SHE'S BUILT FOR US AND TAKES THE PATH OUT, YOU JUST HIDE IT AWAY FROM THE REST OF US?
YOU REALLY THINK ANY OF THEM ARE GOING TO BUY THAT NONSENSE?
I THINK THAT'S UP TO THEM, DON'T YOU?
VOTE CASE
YOU REALLY WANT TO KNOW WHAT THIS IS ABOUT?

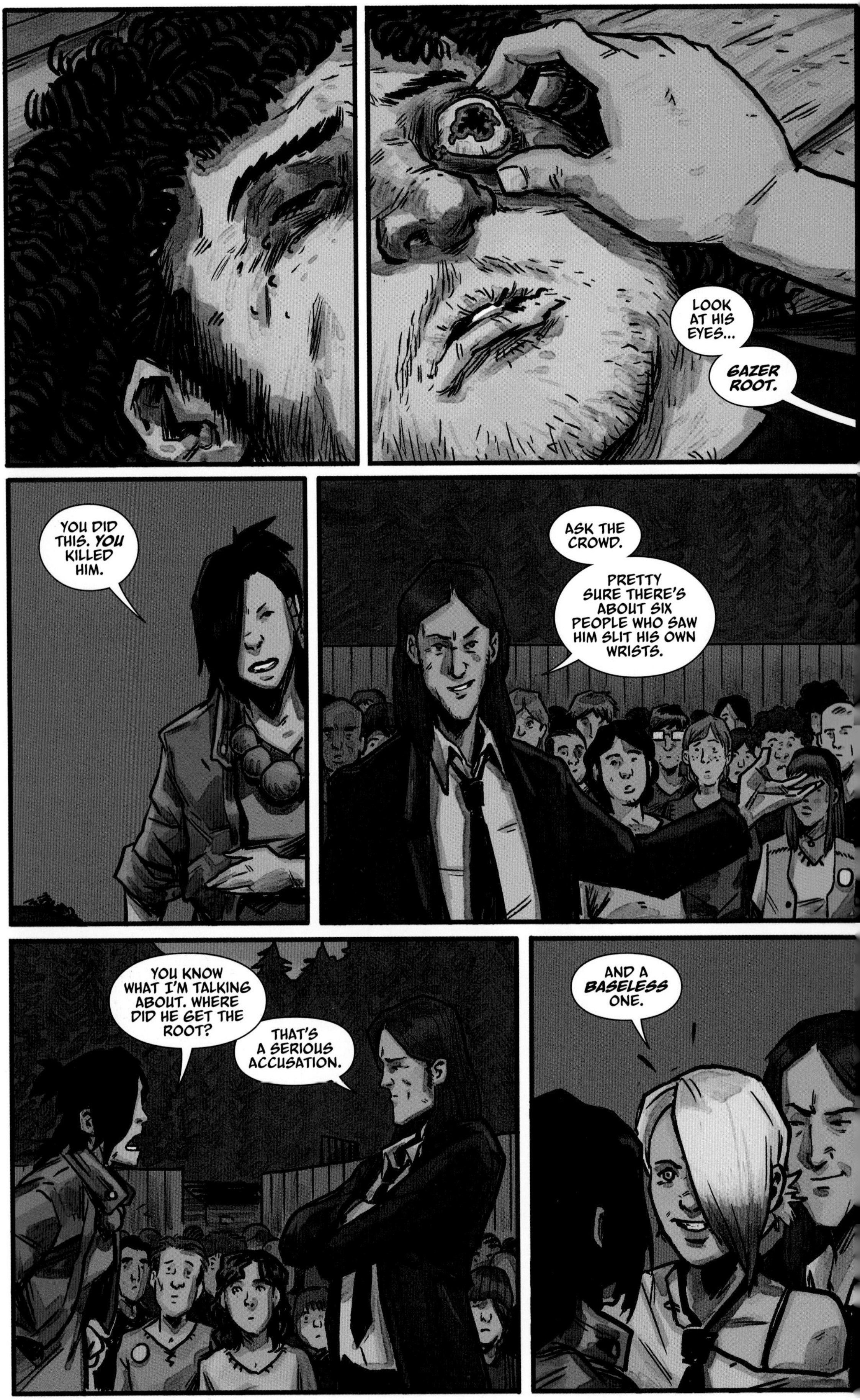
LOOK AT HIS EYES...
GAZER ROOT.
YOU DID THIS. YOU KILLED HIM.
ASK THE CROWD.
PRETTY SURE THERE'S ABOUT SIX PEOPLE WHO SAW HIM SLIT HIS OWN WRISTS.
YOU KNOW WHAT I'M TALKING ABOUT. WHERE DID HE GET THE ROOT?
THAT'S A SERIOUS ACCUSATION.
AND A BASELESS ONE.

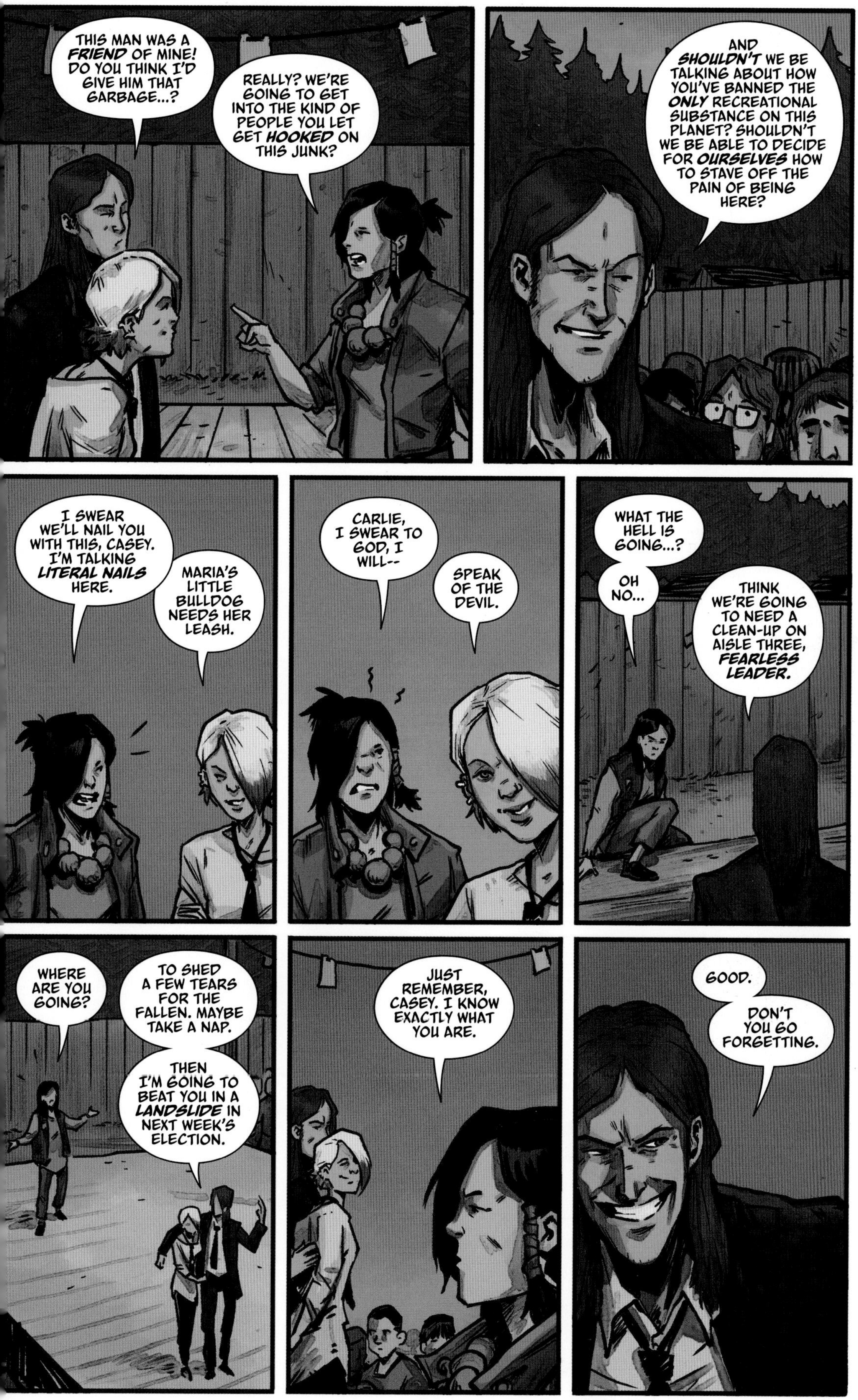

THIS MAN WAS A FRIEND OF MINE! DO YOU THINK I'D GIVE HIM THAT GARBAGE...?
REALLY? WE'RE GOING TO GET INTO THE KIND OF PEOPLE YOU LET GET HOOKED ON THIS JUNK?
AND SHOULDN'T WE BE TALKING ABOUT HOW YOU'VE BANNED THE ONLY RECREATIONAL SUBSTANCE ON THIS PLANET? SHOULDN'T WE BE ABLE TO DECIDE FOR OURSELVES HOW TO STAVE OFF THE PAIN OF BEING HERE?
I SWEAR WE'LL NAIL YOU WITH THIS, CASEY. I'M TALKING LITERAL NAILS HERE.
MARIA'S LITTLE BULLDOG NEEDS HER LEASH.
CARLIE, I SWEAR TO GOD, I WILL--
SPEAK OF THE DEVIL.
WHAT THE HELL IS GOING...?
OH NO...
THINK WE'RE GOING TO NEED A CLEAN-UP ON AISLE THREE, FEARLESS LEADER.
WHERE ARE YOU GOING?
TO SHED A FEW TEARS FOR THE FALLEN. MAYBE TAKE A NAP.
THEN I'M GOING TO BEAT YOU IN A LANDSLIDE IN NEXT WEEK'S ELECTION.
JUST REMEMBER, CASEY. I KNOW EXACTLY WHAT YOU ARE.
GOOD.
DON'T YOU GO FORGETTING.

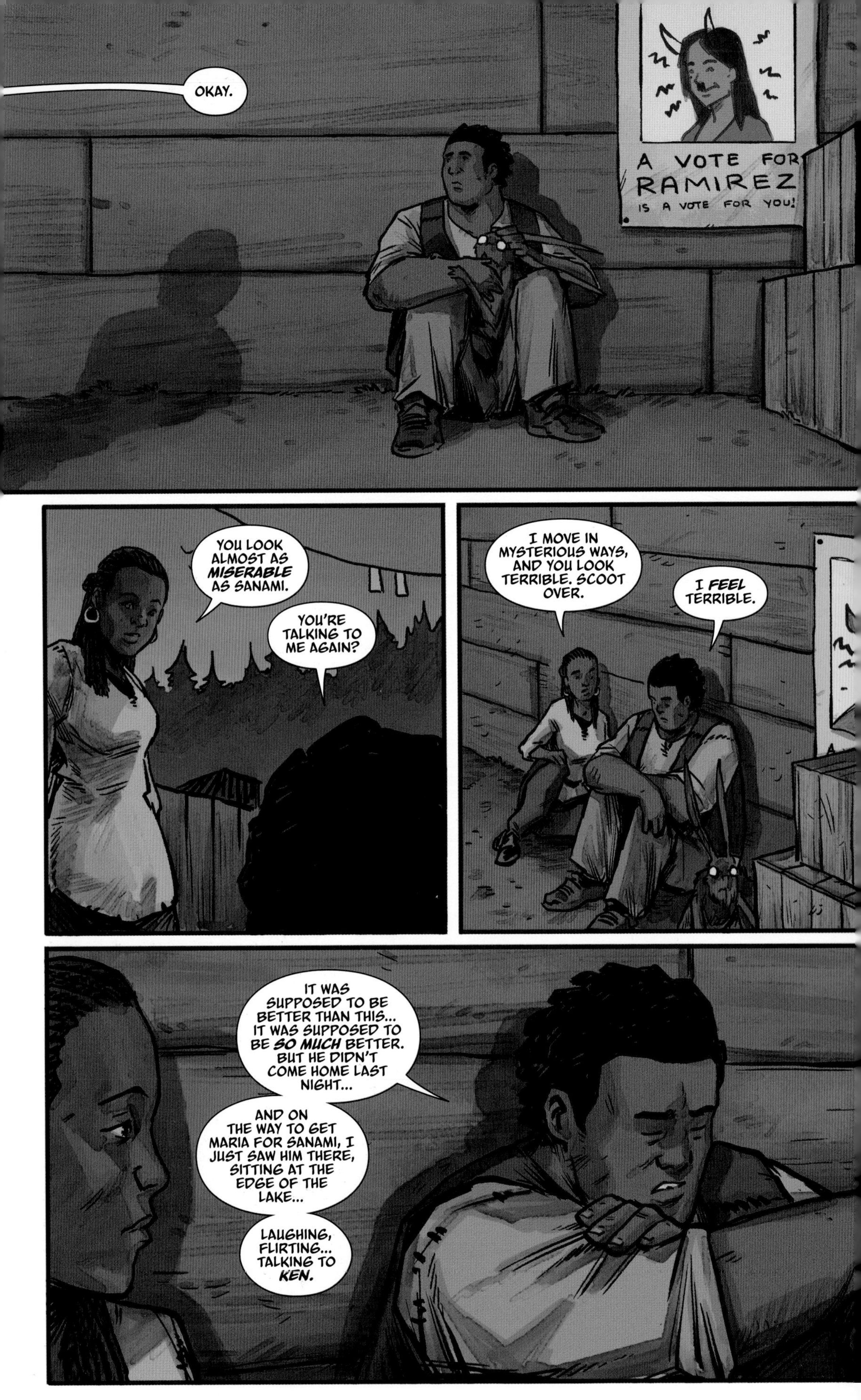
OKAY.
A VOTE FOR RAMIREZ IS A VOTE FOR YOU!
YOU LOOK ALMOST AS *MISERABLE* AS SANAMI.
YOU'RE TALKING TO ME AGAIN?
I MOVE IN MYSTERIOUS WAYS, AND YOU LOOK TERRIBLE. SCOOT OVER.
I *FEEL* TERRIBLE.
IT WAS SUPPOSED TO BE BETTER THAN THIS... IT WAS SUPPOSED TO BE *SO MUCH* BETTER. BUT HE DIDN'T COME HOME LAST NIGHT...
AND ON THE WAY TO GET MARIA FOR SANAMI, I JUST SAW HIM THERE, SITTING AT THE EDGE OF THE LAKE...
LAUGHING, FLIRTING... TALKING TO *KEN.*

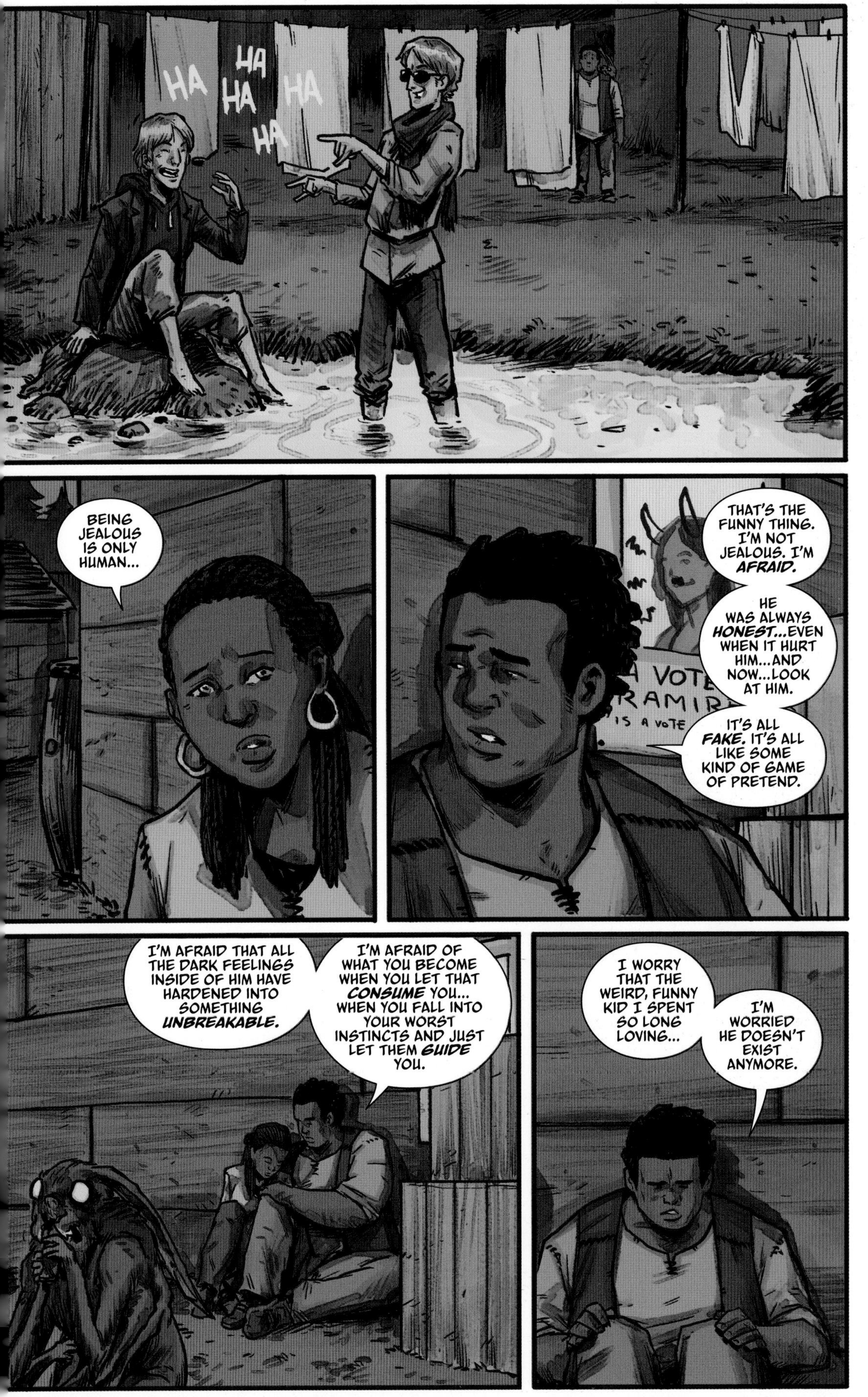
HA HA HA HA HA HA
BEING JEALOUS IS ONLY HUMAN...
THAT'S THE FUNNY THING. I'M NOT JEALOUS. I'M AFRAID.
HE WAS ALWAYS HONEST...EVEN WHEN IT HURT HIM...AND NOW...LOOK AT HIM.
IT'S ALL FAKE. IT'S ALL LIKE SOME KIND OF GAME OF PRETEND.
I'M AFRAID THAT ALL THE DARK FEELINGS INSIDE OF HIM HAVE HARDENED INTO SOMETHING UNBREAKABLE.
I'M AFRAID OF WHAT YOU BECOME WHEN YOU LET THAT CONSUME YOU... WHEN YOU FALL INTO YOUR WORST INSTINCTS AND JUST LET THEM GUIDE YOU.
I WORRY THAT THE WEIRD, FUNNY KID I SPENT SO LONG LOVING...
I'M WORRIED HE DOESN'T EXIST ANYMORE.

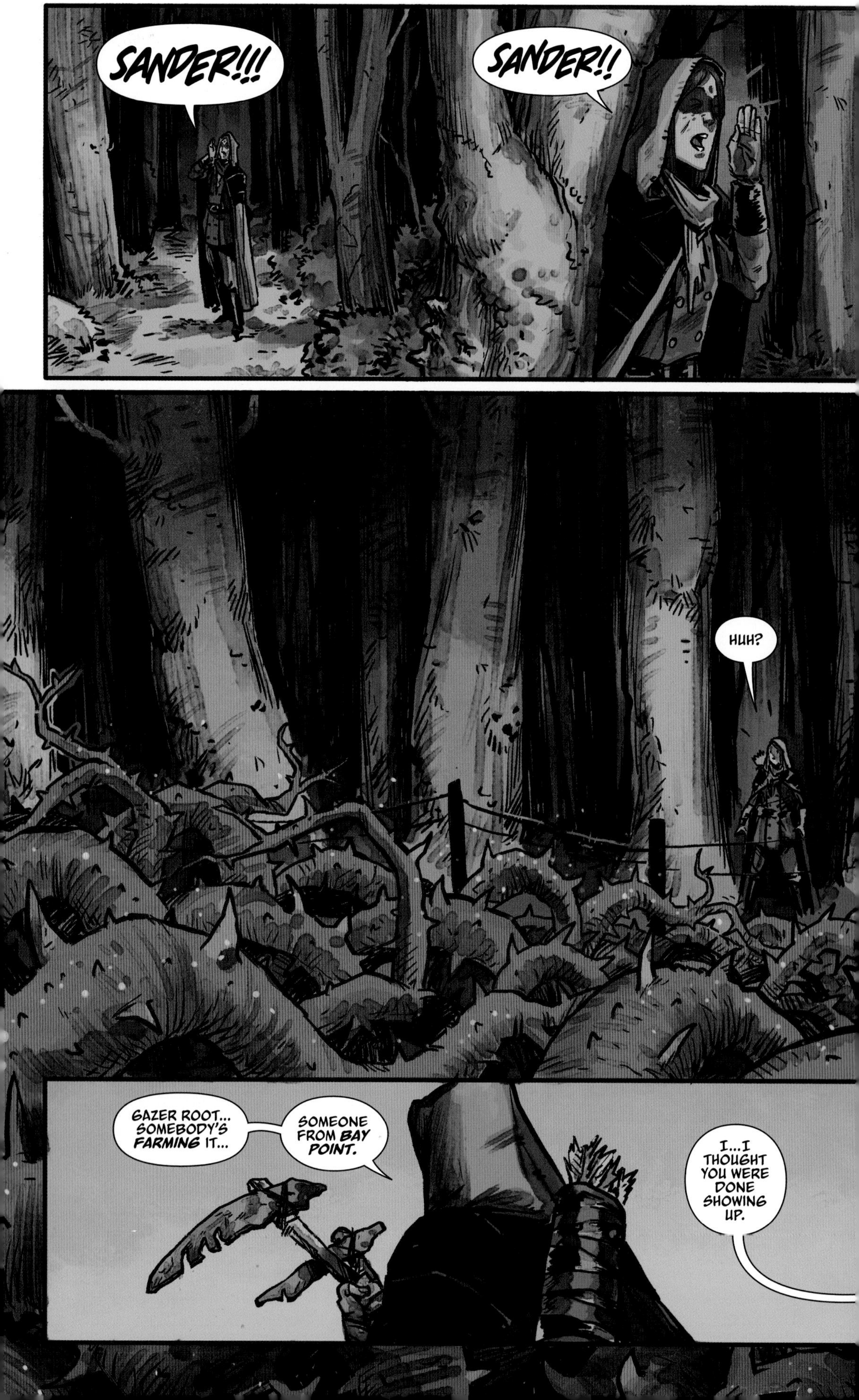
SANDER!!!
SANDER!!
HUH?
GAZER ROOT... SOMEBODY'S FARMING IT...
SOMEONE FROM BAY POINT.
I...I THOUGHT YOU WERE DONE SHOWING UP.

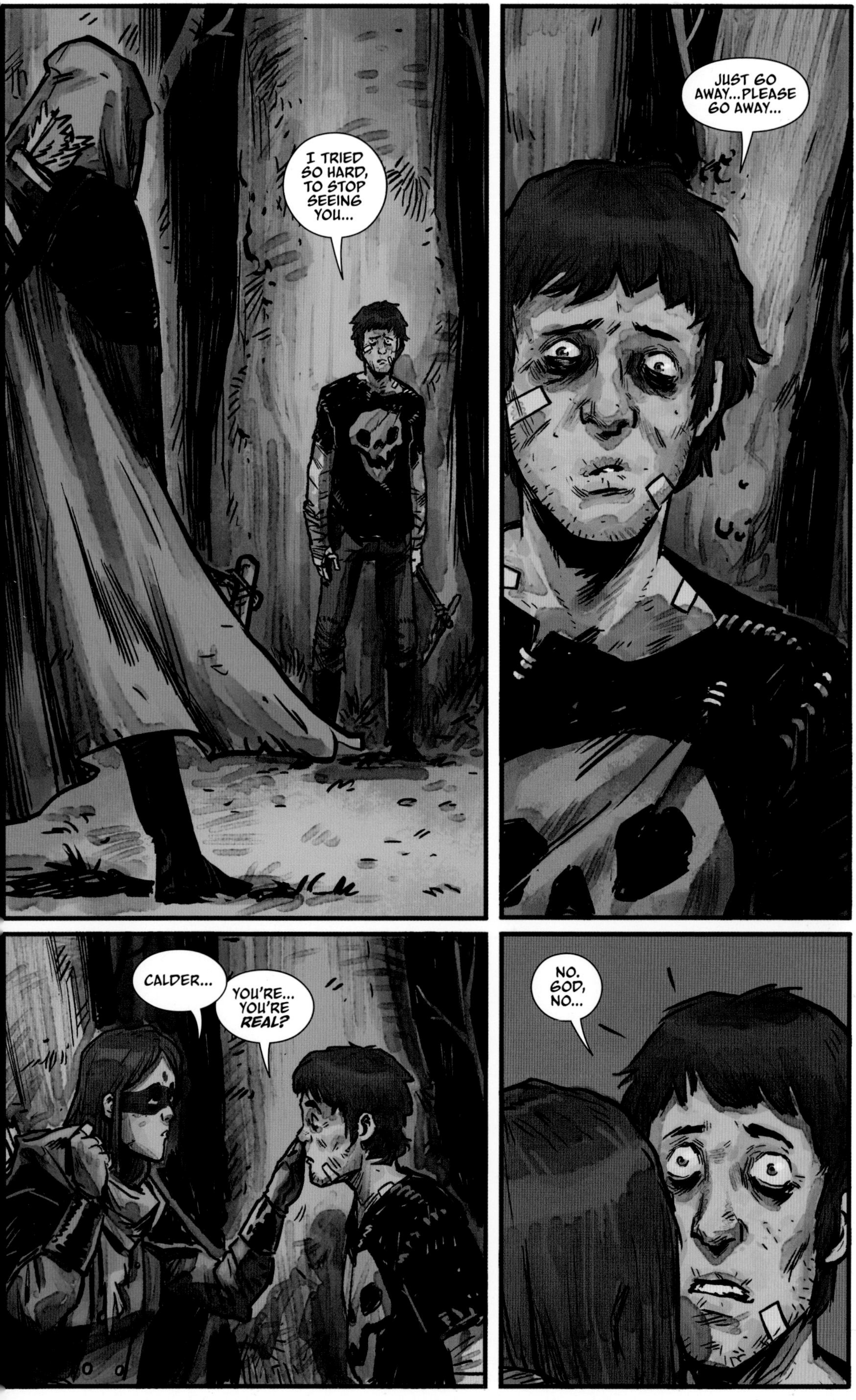
I TRIED SO HARD, TO STOP SEEING YOU...
JUST GO AWAY...PLEASE GO AWAY...
CALDER...
YOU'RE... YOU'RE *REAL?*
NO. GOD, NO...

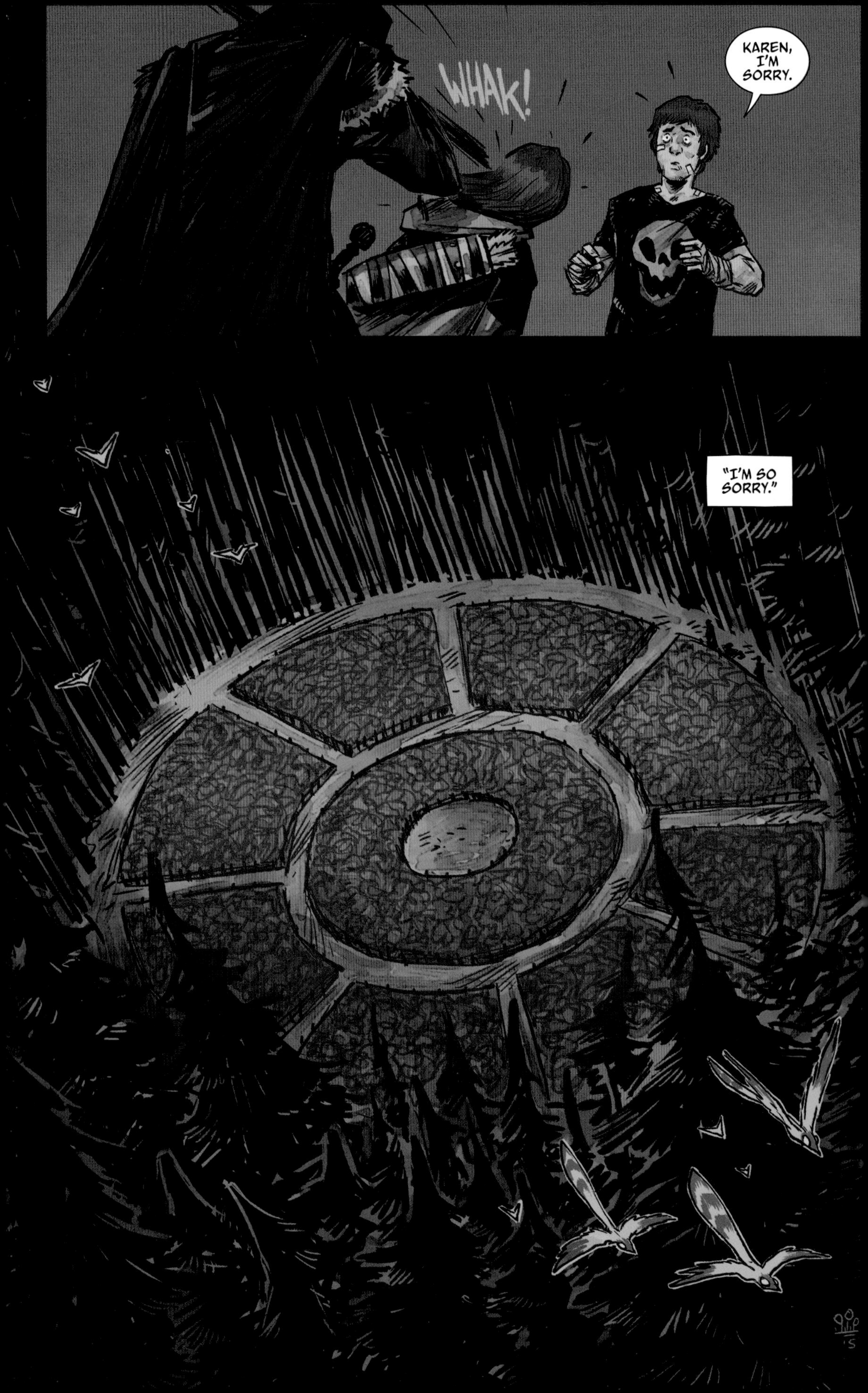

WHAK!
KAREN, I'M SORRY.
"I'M SO SORRY."

CHAPTER
FIFTEEN

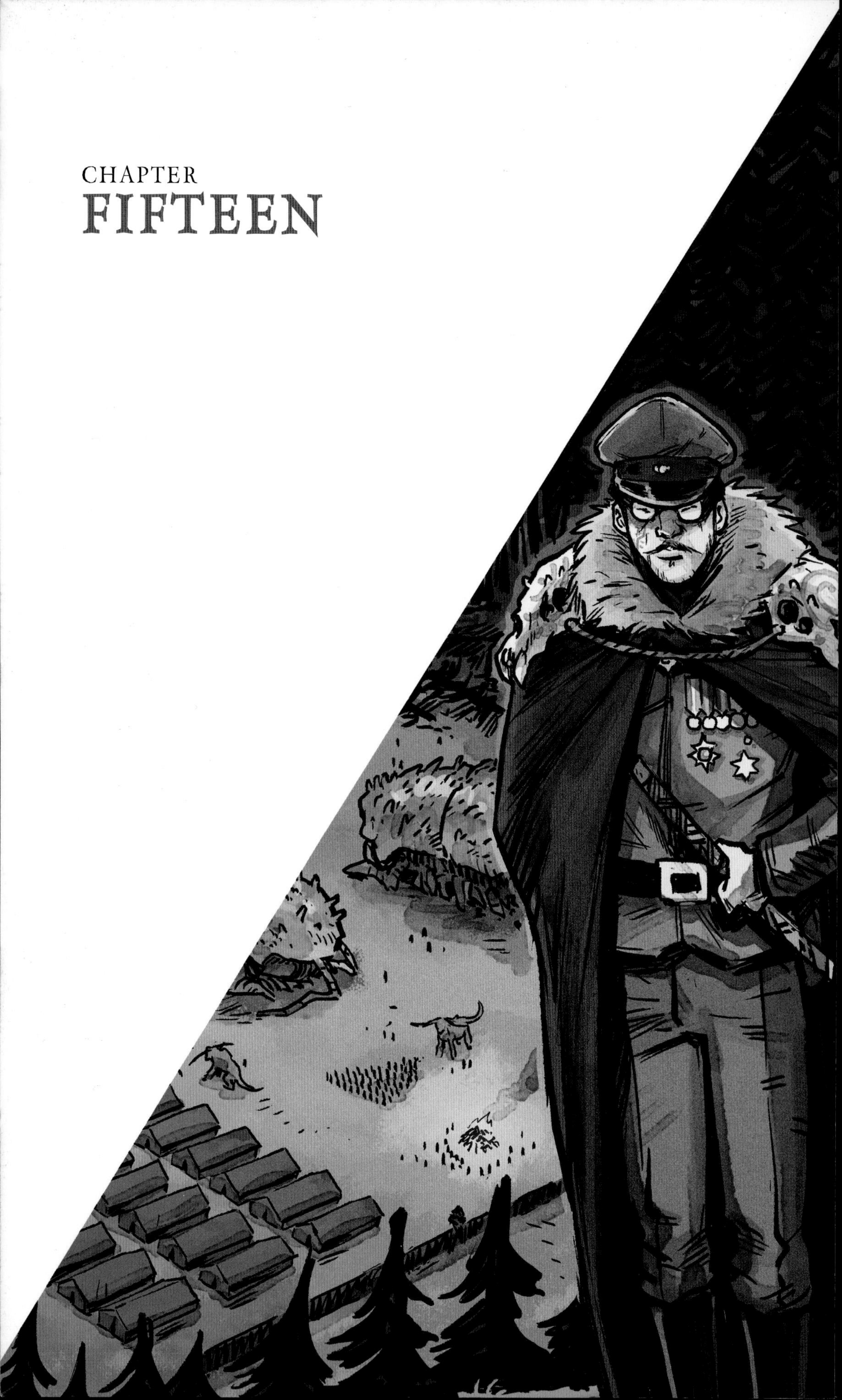

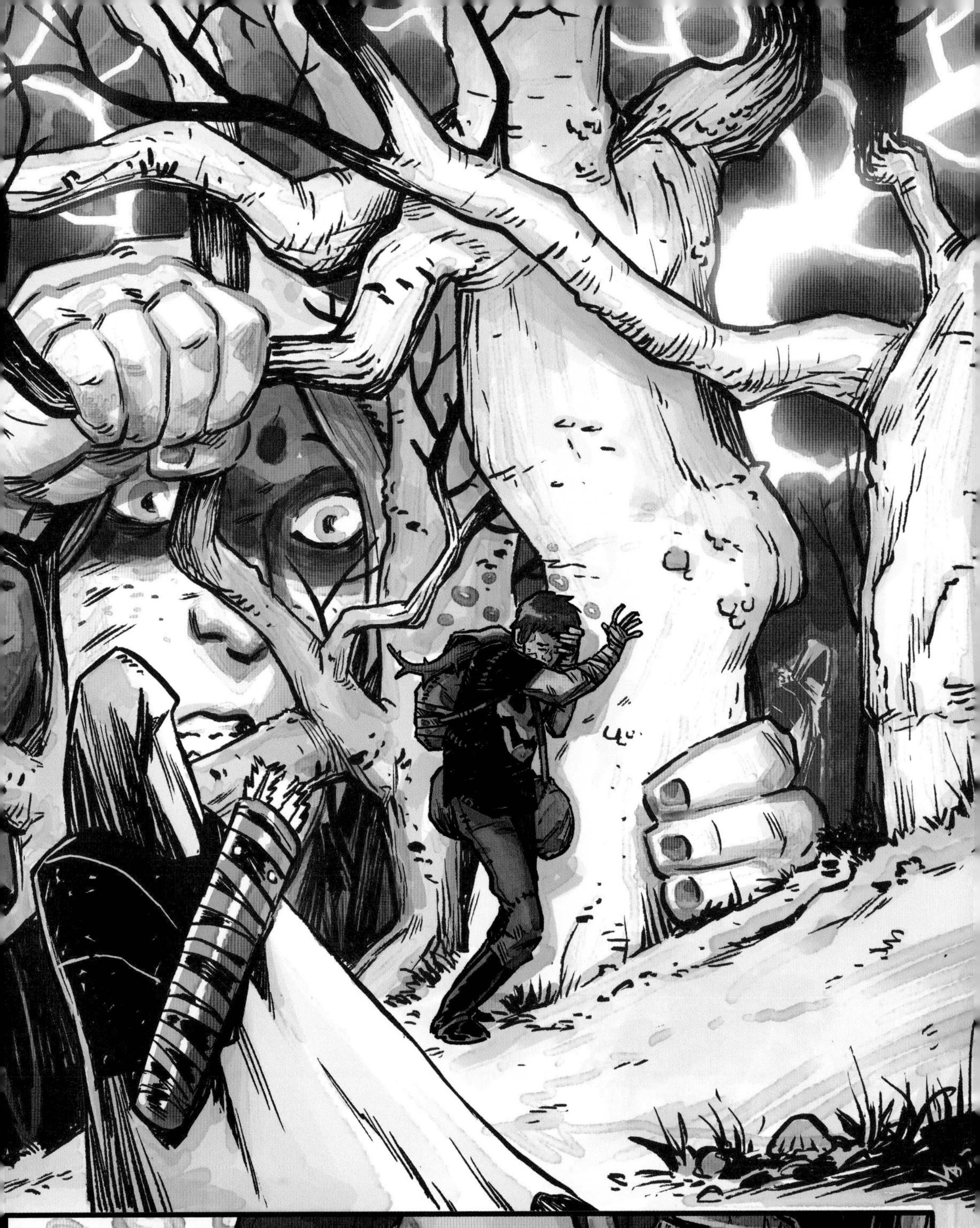

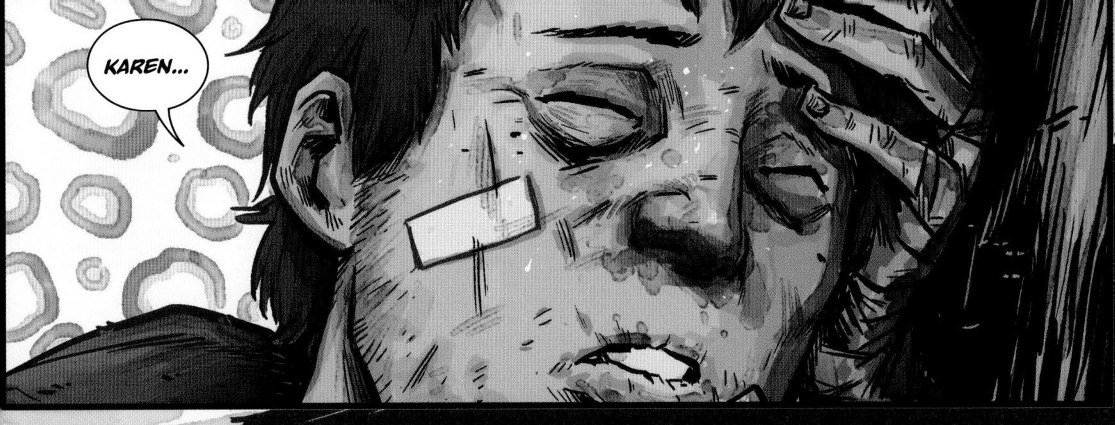
KAREN...

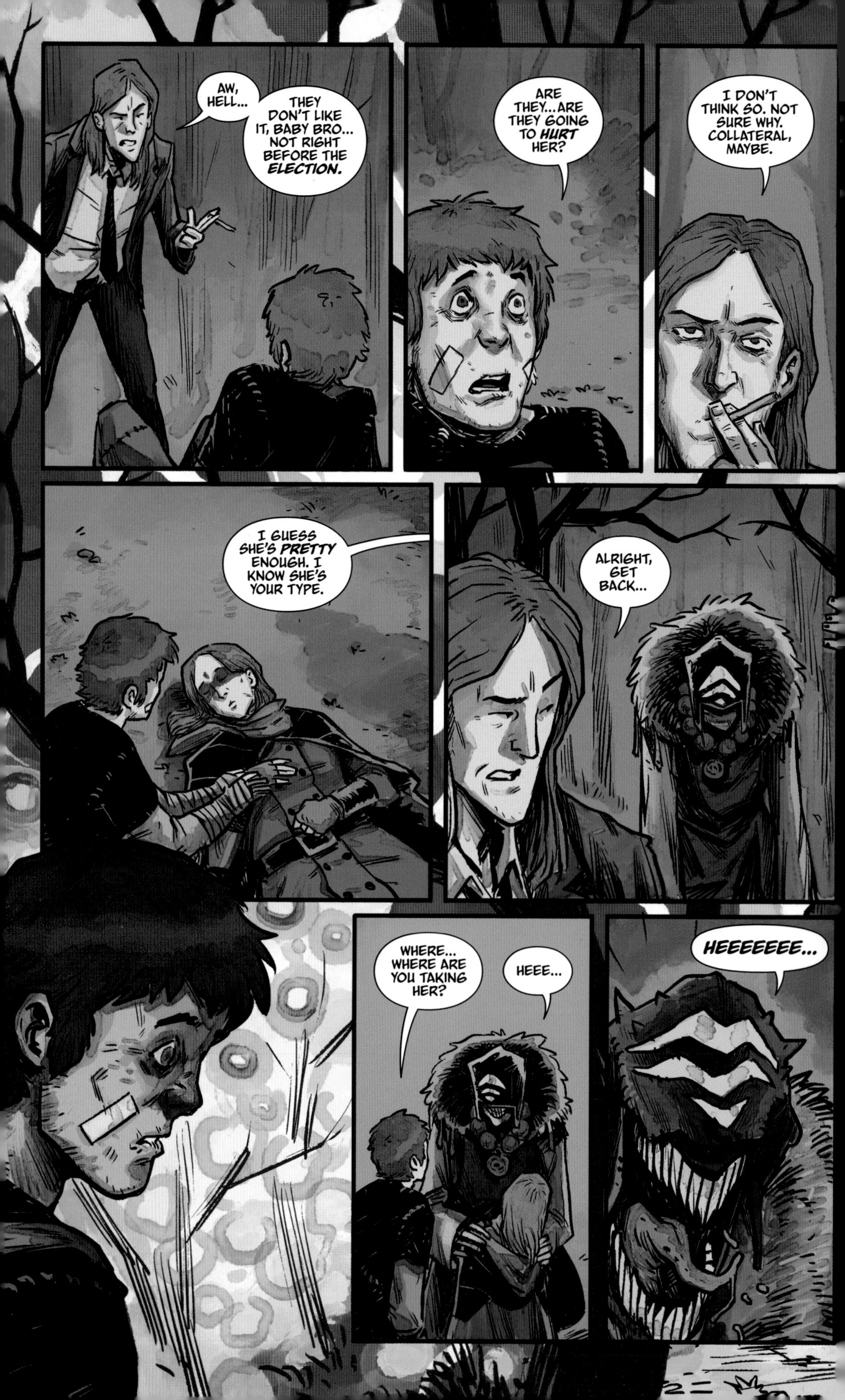
AW, HELL...
THEY DON'T LIKE IT, BABY BRO... NOT RIGHT BEFORE THE ELECTION.
ARE THEY...ARE THEY GOING TO HURT HER?
I DON'T THINK SO. NOT SURE WHY. COLLATERAL, MAYBE.
I GUESS SHE'S PRETTY ENOUGH. I KNOW SHE'S YOUR TYPE.
ALRIGHT, GET BACK...
WHERE... WHERE ARE YOU TAKING HER?
HEEE...
HEEEEEEE...

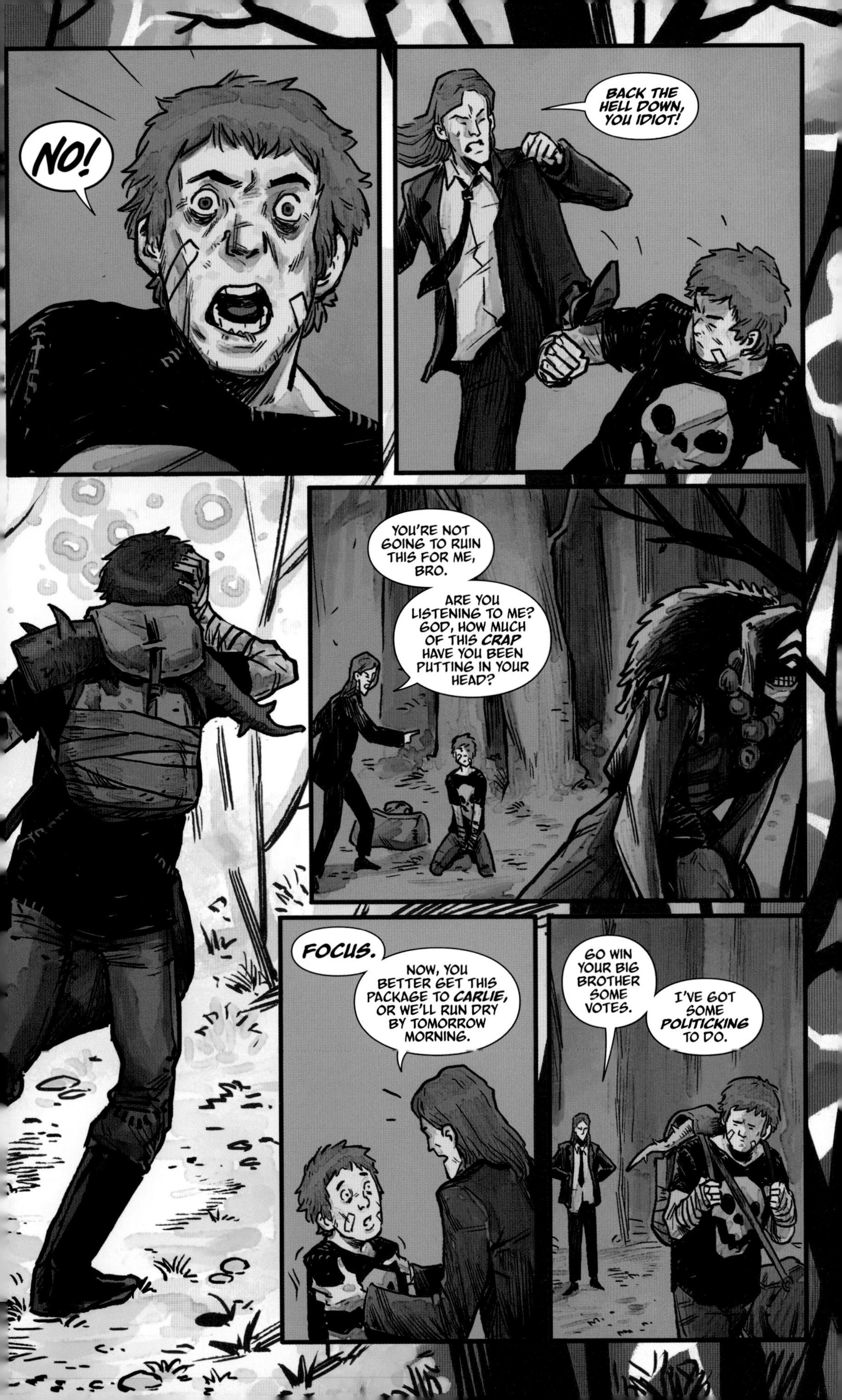

NO!
BACK THE HELL DOWN, YOU IDIOT!
YOU'RE NOT GOING TO RUIN THIS FOR ME, BRO.
ARE YOU LISTENING TO ME? GOD, HOW MUCH OF THIS CRAP HAVE YOU BEEN PUTTING IN YOUR HEAD?
FOCUS.
NOW, YOU BETTER GET THIS PACKAGE TO CARLIE, OR WE'LL RUN DRY BY TOMORROW MORNING.
GO WIN YOUR BIG BROTHER SOME VOTES.
I'VE GOT SOME POLITICKING TO DO.

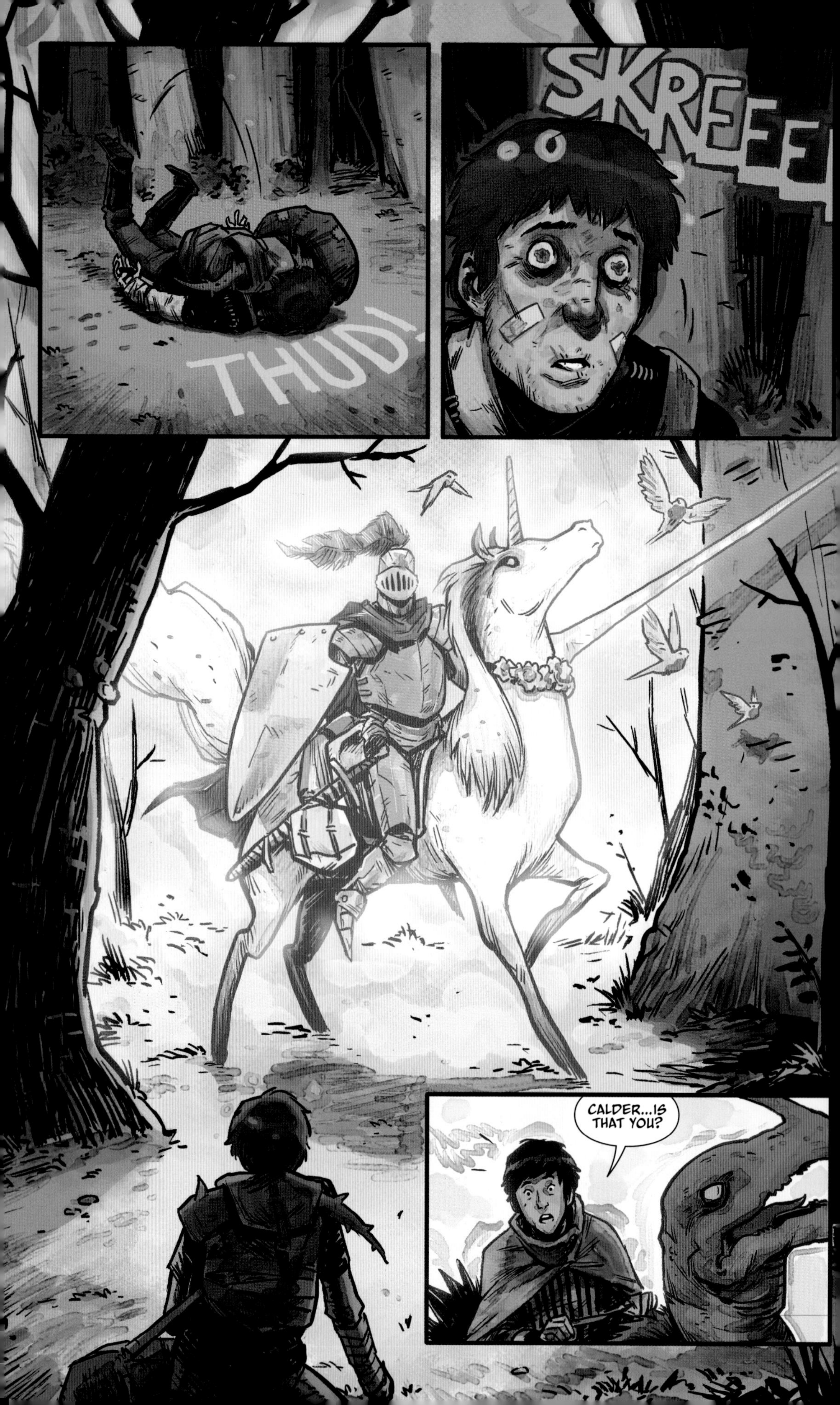
THUD!
SKREEE
CALDER...IS THAT YOU?

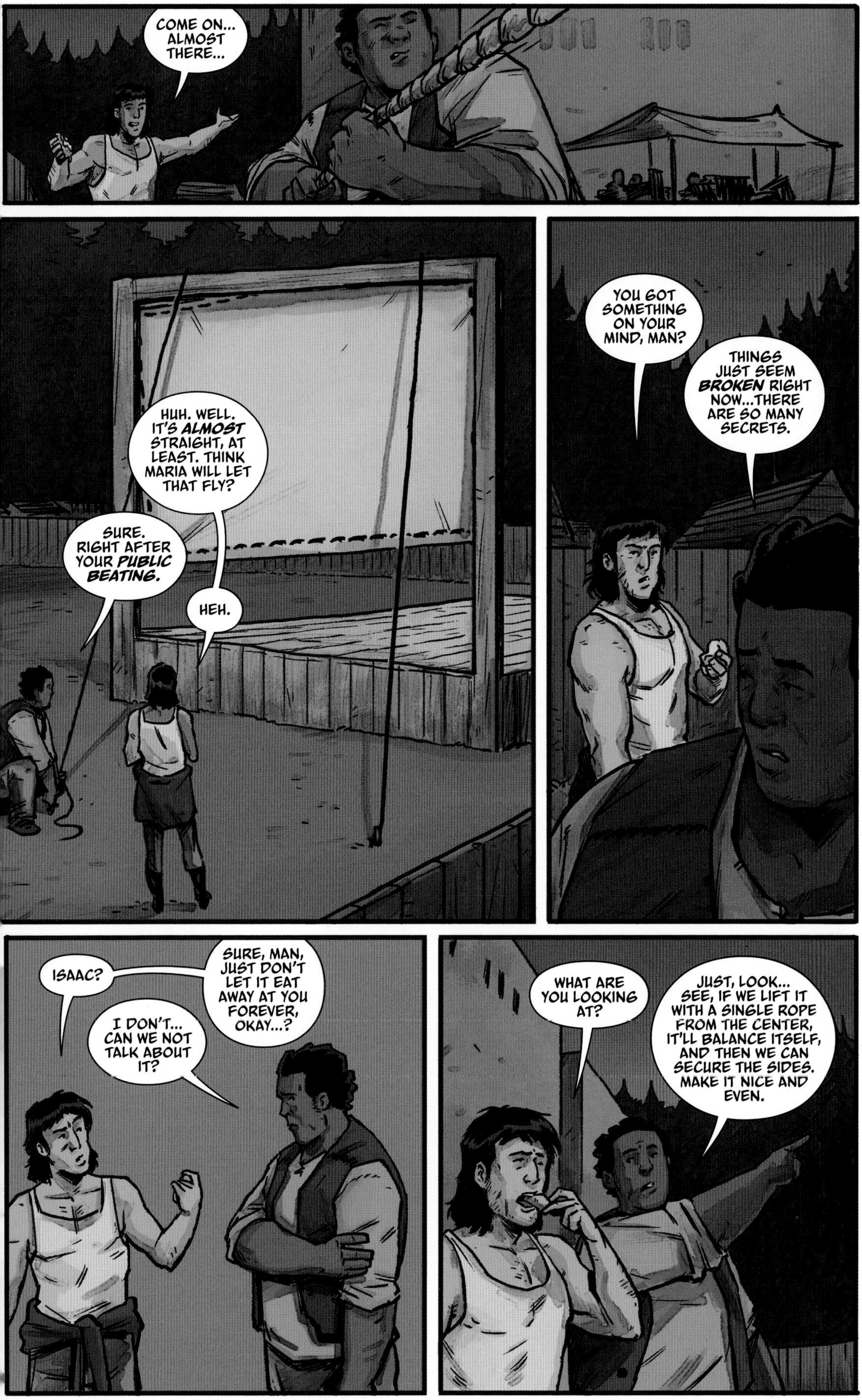
COME ON... ALMOST THERE...
HUH. WELL. IT'S ALMOST STRAIGHT, AT LEAST. THINK MARIA WILL LET THAT FLY?
SURE. RIGHT AFTER YOUR PUBLIC BEATING.
HEH.
YOU GOT SOMETHING ON YOUR MIND, MAN?
THINGS JUST SEEM BROKEN RIGHT NOW...THERE ARE SO MANY SECRETS.
ISAAC?
SURE, MAN, JUST DON'T LET IT EAT AWAY AT YOU FOREVER, OKAY...?
I DON'T... CAN WE NOT TALK ABOUT IT?
WHAT ARE YOU LOOKING AT?
JUST, LOOK... SEE, IF WE LIFT IT WITH A SINGLE ROPE FROM THE CENTER, IT'LL BALANCE ITSELF, AND THEN WE CAN SECURE THE SIDES. MAKE IT NICE AND EVEN.

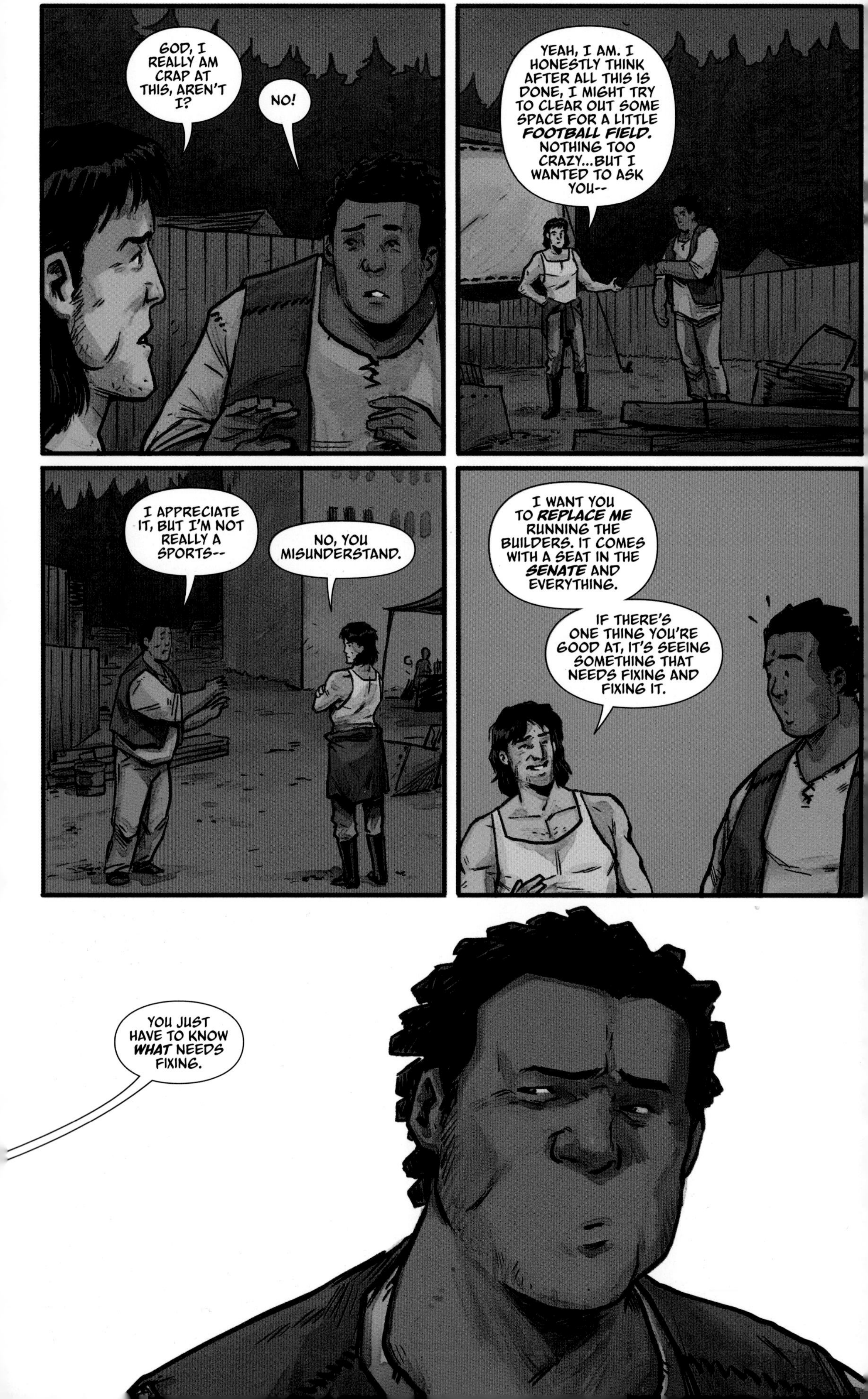
GOD, I REALLY AM CRAP AT THIS, AREN'T I?
NO!
YEAH, I AM. I HONESTLY THINK AFTER ALL THIS IS DONE, I MIGHT TRY TO CLEAR OUT SOME SPACE FOR A LITTLE FOOTBALL FIELD. NOTHING TOO CRAZY...BUT I WANTED TO ASK YOU--
I APPRECIATE IT, BUT I'M NOT REALLY A SPORTS--
NO, YOU MISUNDERSTAND.
I WANT YOU TO REPLACE ME RUNNING THE BUILDERS. IT COMES WITH A SEAT IN THE SENATE AND EVERYTHING.
IF THERE'S ONE THING YOU'RE GOOD AT, IT'S SEEING SOMETHING THAT NEEDS FIXING AND FIXING IT.
YOU JUST HAVE TO KNOW WHAT NEEDS FIXING.

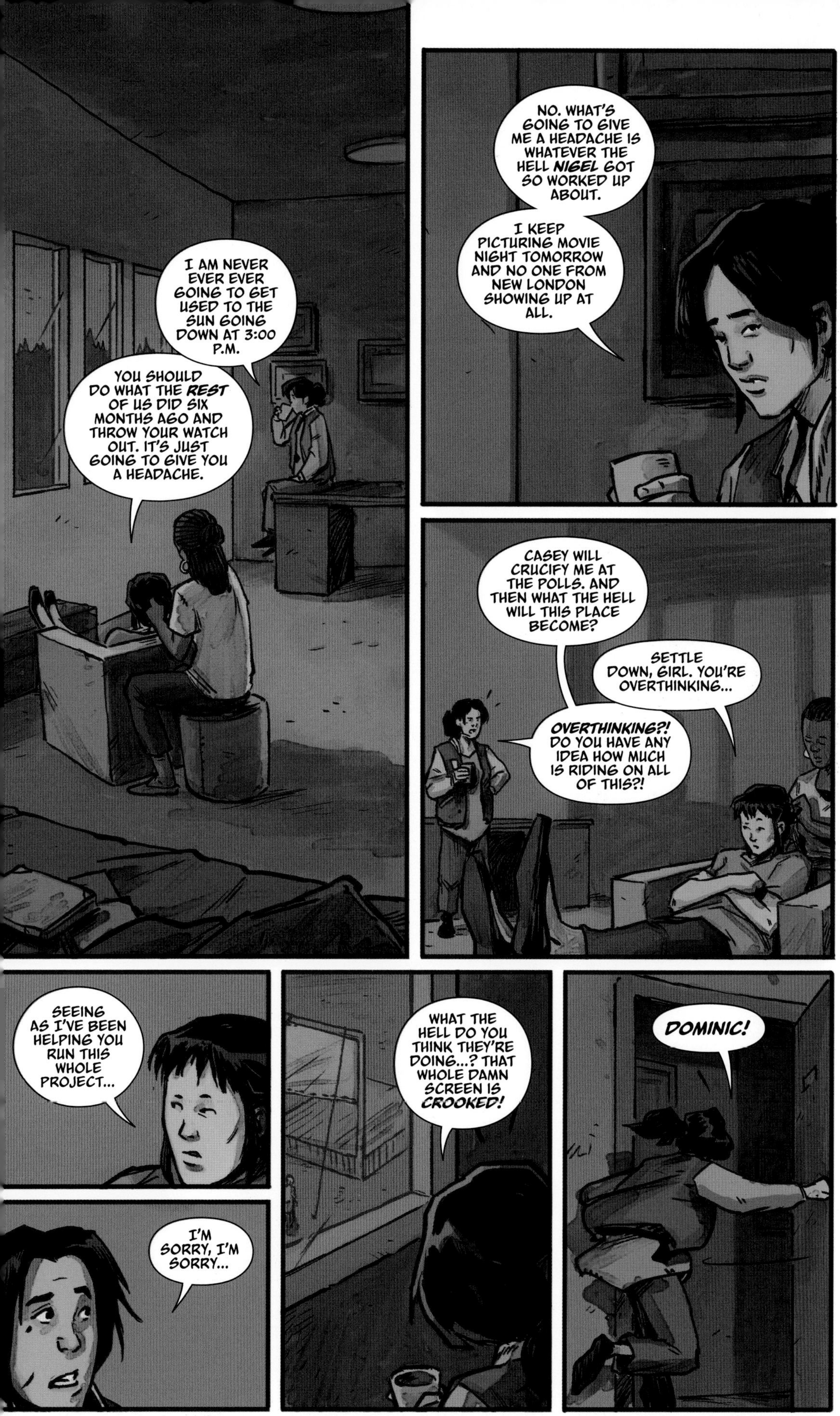
I AM NEVER EVER EVER GOING TO GET USED TO THE SUN GOING DOWN AT 3:00 P.M.
YOU SHOULD DO WHAT THE REST OF US DID SIX MONTHS AGO AND THROW YOUR WATCH OUT. IT'S JUST GOING TO GIVE YOU A HEADACHE.
NO. WHAT'S GOING TO GIVE ME A HEADACHE IS WHATEVER THE HELL NIGEL GOT SO WORKED UP ABOUT.
I KEEP PICTURING MOVIE NIGHT TOMORROW AND NO ONE FROM NEW LONDON SHOWING UP AT ALL.
CASEY WILL CRUCIFY ME AT THE POLLS. AND THEN WHAT THE HELL WILL THIS PLACE BECOME?
SETTLE DOWN, GIRL. YOU'RE OVERTHINKING...
OVERTHINKING?! DO YOU HAVE ANY IDEA HOW MUCH IS RIDING ON ALL OF THIS?!
SEEING AS I'VE BEEN HELPING YOU RUN THIS WHOLE PROJECT...
I'M SORRY, I'M SORRY...
WHAT THE HELL DO YOU THINK THEY'RE DOING...? THAT WHOLE DAMN SCREEN IS CROOKED!
DOMINIC!

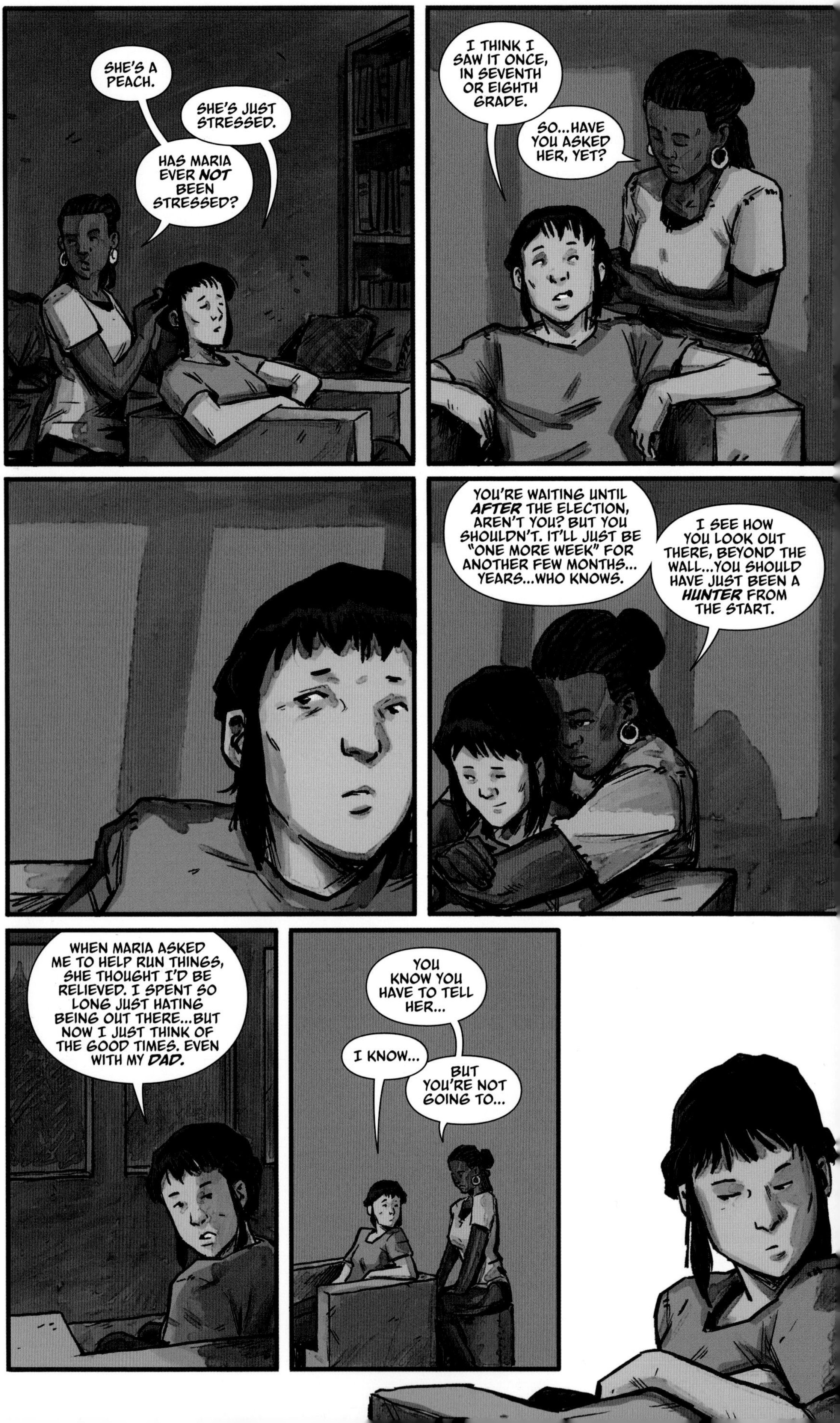
SHE'S A PEACH.
SHE'S JUST STRESSED.
HAS MARIA EVER NOT BEEN STRESSED?
I THINK I SAW IT ONCE, IN SEVENTH OR EIGHTH GRADE.
SO...HAVE YOU ASKED HER, YET?
YOU'RE WAITING UNTIL AFTER THE ELECTION, AREN'T YOU? BUT YOU SHOULDN'T. IT'LL JUST BE "ONE MORE WEEK" FOR ANOTHER FEW MONTHS... YEARS...WHO KNOWS.
I SEE HOW YOU LOOK OUT THERE, BEYOND THE WALL...YOU SHOULD HAVE JUST BEEN A HUNTER FROM THE START.
WHEN MARIA ASKED ME TO HELP RUN THINGS, SHE THOUGHT I'D BE RELIEVED. I SPENT SO LONG JUST HATING BEING OUT THERE...BUT NOW I JUST THINK OF THE GOOD TIMES. EVEN WITH MY DAD.
YOU KNOW YOU HAVE TO TELL HER...
I KNOW...
BUT YOU'RE NOT GOING TO...

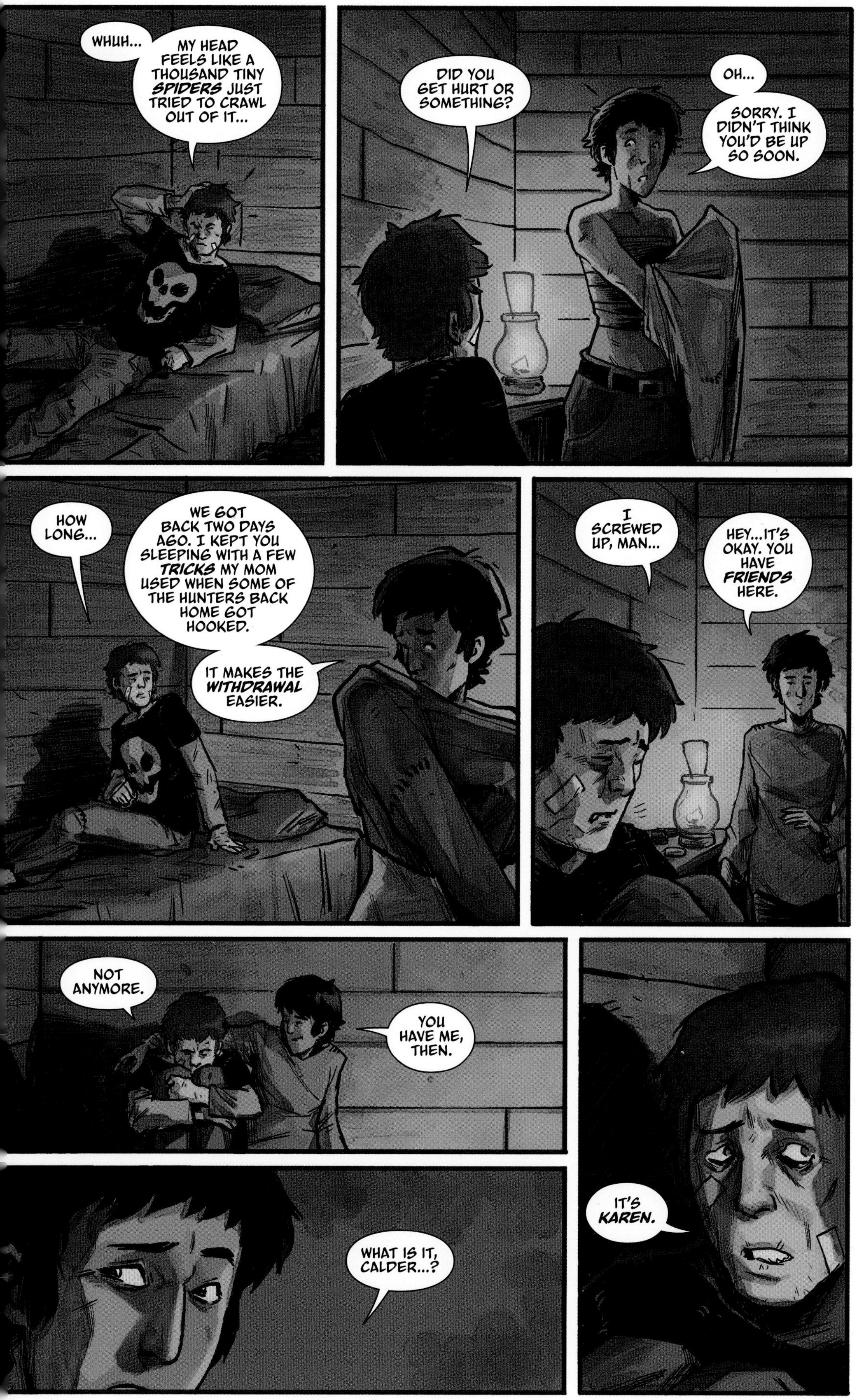
WHUH...
MY HEAD FEELS LIKE A THOUSAND TINY SPIDERS JUST TRIED TO CRAWL OUT OF IT...
DID YOU GET HURT OR SOMETHING?
OH...
SORRY. I DIDN'T THINK YOU'D BE UP SO SOON.
HOW LONG...
WE GOT BACK TWO DAYS AGO. I KEPT YOU SLEEPING WITH A FEW TRICKS MY MOM USED WHEN SOME OF THE HUNTERS BACK HOME GOT HOOKED.
IT MAKES THE WITHDRAWAL EASIER.
I SCREWED UP, MAN...
HEY...IT'S OKAY. YOU HAVE FRIENDS HERE.
NOT ANYMORE.
YOU HAVE ME, THEN.
WHAT IS IT, CALDER...?
IT'S KAREN.

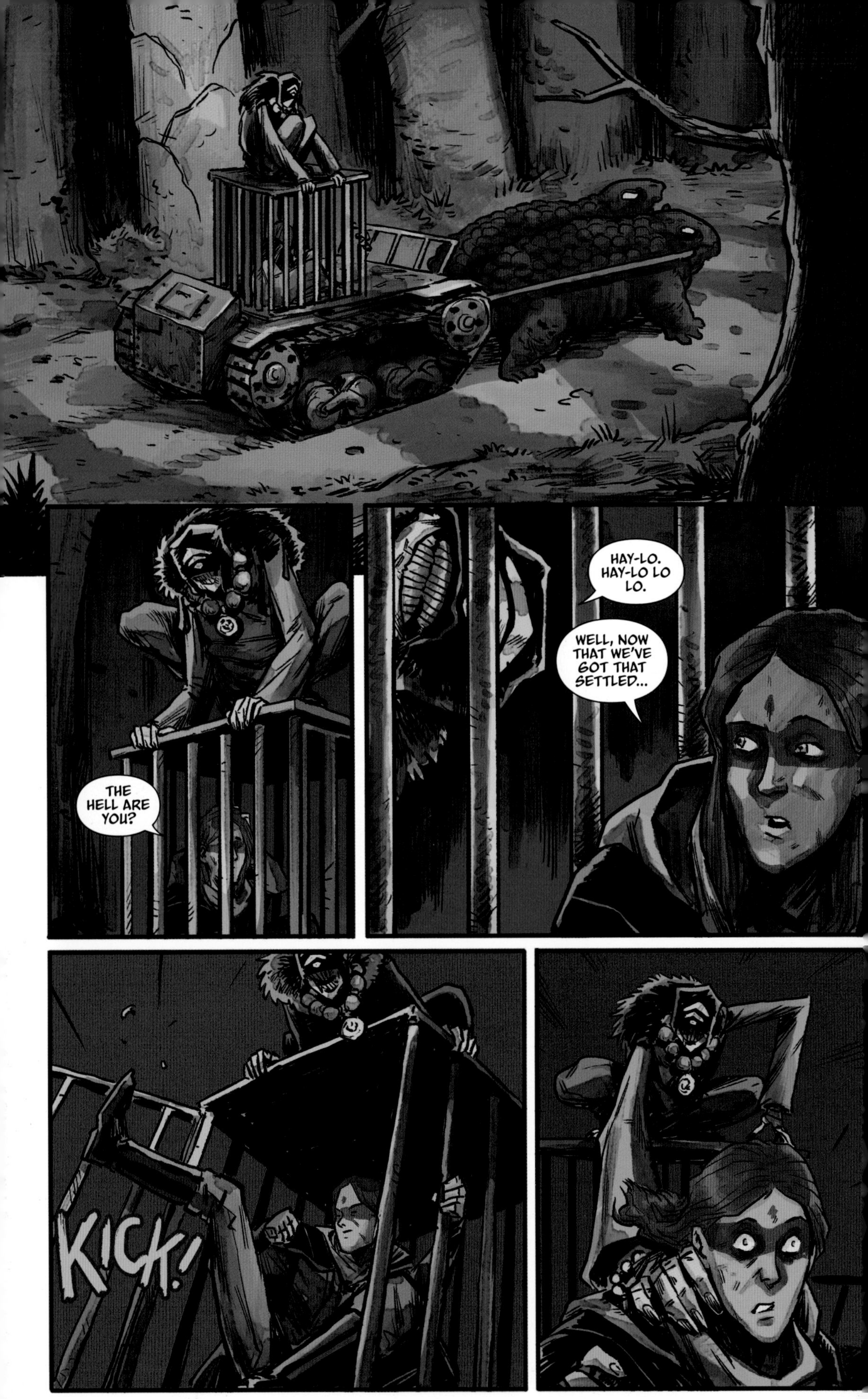
THE HELL ARE YOU?
HAY-LO. HAY-LO LO LO.
WELL, NOW THAT WE'VE GOT THAT SETTLED...
KICK!

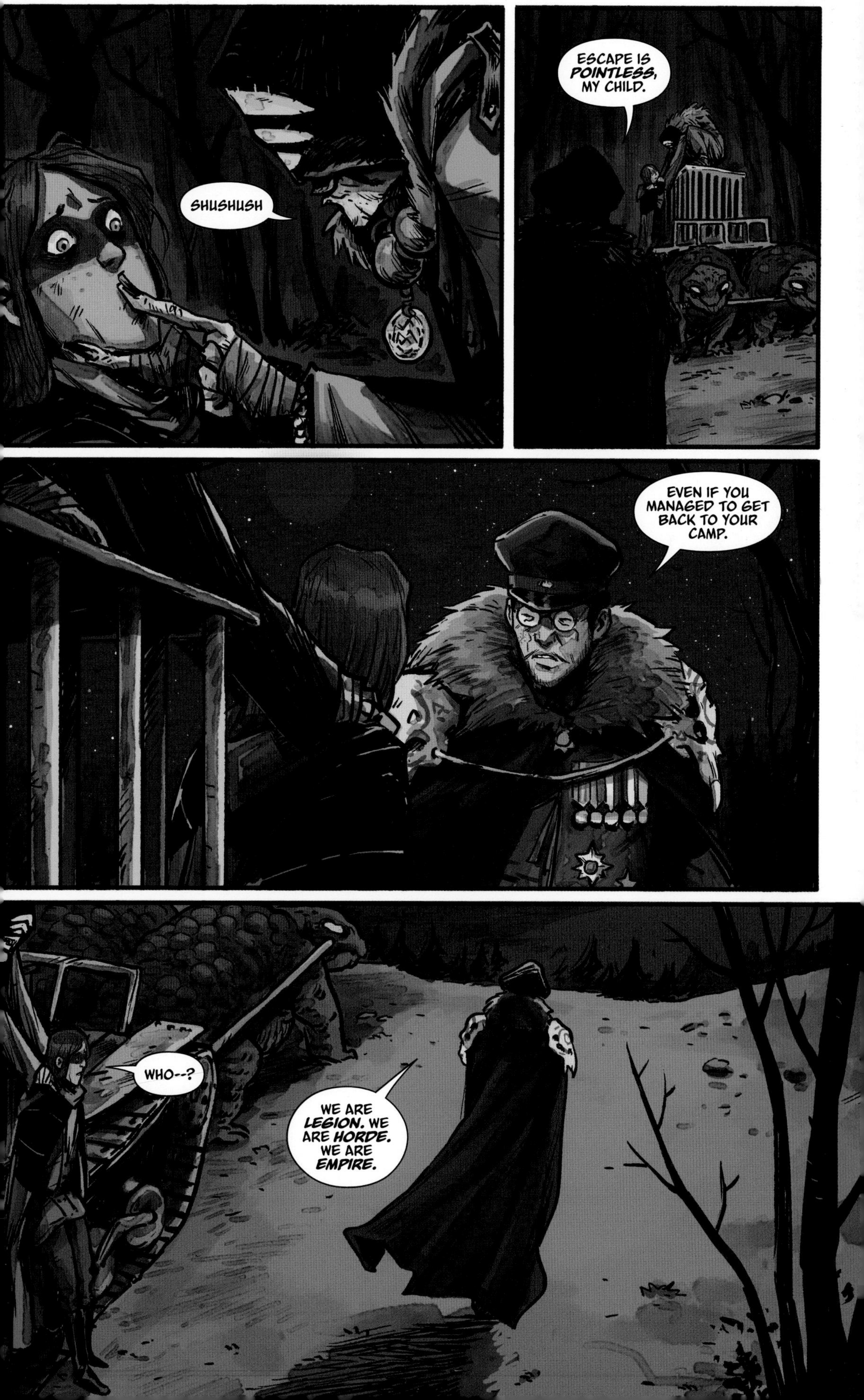
SHUSHUSH
ESCAPE IS POINTLESS, MY CHILD.
EVEN IF YOU MANAGED TO GET BACK TO YOUR CAMP.
WHO--?
WE ARE LEGION. WE ARE HORDE. WE ARE EMPIRE.

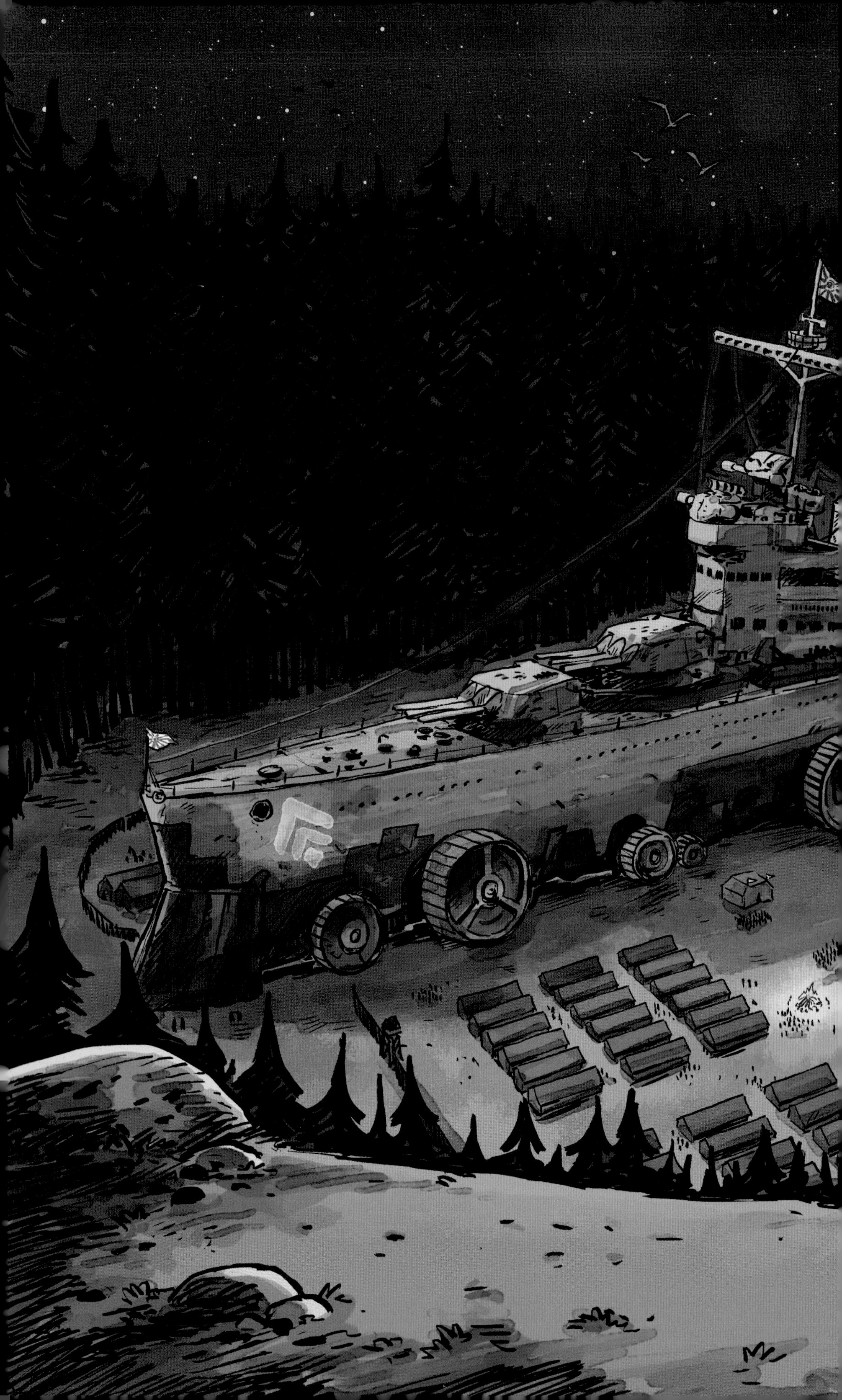

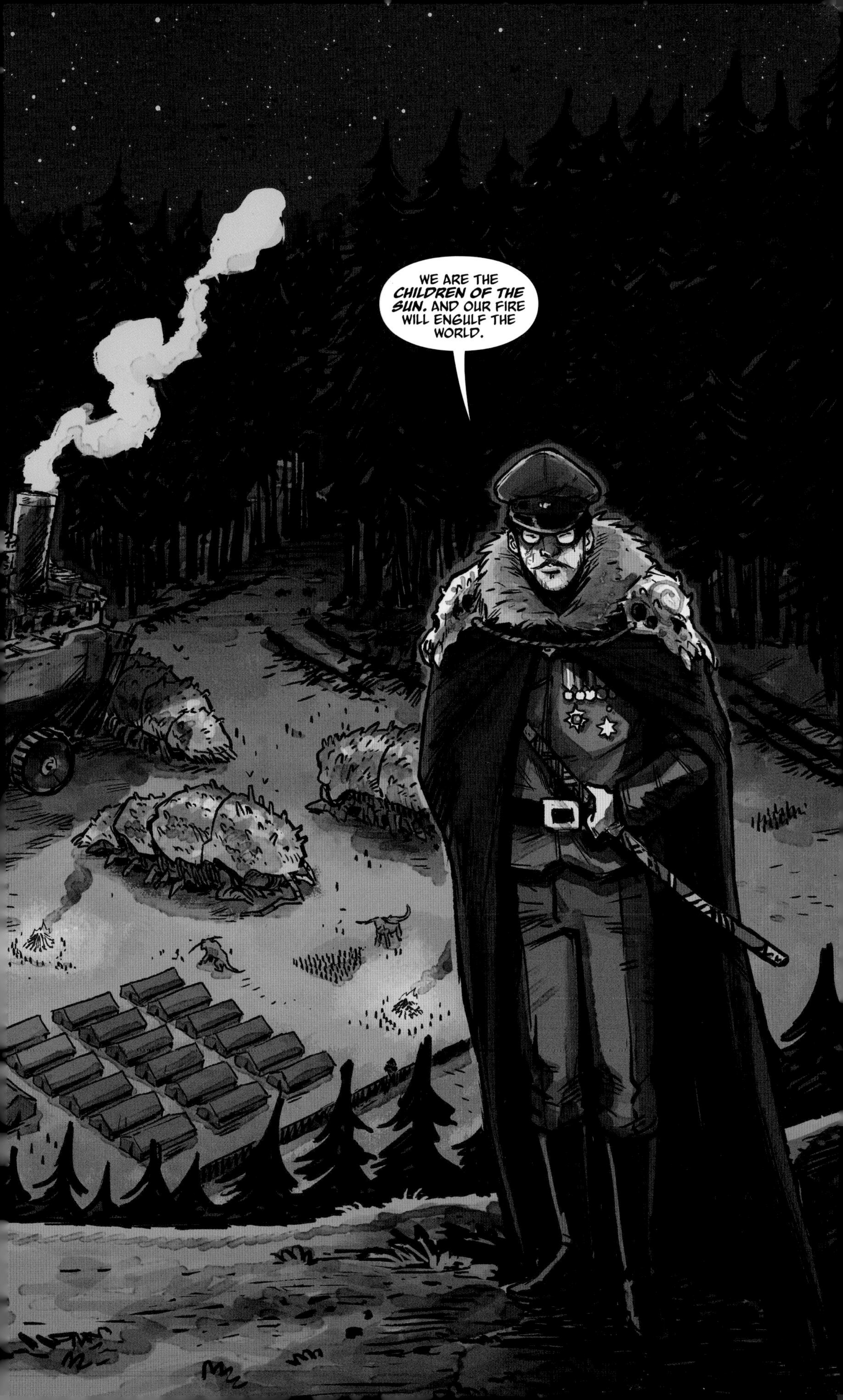
WE ARE THE ***CHILDREN OF THE SUN.*** AND OUR FIRE WILL ENGULF THE WORLD.

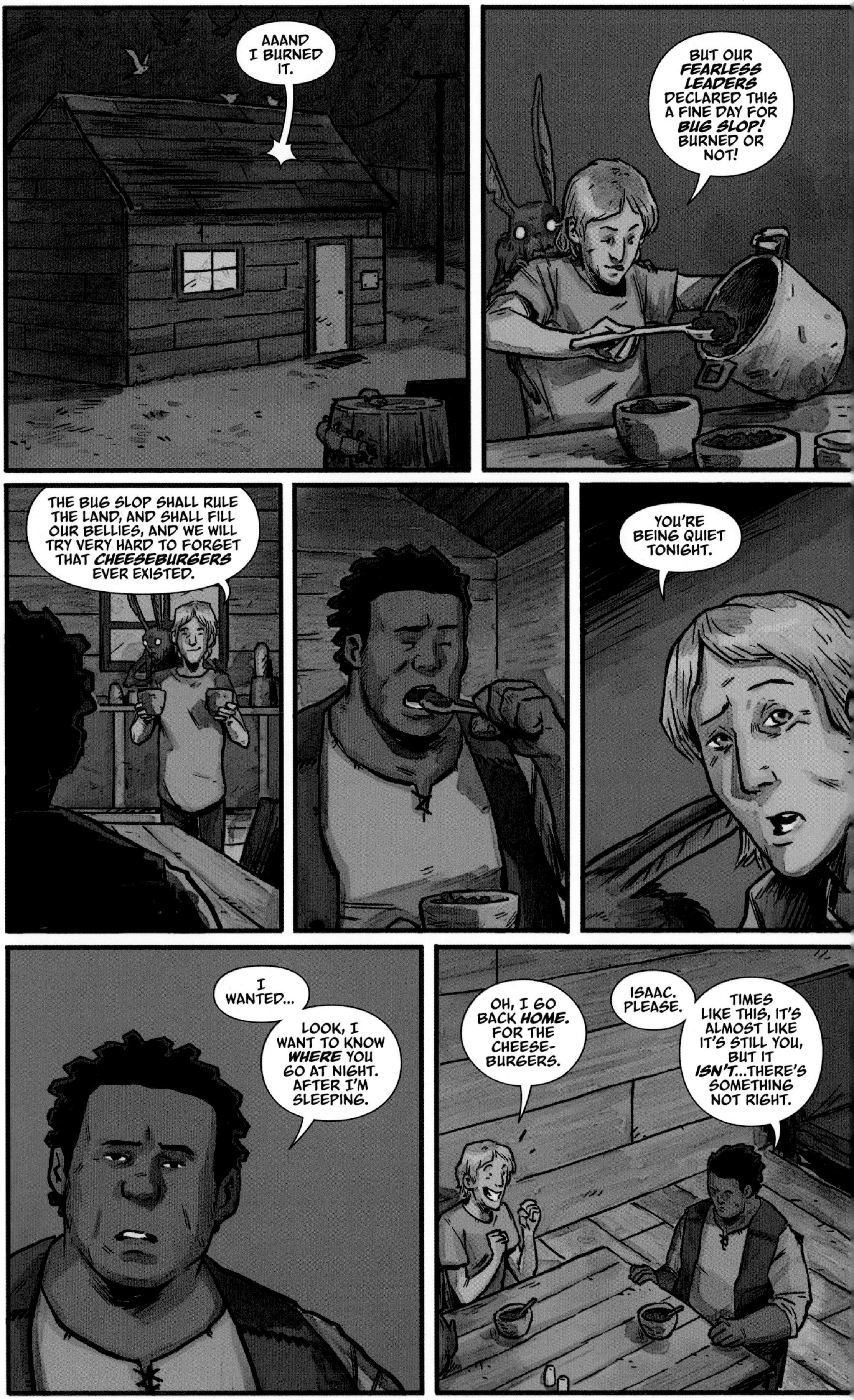
AAAND I BURNED IT.
BUT OUR FEARLESS LEADERS DECLARED THIS A FINE DAY FOR BUG SLOP! BURNED OR NOT!
THE BUG SLOP SHALL RULE THE LAND, AND SHALL FILL OUR BELLIES, AND WE WILL TRY VERY HARD TO FORGET THAT CHEESEBURGERS EVER EXISTED.
YOU'RE BEING QUIET TONIGHT.
I WANTED...
LOOK, I WANT TO KNOW WHERE YOU GO AT NIGHT. AFTER I'M SLEEPING.
OH, I GO BACK HOME. FOR THE CHEESE-BURGERS.
ISAAC. PLEASE.
TIMES LIKE THIS, IT'S ALMOST LIKE IT'S STILL YOU, BUT IT ISN'T...THERE'S SOMETHING NOT RIGHT.

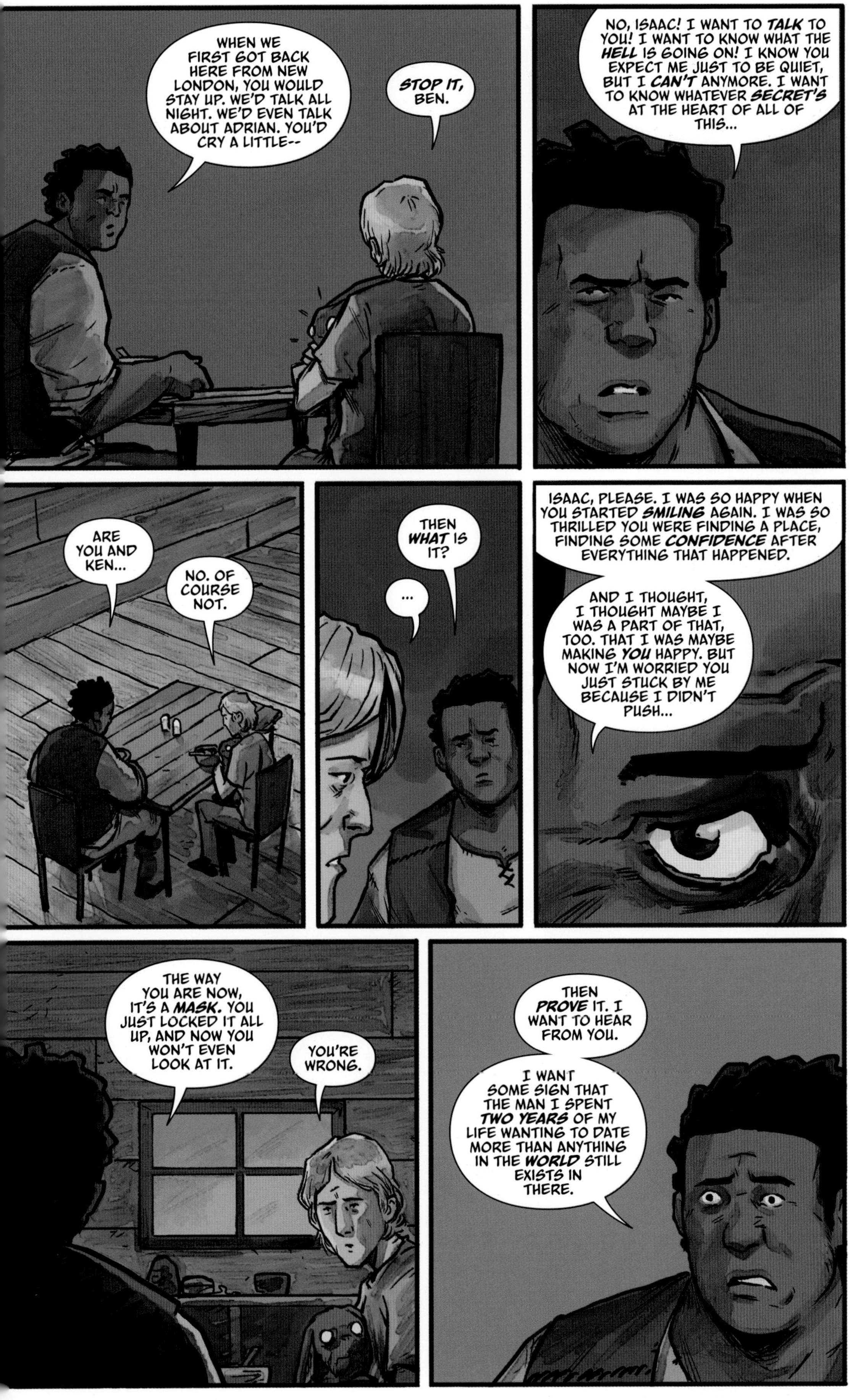
WHEN WE FIRST GOT BACK HERE FROM NEW LONDON, YOU WOULD STAY UP. WE'D TALK ALL NIGHT. WE'D EVEN TALK ABOUT ADRIAN. YOU'D CRY A LITTLE--
STOP IT, BEN.
NO, ISAAC! I WANT TO TALK TO YOU! I WANT TO KNOW WHAT THE HELL IS GOING ON! I KNOW YOU EXPECT ME JUST TO BE QUIET, BUT I CAN'T ANYMORE. I WANT TO KNOW WHATEVER SECRET'S AT THE HEART OF ALL OF THIS...
ARE YOU AND KEN...
NO. OF COURSE NOT.
THEN WHAT IS IT?
...
ISAAC, PLEASE. I WAS SO HAPPY WHEN YOU STARTED SMILING AGAIN. I WAS SO THRILLED YOU WERE FINDING A PLACE, FINDING SOME CONFIDENCE AFTER EVERYTHING THAT HAPPENED.
AND I THOUGHT, I THOUGHT MAYBE I WAS A PART OF THAT, TOO. THAT I WAS MAYBE MAKING YOU HAPPY. BUT NOW I'M WORRIED YOU JUST STUCK BY ME BECAUSE I DIDN'T PUSH...
THE WAY YOU ARE NOW, IT'S A MASK. YOU JUST LOCKED IT ALL UP, AND NOW YOU WON'T EVEN LOOK AT IT.
YOU'RE WRONG.
THEN PROVE IT. I WANT TO HEAR FROM YOU.
I WANT SOME SIGN THAT THE MAN I SPENT TWO YEARS OF MY LIFE WANTING TO DATE MORE THAN ANYTHING IN THE WORLD STILL EXISTS IN THERE.

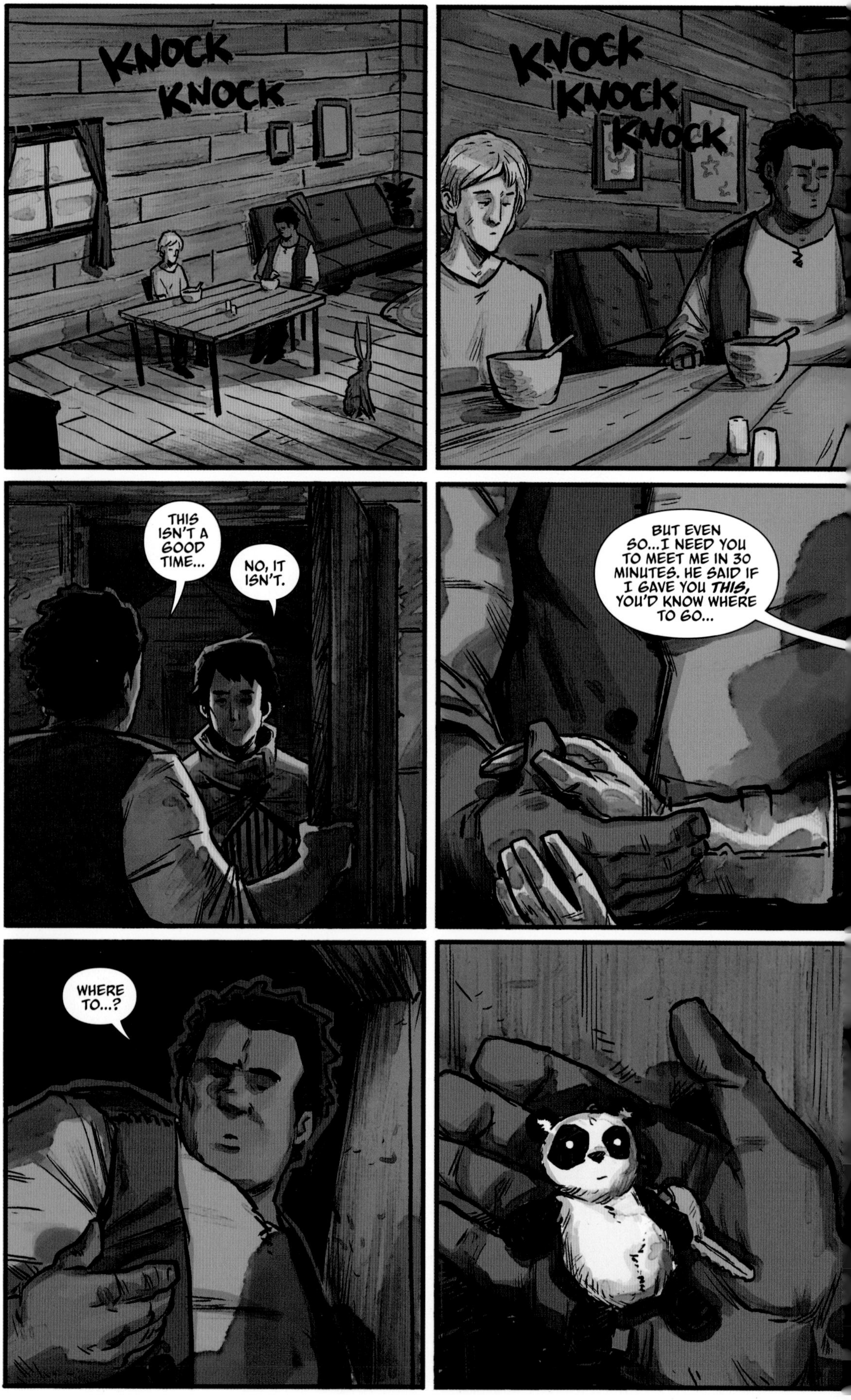
KNOCK
KNOCK
KNOCK
KNOCK
KNOCK
THIS ISN'T A GOOD TIME...
NO, IT ISN'T.
BUT EVEN SO...I NEED YOU TO MEET ME IN 30 MINUTES. HE SAID IF I GAVE YOU THIS, YOU'D KNOW WHERE TO GO...
WHERE TO...?

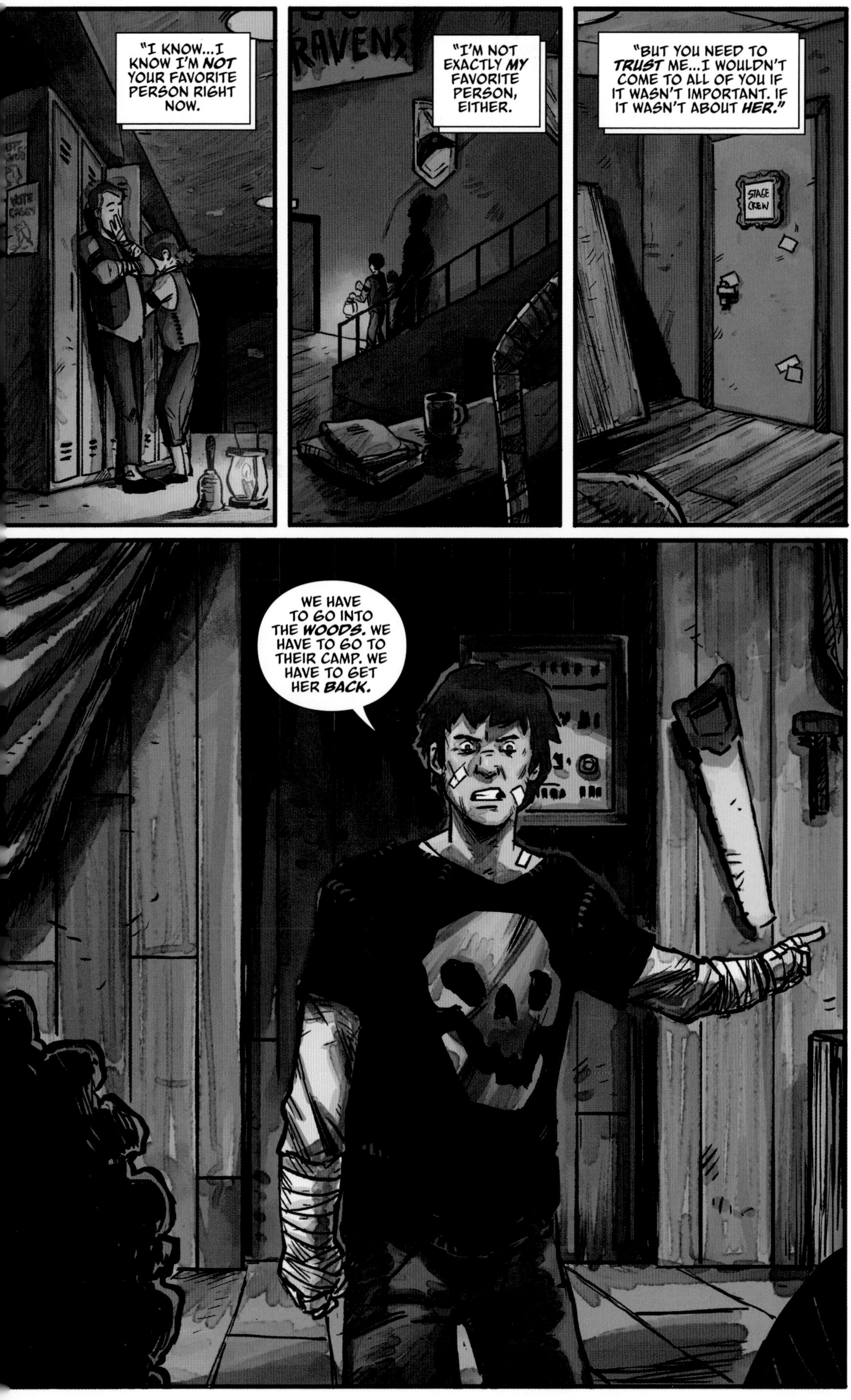
"I KNOW...I KNOW I'M NOT YOUR FAVORITE PERSON RIGHT NOW.
RAVENS
"I'M NOT EXACTLY MY FAVORITE PERSON, EITHER.
"BUT YOU NEED TO TRUST ME...I WOULDN'T COME TO ALL OF YOU IF IT WASN'T IMPORTANT. IF IT WASN'T ABOUT HER."
STAGE CREW
WE HAVE TO GO INTO THE WOODS. WE HAVE TO GO TO THEIR CAMP. WE HAVE TO GET HER BACK.

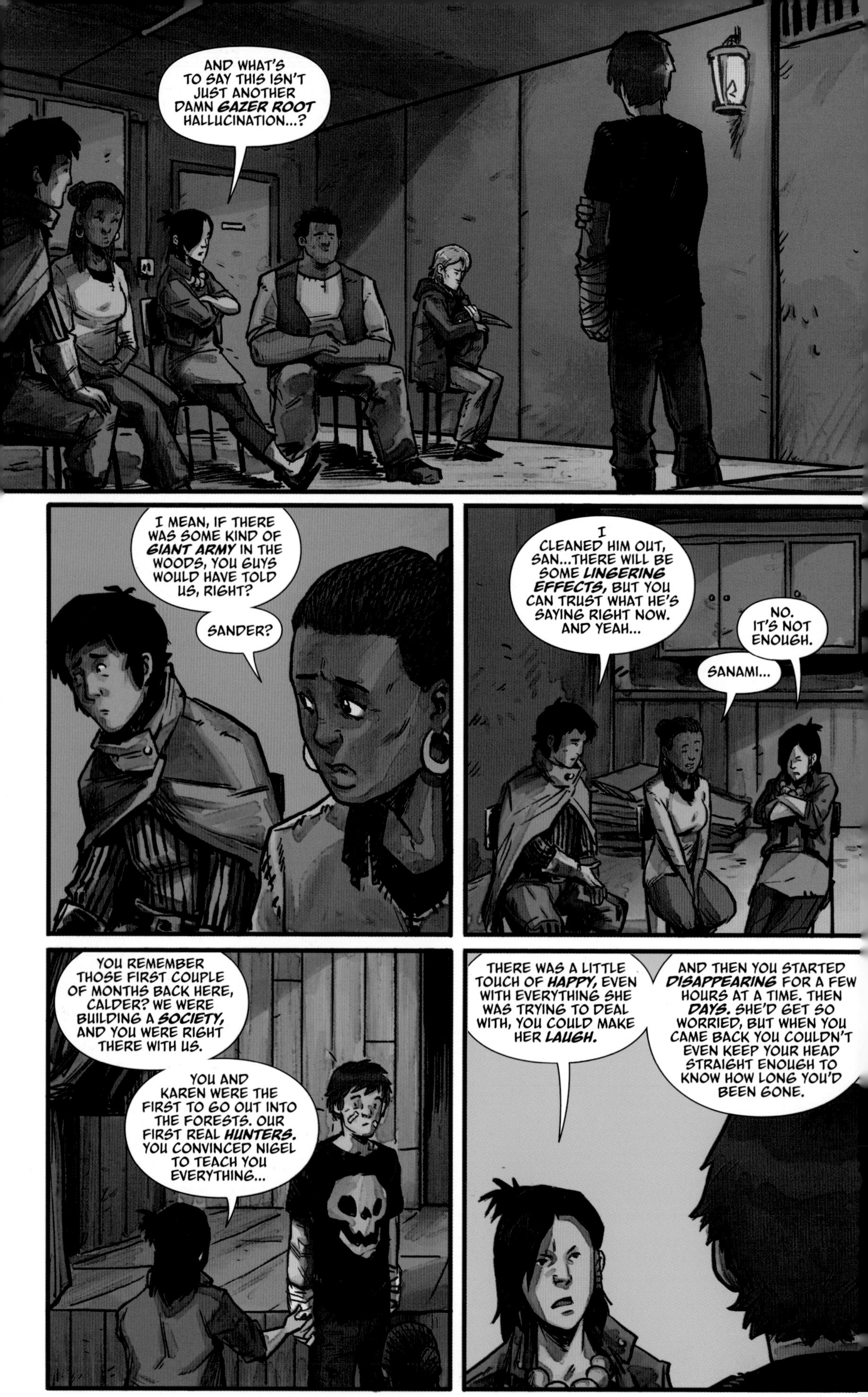
AND WHAT'S TO SAY THIS ISN'T JUST ANOTHER DAMN GAZER ROOT HALLUCINATION...?
I MEAN, IF THERE WAS SOME KIND OF GIANT ARMY IN THE WOODS, YOU GUYS WOULD HAVE TOLD US, RIGHT?
SANDER?
I CLEANED HIM OUT, SAN...THERE WILL BE SOME LINGERING EFFECTS, BUT YOU CAN TRUST WHAT HE'S SAYING RIGHT NOW. AND YEAH...
NO. IT'S NOT ENOUGH.
SANAMI...
YOU REMEMBER THOSE FIRST COUPLE OF MONTHS BACK HERE, CALDER? WE WERE BUILDING A SOCIETY, AND YOU WERE RIGHT THERE WITH US.
YOU AND KAREN WERE THE FIRST TO GO OUT INTO THE FORESTS. OUR FIRST REAL HUNTERS. YOU CONVINCED NIGEL TO TEACH YOU EVERYTHING...
THERE WAS A LITTLE TOUCH OF HAPPY, EVEN WITH EVERYTHING SHE WAS TRYING TO DEAL WITH, YOU COULD MAKE HER LAUGH.
AND THEN YOU STARTED DISAPPEARING FOR A FEW HOURS AT A TIME. THEN DAYS. SHE'D GET SO WORRIED, BUT WHEN YOU CAME BACK YOU COULDN'T EVEN KEEP YOUR HEAD STRAIGHT ENOUGH TO KNOW HOW LONG YOU'D BEEN GONE.

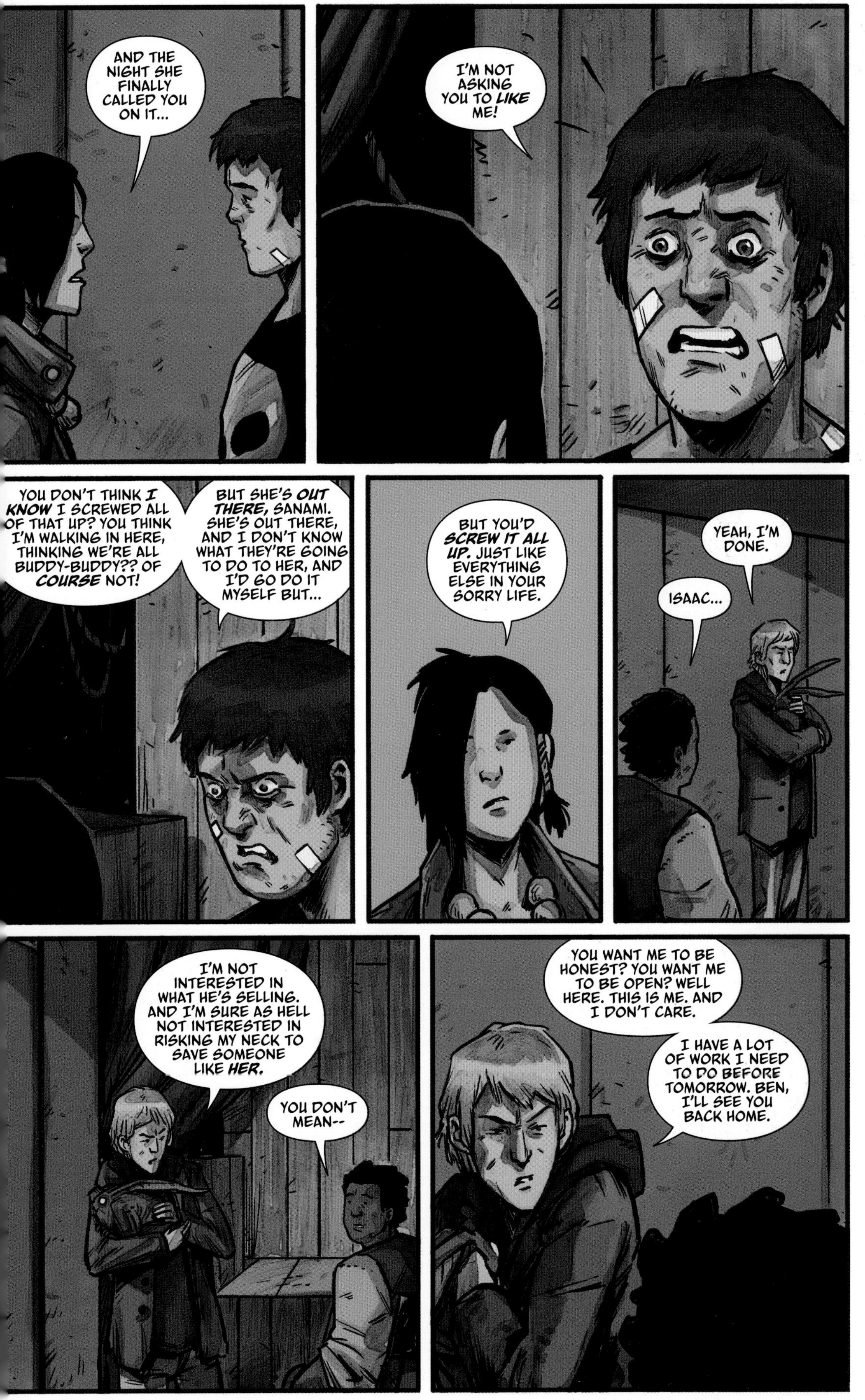
AND THE NIGHT SHE FINALLY CALLED YOU ON IT...
I'M NOT ASKING YOU TO LIKE ME!
YOU DON'T THINK I KNOW I SCREWED ALL OF THAT UP? YOU THINK I'M WALKING IN HERE, THINKING WE'RE ALL BUDDY-BUDDY?? OF COURSE NOT!
BUT SHE'S OUT THERE, SANAMI. SHE'S OUT THERE, AND I DON'T KNOW WHAT THEY'RE GOING TO DO TO HER, AND I'D GO DO IT MYSELF BUT...
BUT YOU'D SCREW IT ALL UP. JUST LIKE EVERYTHING ELSE IN YOUR SORRY LIFE.
YEAH, I'M DONE.
ISAAC...
I'M NOT INTERESTED IN WHAT HE'S SELLING. AND I'M SURE AS HELL NOT INTERESTED IN RISKING MY NECK TO SAVE SOMEONE LIKE HER.
YOU DON'T MEAN--
YOU WANT ME TO BE HONEST? YOU WANT ME TO BE OPEN? WELL HERE. THIS IS ME. AND I DON'T CARE.
I HAVE A LOT OF WORK I NEED TO DO BEFORE TOMORROW. BEN, I'LL SEE YOU BACK HOME.

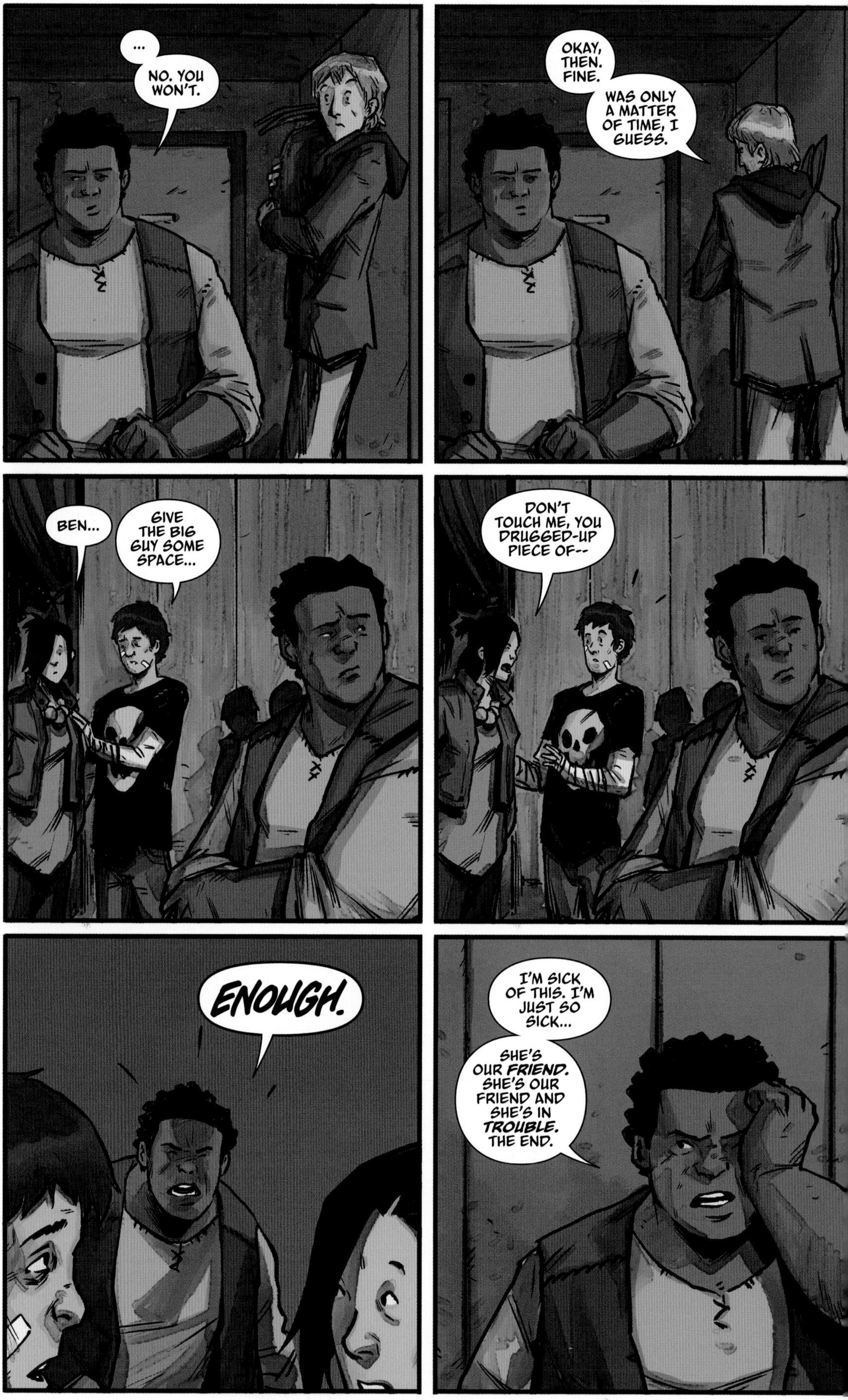
...
NO. YOU WON'T.
OKAY, THEN. FINE.
WAS ONLY A MATTER OF TIME, I GUESS.
BEN...
GIVE THE BIG GUY SOME SPACE...
DON'T TOUCH ME, YOU DRUGGED-UP PIECE OF--
ENOUGH.
I'M SICK OF THIS. I'M JUST SO SICK...
SHE'S OUR FRIEND. SHE'S OUR FRIEND AND SHE'S IN TROUBLE. THE END.

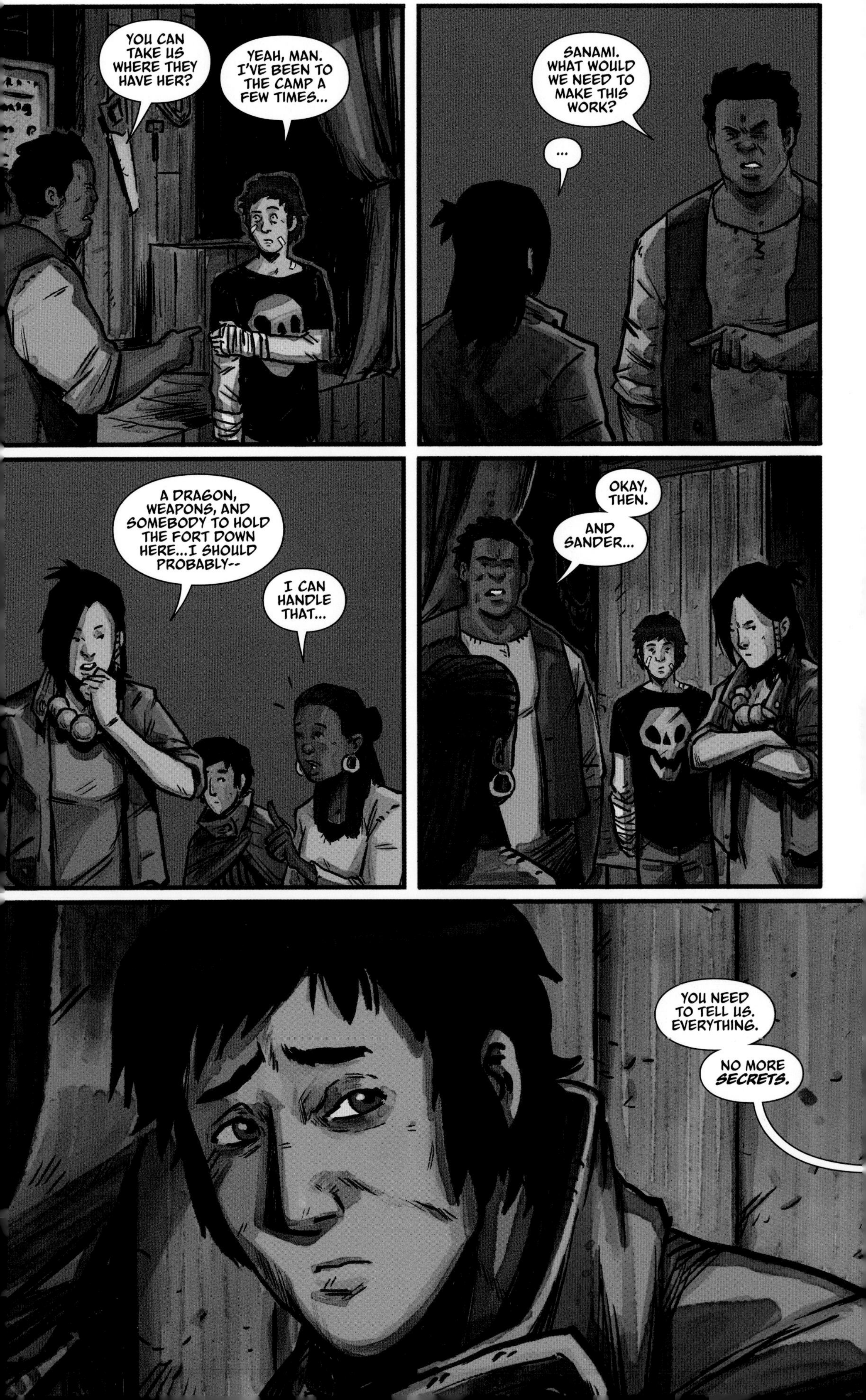
YOU CAN TAKE US WHERE THEY HAVE HER?
YEAH, MAN. I'VE BEEN TO THE CAMP A FEW TIMES...
SANAMI. WHAT WOULD WE NEED TO MAKE THIS WORK?
...
A DRAGON, WEAPONS, AND SOMEBODY TO HOLD THE FORT DOWN HERE...I SHOULD PROBABLY--
I CAN HANDLE THAT...
OKAY, THEN.
AND SANDER...
YOU NEED TO TELL US. EVERYTHING.
NO MORE *SECRETS.*

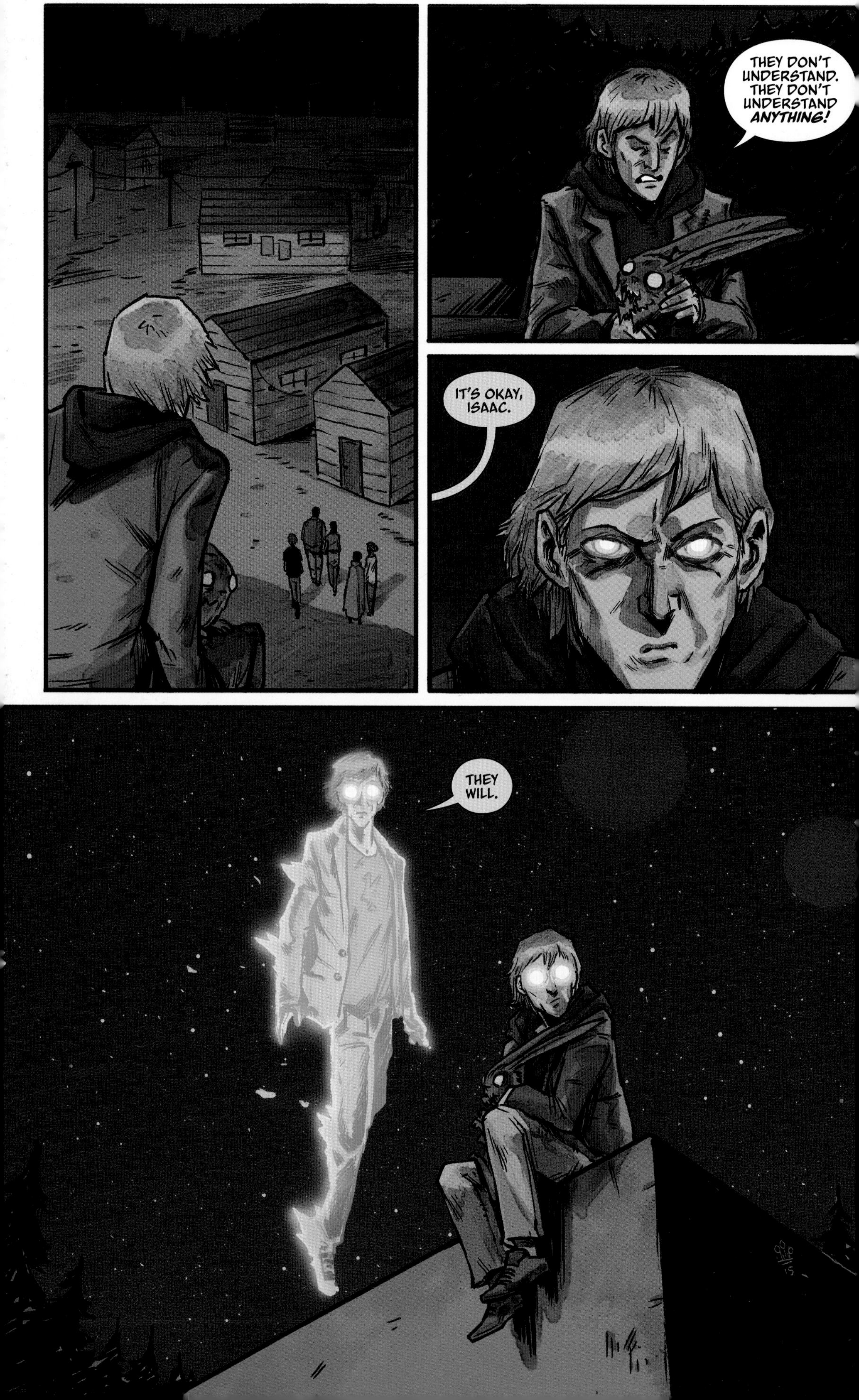
THEY DON'T UNDERSTAND. THEY DON'T UNDERSTAND ANYTHING!
IT'S OKAY, ISAAC.
THEY WILL.

CHAPTER SIXTEEN

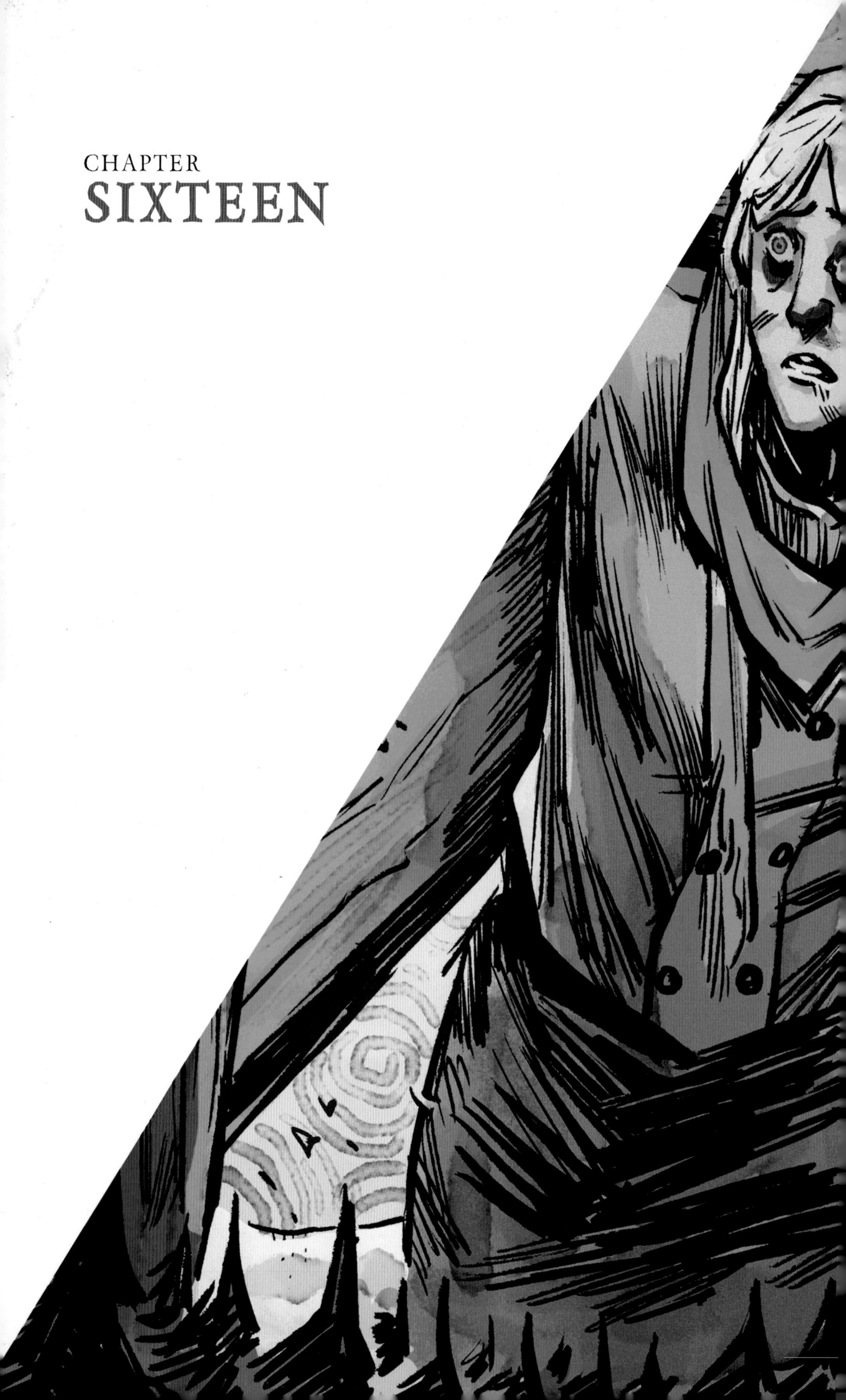

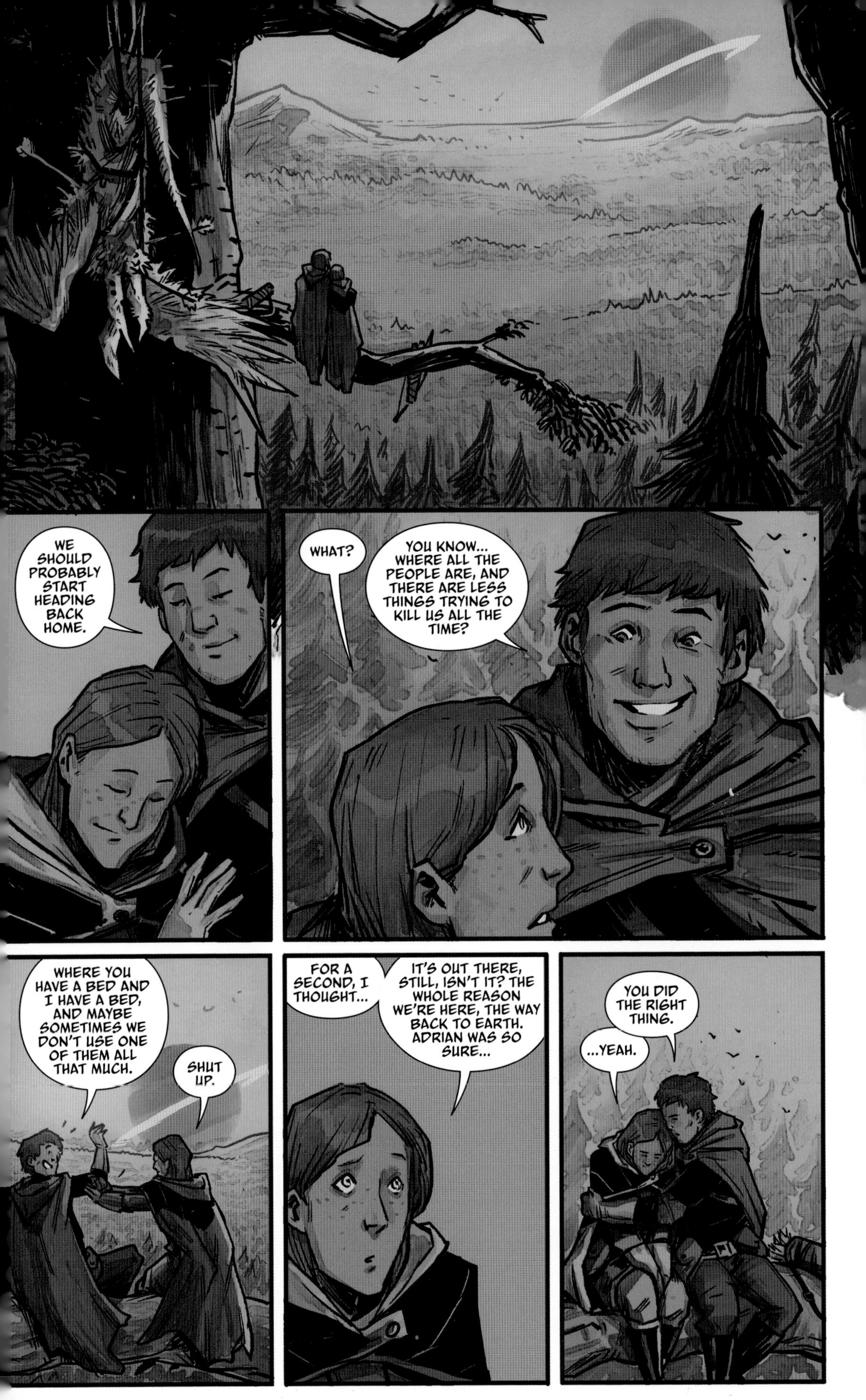

WE SHOULD PROBABLY START HEADING BACK HOME.
WHAT?
YOU KNOW... WHERE ALL THE PEOPLE ARE, AND THERE ARE LESS THINGS TRYING TO KILL US ALL THE TIME?
WHERE YOU HAVE A BED AND I HAVE A BED, AND MAYBE SOMETIMES WE DON'T USE ONE OF THEM ALL THAT MUCH.
SHUT UP.
FOR A SECOND, I THOUGHT...
IT'S OUT THERE, STILL, ISN'T IT? THE WHOLE REASON WE'RE HERE, THE WAY BACK TO EARTH. ADRIAN WAS SO SURE...
YOU DID THE RIGHT THING.
...YEAH.

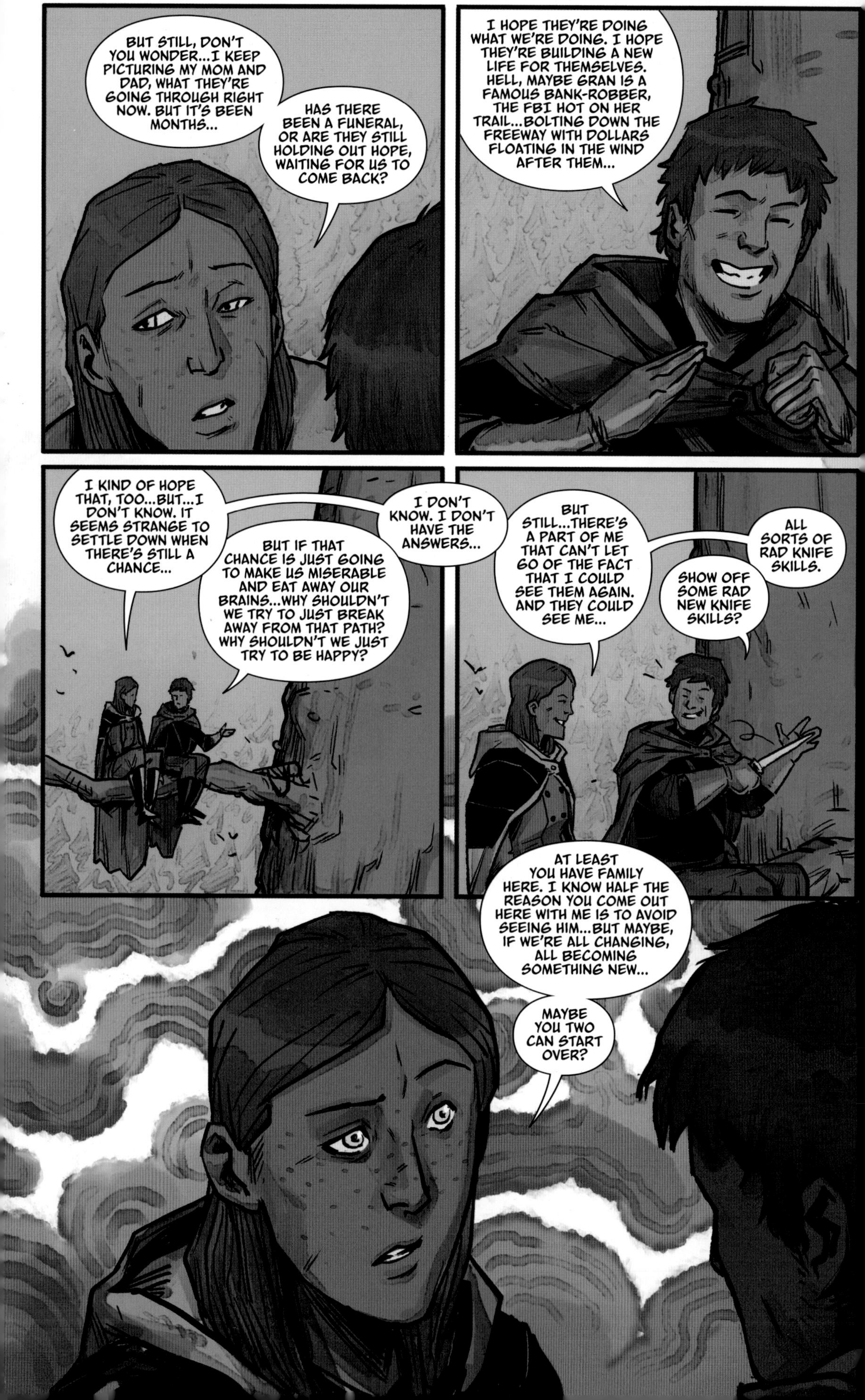
BUT STILL, DON'T YOU WONDER...I KEEP PICTURING MY MOM AND DAD, WHAT THEY'RE GOING THROUGH RIGHT NOW. BUT IT'S BEEN MONTHS...
HAS THERE BEEN A FUNERAL, OR ARE THEY STILL HOLDING OUT HOPE, WAITING FOR US TO COME BACK?
I HOPE THEY'RE DOING WHAT WE'RE DOING. I HOPE THEY'RE BUILDING A NEW LIFE FOR THEMSELVES. HELL, MAYBE GRAN IS A FAMOUS BANK-ROBBER, THE FBI HOT ON HER TRAIL...BOLTING DOWN THE FREEWAY WITH DOLLARS FLOATING IN THE WIND AFTER THEM...
I KIND OF HOPE THAT, TOO...BUT...I DON'T KNOW. IT SEEMS STRANGE TO SETTLE DOWN WHEN THERE'S STILL A CHANCE...
BUT IF THAT CHANCE IS JUST GOING TO MAKE US MISERABLE AND EAT AWAY OUR BRAINS...WHY SHOULDN'T WE TRY TO JUST BREAK AWAY FROM THAT PATH? WHY SHOULDN'T WE JUST TRY TO BE HAPPY?
I DON'T KNOW. I DON'T HAVE THE ANSWERS...
BUT STILL...THERE'S A PART OF ME THAT CAN'T LET GO OF THE FACT THAT I COULD SEE THEM AGAIN. AND THEY COULD SEE ME...
SHOW OFF SOME RAD NEW KNIFE SKILLS?
ALL SORTS OF RAD KNIFE SKILLS.
AT LEAST YOU HAVE FAMILY HERE. I KNOW HALF THE REASON YOU COME OUT HERE WITH ME IS TO AVOID SEEING HIM...BUT MAYBE, IF WE'RE ALL CHANGING, ALL BECOMING SOMETHING NEW...
MAYBE YOU TWO CAN START OVER?

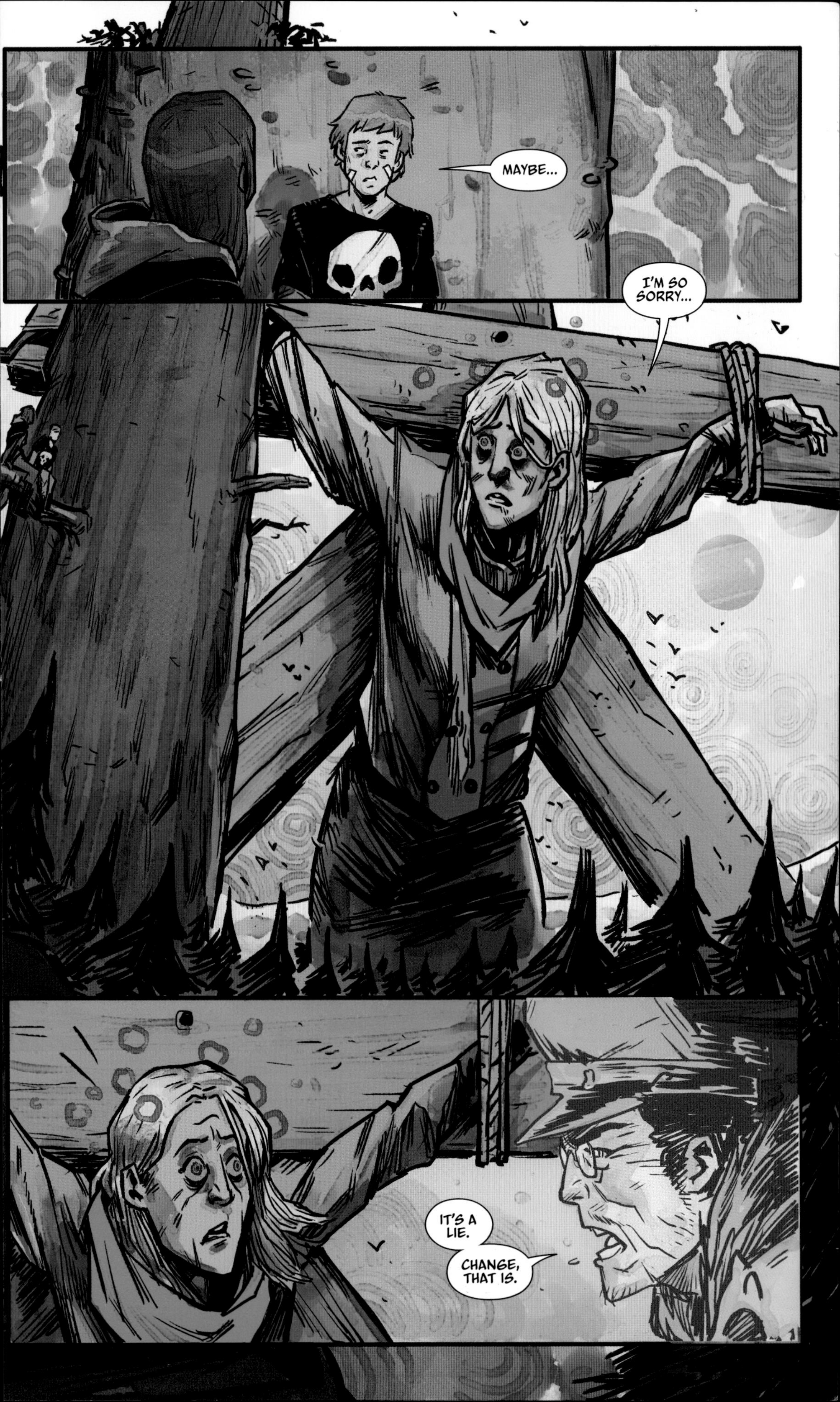
MAYBE...
I'M SO SORRY...
IT'S A LIE.
CHANGE, THAT IS.

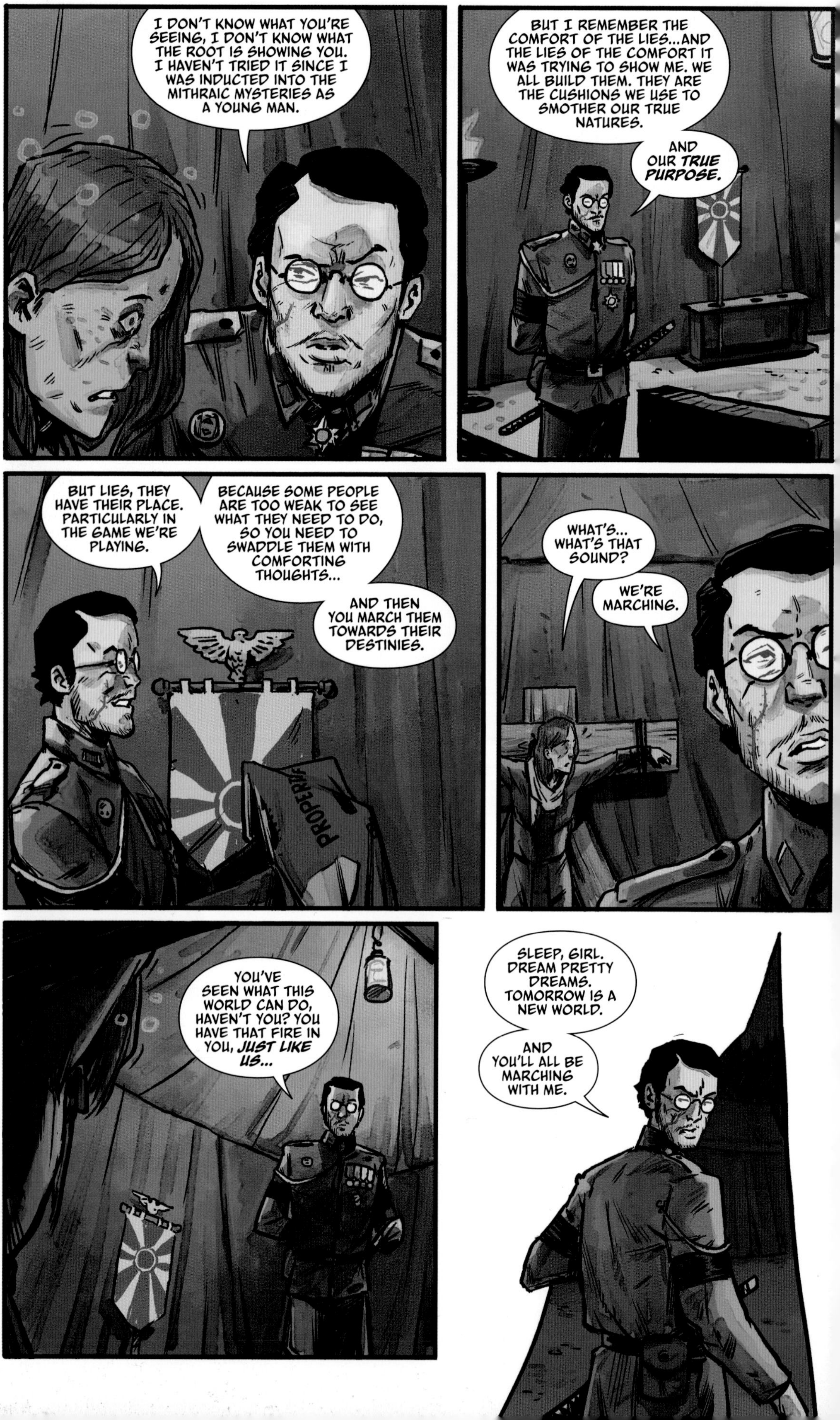
I DON'T KNOW WHAT YOU'RE SEEING, I DON'T KNOW WHAT THE ROOT IS SHOWING YOU. I HAVEN'T TRIED IT SINCE I WAS INDUCTED INTO THE MITHRAIC MYSTERIES AS A YOUNG MAN.
BUT I REMEMBER THE COMFORT OF THE LIES...AND THE LIES OF THE COMFORT IT WAS TRYING TO SHOW ME. WE ALL BUILD THEM. THEY ARE THE CUSHIONS WE USE TO SMOTHER OUR TRUE NATURES.
AND OUR TRUE PURPOSE.
BUT LIES, THEY HAVE THEIR PLACE. PARTICULARLY IN THE GAME WE'RE PLAYING.
BECAUSE SOME PEOPLE ARE TOO WEAK TO SEE WHAT THEY NEED TO DO, SO YOU NEED TO SWADDLE THEM WITH COMFORTING THOUGHTS...
AND THEN YOU MARCH THEM TOWARDS THEIR DESTINIES.
WHAT'S... WHAT'S THAT SOUND?
WE'RE MARCHING.
YOU'VE SEEN WHAT THIS WORLD CAN DO, HAVEN'T YOU? YOU HAVE THAT FIRE IN YOU, JUST LIKE US...
SLEEP, GIRL. DREAM PRETTY DREAMS. TOMORROW IS A NEW WORLD.
AND YOU'LL ALL BE MARCHING WITH ME.

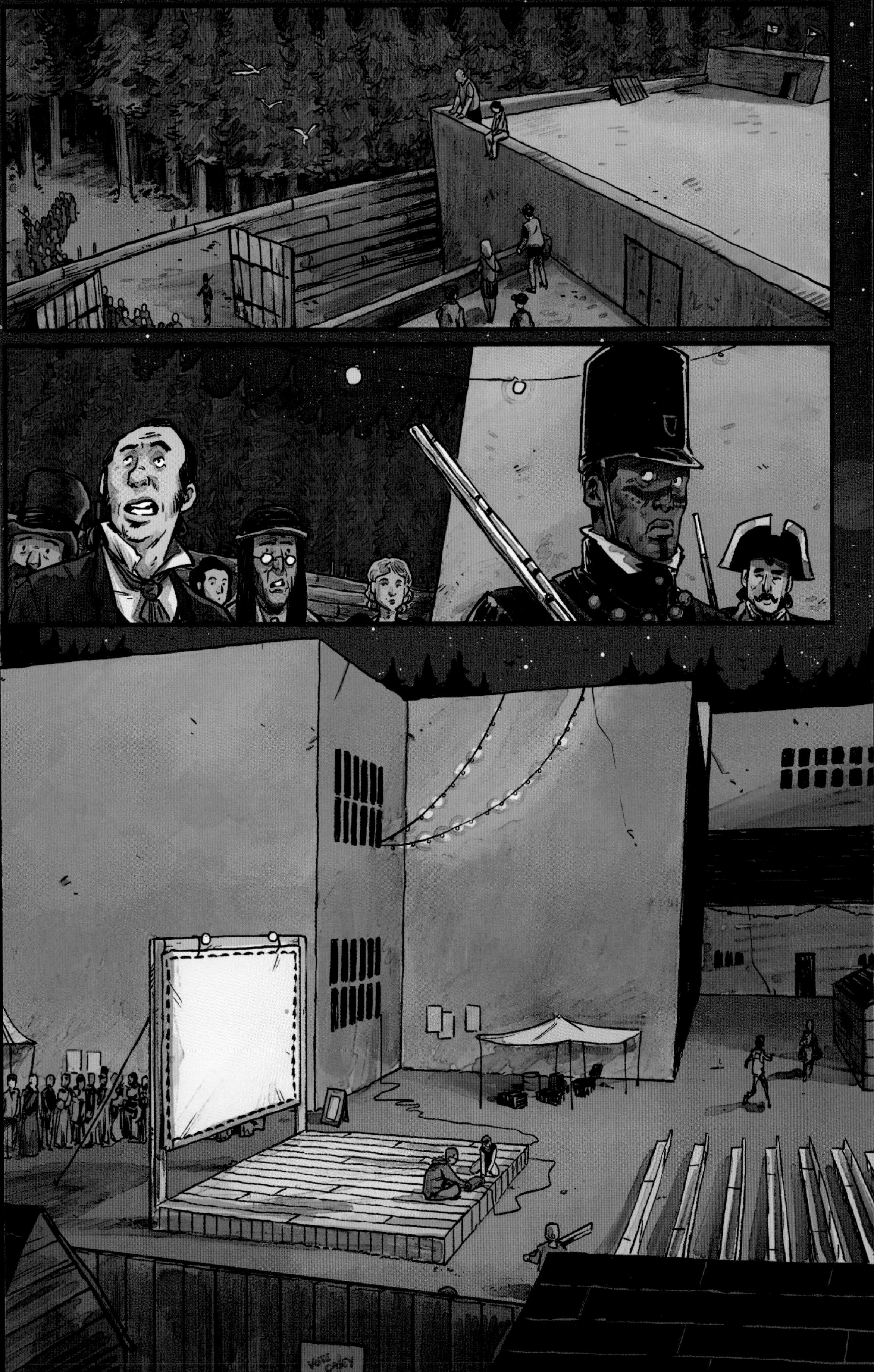
VOTE CASEY

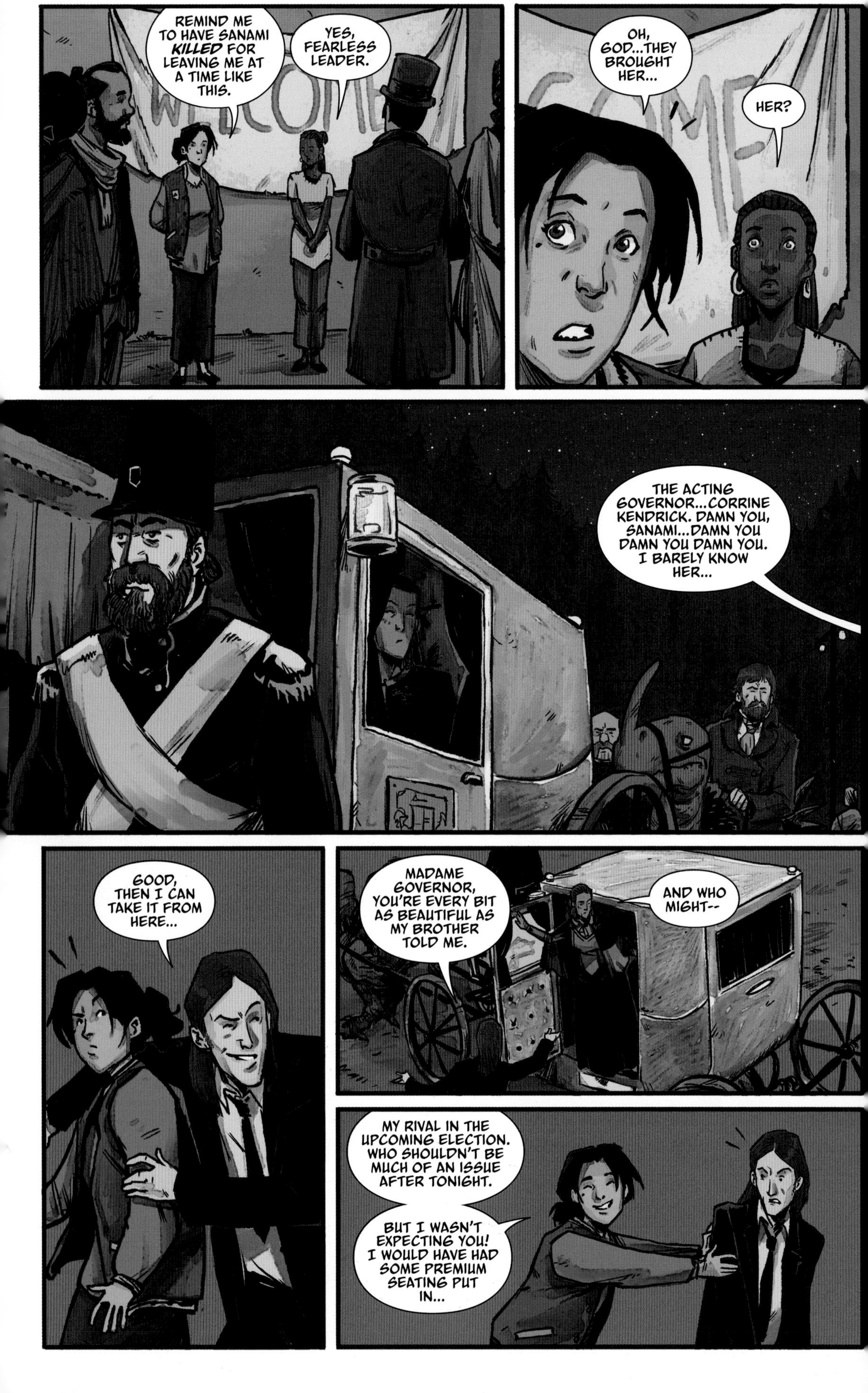

REMIND ME TO HAVE SANAMI *KILLED* FOR LEAVING ME AT A TIME LIKE THIS.
YES, FEARLESS LEADER.
OH, GOD...THEY BROUGHT HER...
HER?
THE ACTING GOVERNOR...CORRINE KENDRICK. DAMN YOU, SANAMI...DAMN YOU DAMN YOU DAMN YOU. I BARELY KNOW HER...
GOOD, THEN I CAN TAKE IT FROM HERE...
MADAME GOVERNOR, YOU'RE EVERY BIT AS BEAUTIFUL AS MY BROTHER TOLD ME.
AND WHO MIGHT--
MY RIVAL IN THE UPCOMING ELECTION. WHO SHOULDN'T BE MUCH OF AN ISSUE AFTER TONIGHT.
BUT I WASN'T EXPECTING YOU! I WOULD HAVE HAD SOME PREMIUM SEATING PUT IN...

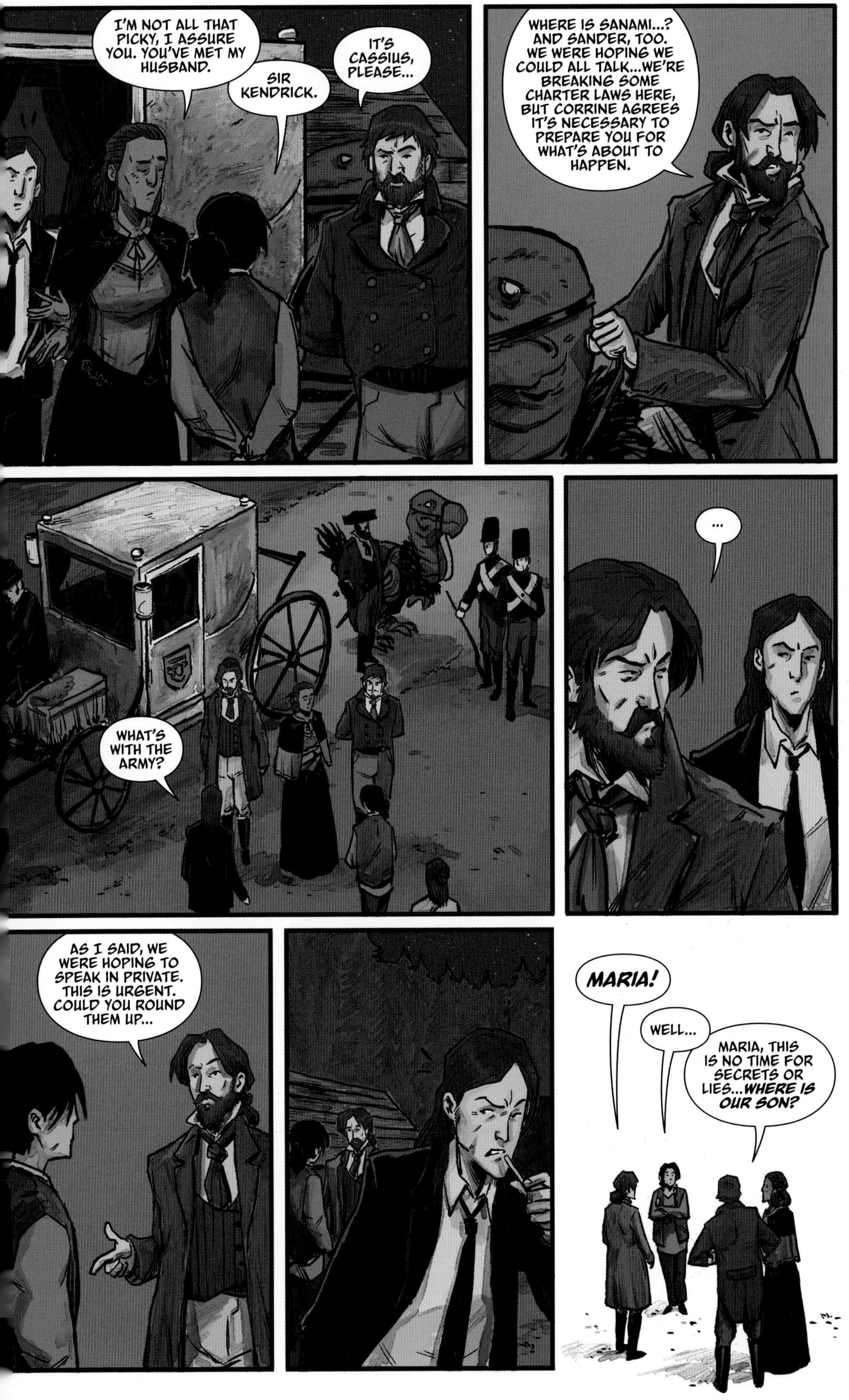
I'M NOT ALL THAT PICKY, I ASSURE YOU. YOU'VE MET MY HUSBAND.
SIR KENDRICK.
IT'S CASSIUS, PLEASE...
WHERE IS SANAMI...? AND SANDER, TOO. WE WERE HOPING WE COULD ALL TALK...WE'RE BREAKING SOME CHARTER LAWS HERE, BUT CORRINE AGREES IT'S NECESSARY TO PREPARE YOU FOR WHAT'S ABOUT TO HAPPEN.
WHAT'S WITH THE ARMY?
...
AS I SAID, WE WERE HOPING TO SPEAK IN PRIVATE. THIS IS URGENT. COULD YOU ROUND THEM UP...
MARIA!
WELL...
MARIA, THIS IS NO TIME FOR SECRETS OR LIES...WHERE IS OUR SON?

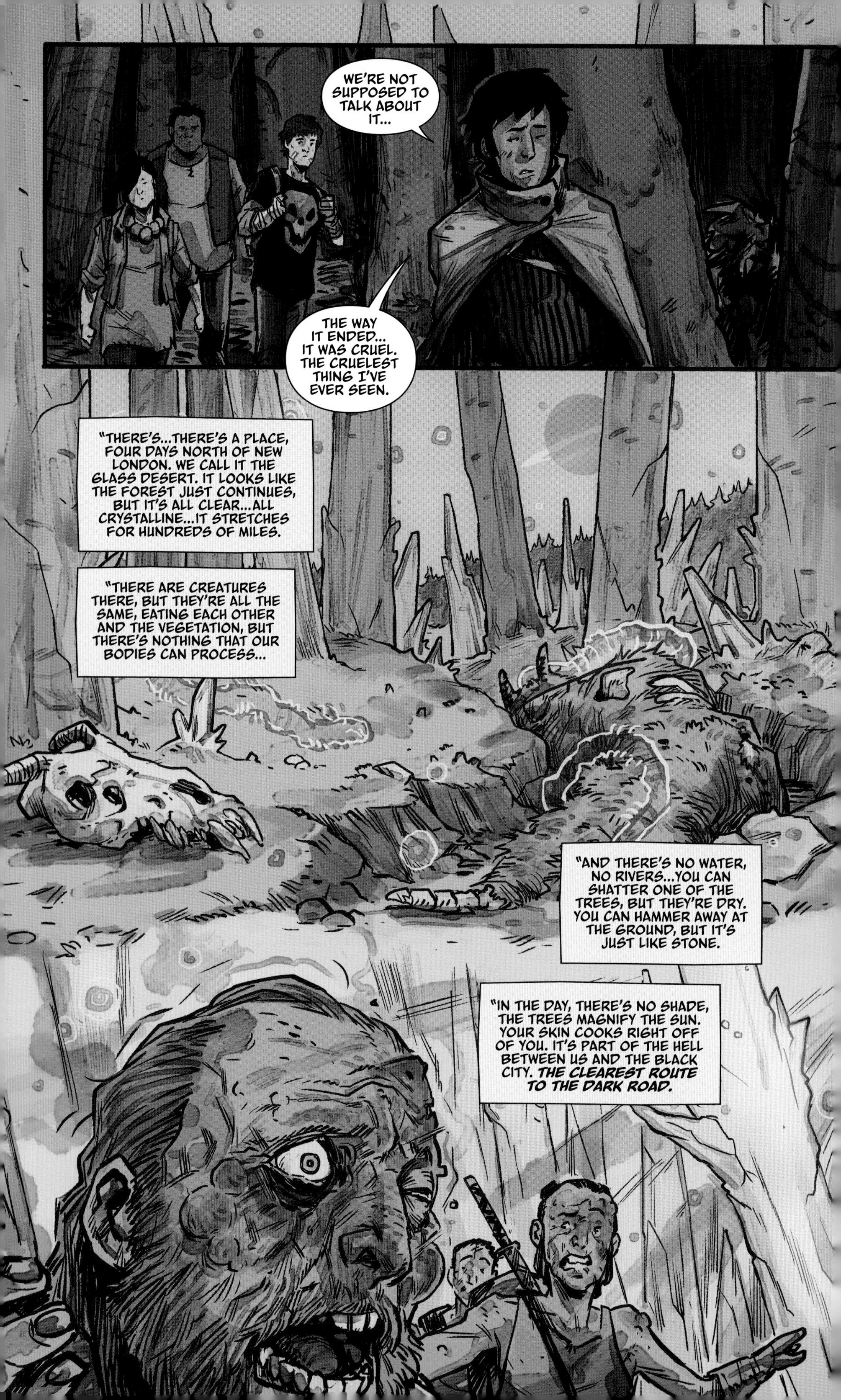

WE'RE NOT SUPPOSED TO TALK ABOUT IT...
THE WAY IT ENDED... IT WAS CRUEL. THE CRUELEST THING I'VE EVER SEEN.
"THERE'S...THERE'S A PLACE, FOUR DAYS NORTH OF NEW LONDON. WE CALL IT THE GLASS DESERT. IT LOOKS LIKE THE FOREST JUST CONTINUES, BUT IT'S ALL CLEAR...ALL CRYSTALLINE...IT STRETCHES FOR HUNDREDS OF MILES.
"THERE ARE CREATURES THERE, BUT THEY'RE ALL THE SAME, EATING EACH OTHER AND THE VEGETATION, BUT THERE'S NOTHING THAT OUR BODIES CAN PROCESS...
"AND THERE'S NO WATER, NO RIVERS...YOU CAN SHATTER ONE OF THE TREES, BUT THEY'RE DRY. YOU CAN HAMMER AWAY AT THE GROUND, BUT IT'S JUST LIKE STONE.
"IN THE DAY, THERE'S NO SHADE, THE TREES MAGNIFY THE SUN. YOUR SKIN COOKS RIGHT OFF OF YOU. IT'S PART OF THE HELL BETWEEN US AND THE BLACK CITY. *THE CLEAREST ROUTE TO THE DARK ROAD.*

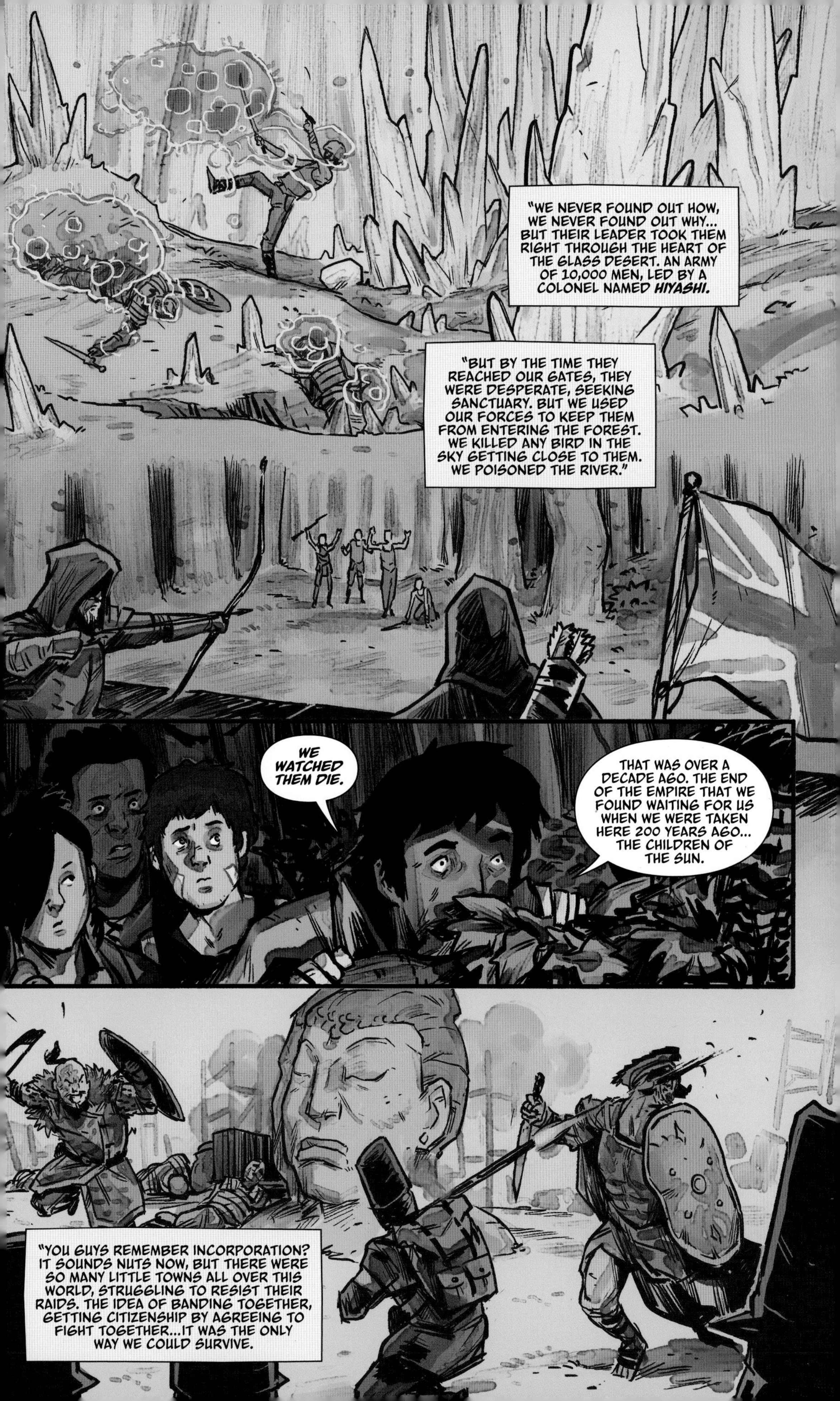
"WE NEVER FOUND OUT HOW, WE NEVER FOUND OUT WHY... BUT THEIR LEADER TOOK THEM RIGHT THROUGH THE HEART OF THE GLASS DESERT. AN ARMY OF 10,000 MEN, LED BY A COLONEL NAMED HIYASHI.
"BUT BY THE TIME THEY REACHED OUR GATES, THEY WERE DESPERATE, SEEKING SANCTUARY. BUT WE USED OUR FORCES TO KEEP THEM FROM ENTERING THE FOREST. WE KILLED ANY BIRD IN THE SKY GETTING CLOSE TO THEM. WE POISONED THE RIVER."
WE WATCHED THEM DIE.
THAT WAS OVER A DECADE AGO. THE END OF THE EMPIRE THAT WE FOUND WAITING FOR US WHEN WE WERE TAKEN HERE 200 YEARS AGO... THE CHILDREN OF THE SUN.
"YOU GUYS REMEMBER INCORPORATION? IT SOUNDS NUTS NOW, BUT THERE WERE SO MANY LITTLE TOWNS ALL OVER THIS WORLD, STRUGGLING TO RESIST THEIR RAIDS. THE IDEA OF BANDING TOGETHER, GETTING CITIZENSHIP BY AGREEING TO FIGHT TOGETHER...IT WAS THE ONLY WAY WE COULD SURVIVE.

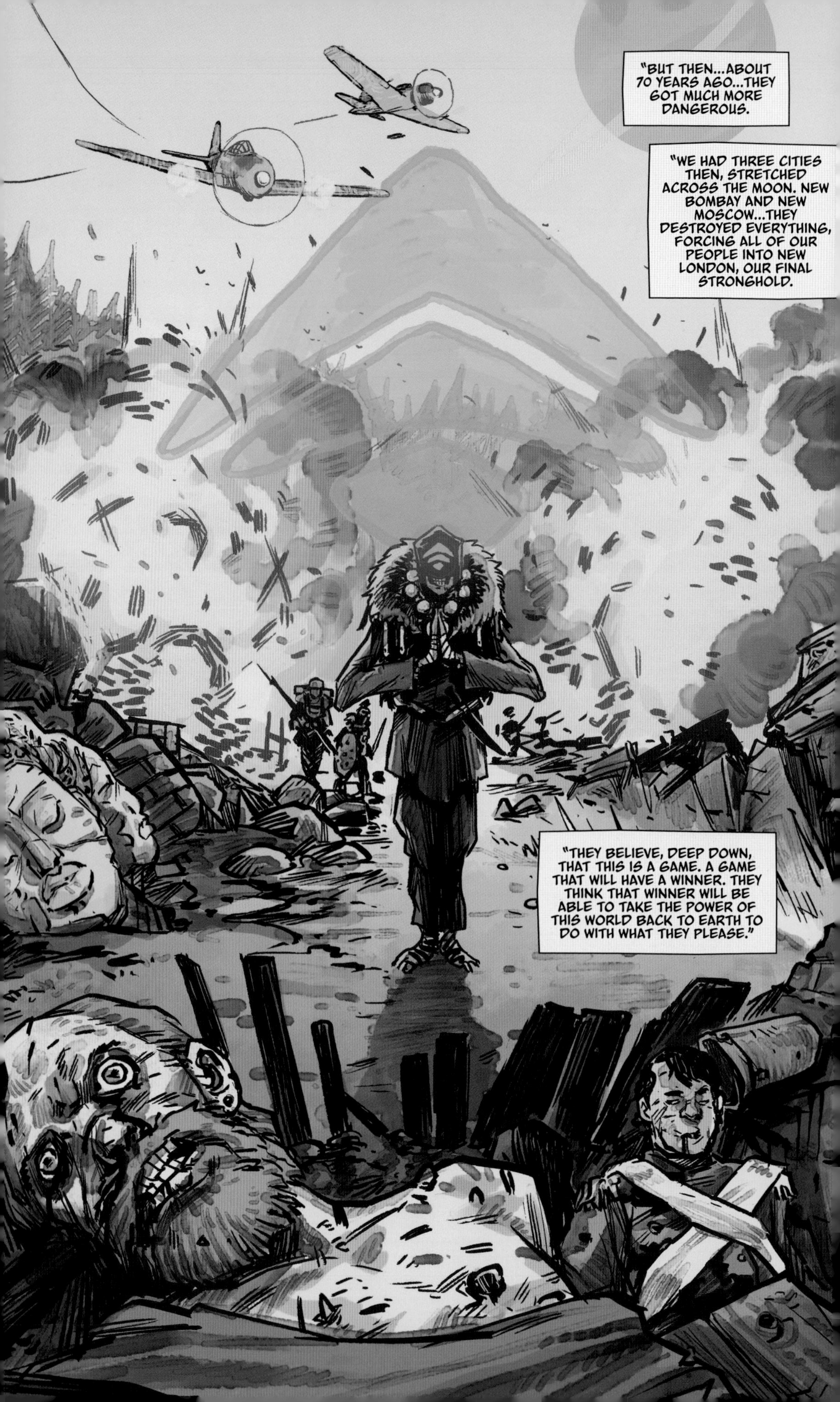
"BUT THEN...ABOUT 70 YEARS AGO...THEY GOT MUCH MORE DANGEROUS.
"WE HAD THREE CITIES THEN, STRETCHED ACROSS THE MOON. NEW BOMBAY AND NEW MOSCOW...THEY DESTROYED EVERYTHING, FORCING ALL OF OUR PEOPLE INTO NEW LONDON, OUR FINAL STRONGHOLD.
"THEY BELIEVE, DEEP DOWN, THAT THIS IS A GAME. A GAME THAT WILL HAVE A WINNER. THEY THINK THAT WINNER WILL BE ABLE TO TAKE THE POWER OF THIS WORLD BACK TO EARTH TO DO WITH WHAT THEY PLEASE."

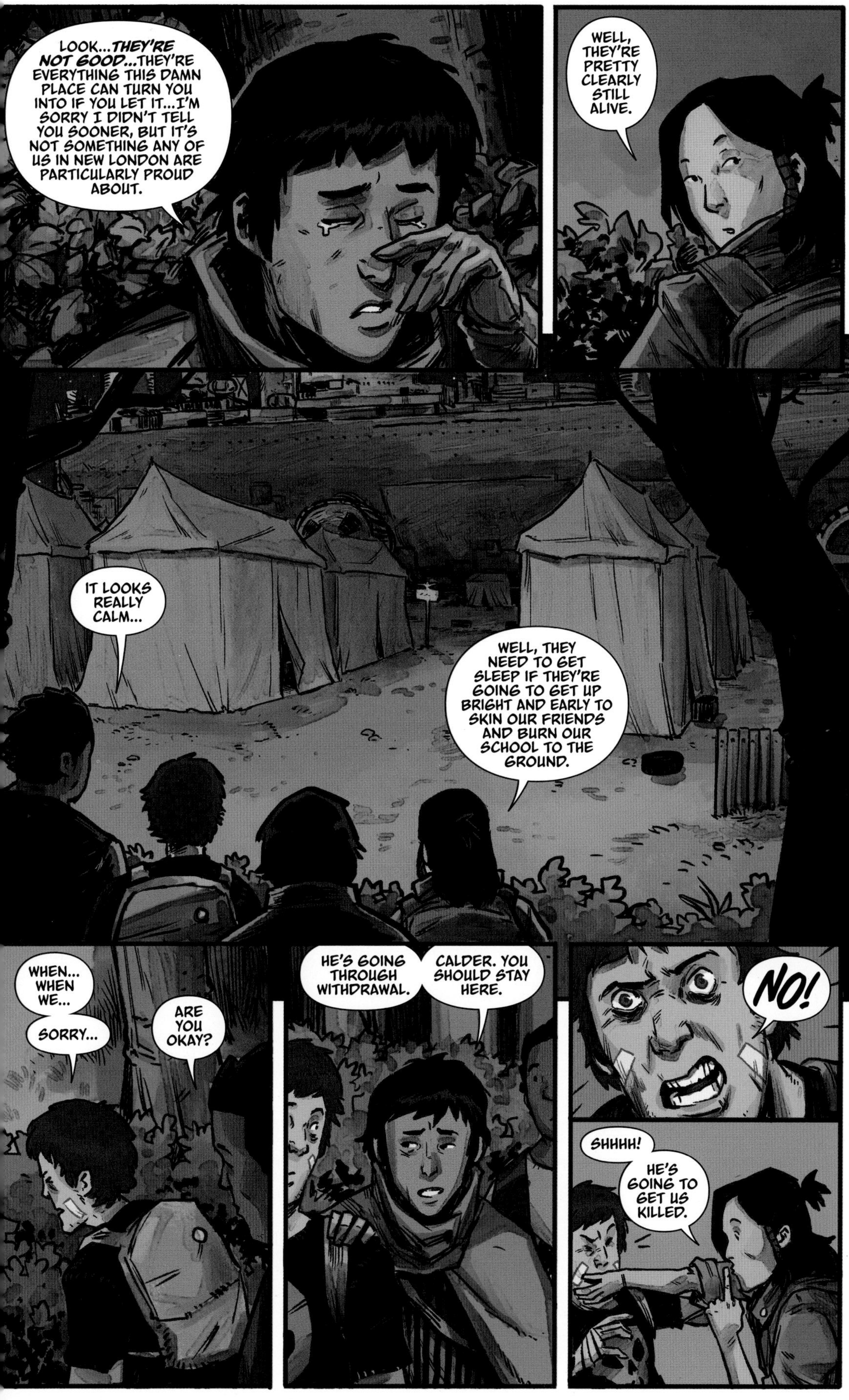
LOOK...THEY'RE NOT GOOD...THEY'RE EVERYTHING THIS DAMN PLACE CAN TURN YOU INTO IF YOU LET IT...I'M SORRY I DIDN'T TELL YOU SOONER, BUT IT'S NOT SOMETHING ANY OF US IN NEW LONDON ARE PARTICULARLY PROUD ABOUT.
WELL, THEY'RE PRETTY CLEARLY STILL ALIVE.
IT LOOKS REALLY CALM...
WELL, THEY NEED TO GET SLEEP IF THEY'RE GOING TO GET UP BRIGHT AND EARLY TO SKIN OUR FRIENDS AND BURN OUR SCHOOL TO THE GROUND.
WHEN... WHEN WE...
SORRY...
ARE YOU OKAY?
HE'S GOING THROUGH WITHDRAWAL.
CALDER. YOU SHOULD STAY HERE.
NO!
SHHHH!
HE'S GOING TO GET US KILLED.

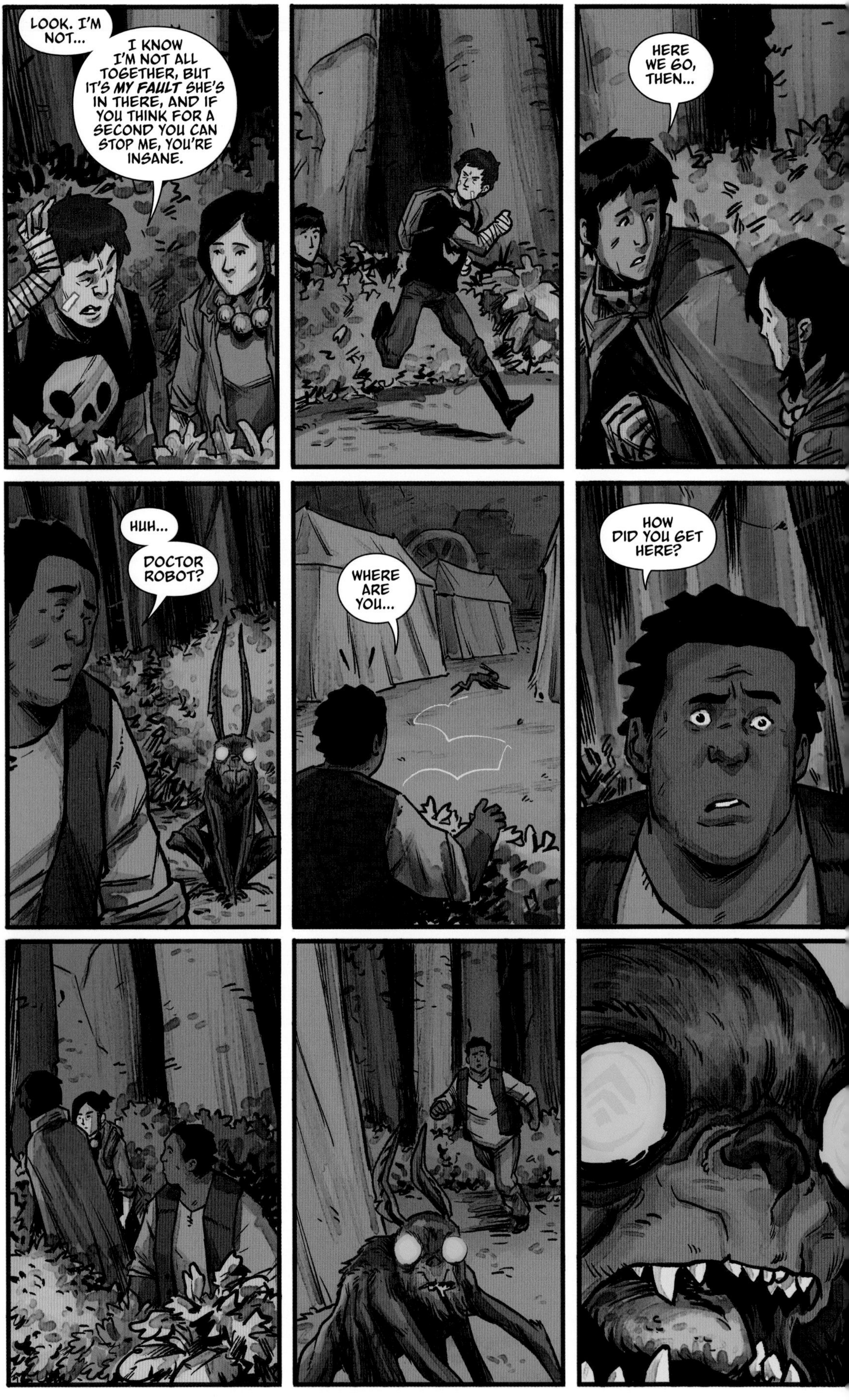
LOOK. I'M NOT...
I KNOW I'M NOT ALL TOGETHER, BUT IT'S *MY FAULT* SHE'S IN THERE, AND IF YOU THINK FOR A SECOND YOU CAN STOP ME, YOU'RE INSANE.
HERE WE GO, THEN...
HUH...
DOCTOR ROBOT?
WHERE ARE YOU...
HOW DID YOU GET HERE?

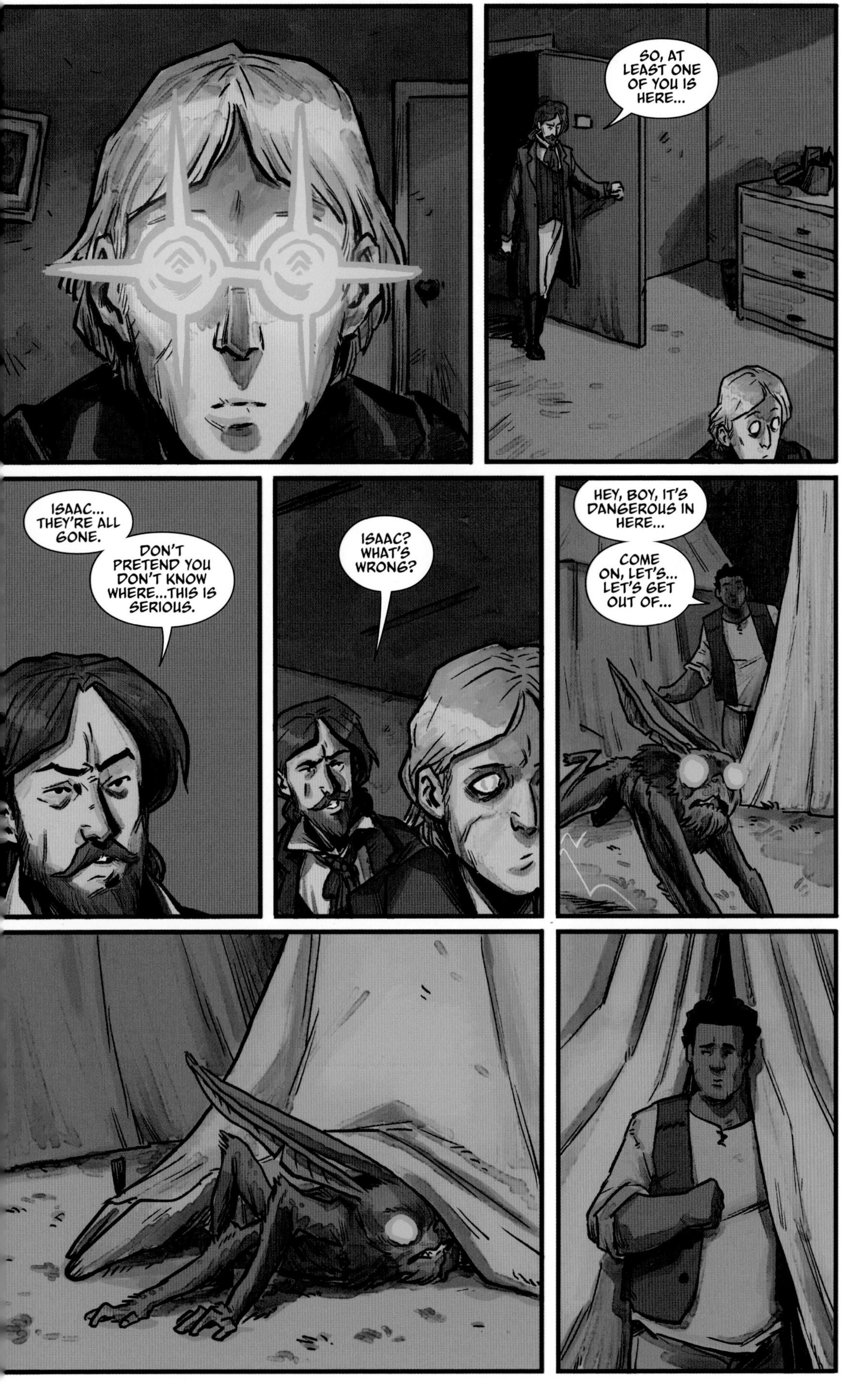
SO, AT LEAST ONE OF YOU IS HERE...
ISAAC... THEY'RE ALL GONE.
DON'T PRETEND YOU DON'T KNOW WHERE...THIS IS SERIOUS.
ISAAC? WHAT'S WRONG?
HEY, BOY, IT'S DANGEROUS IN HERE...
COME ON, LET'S... LET'S GET OUT OF...

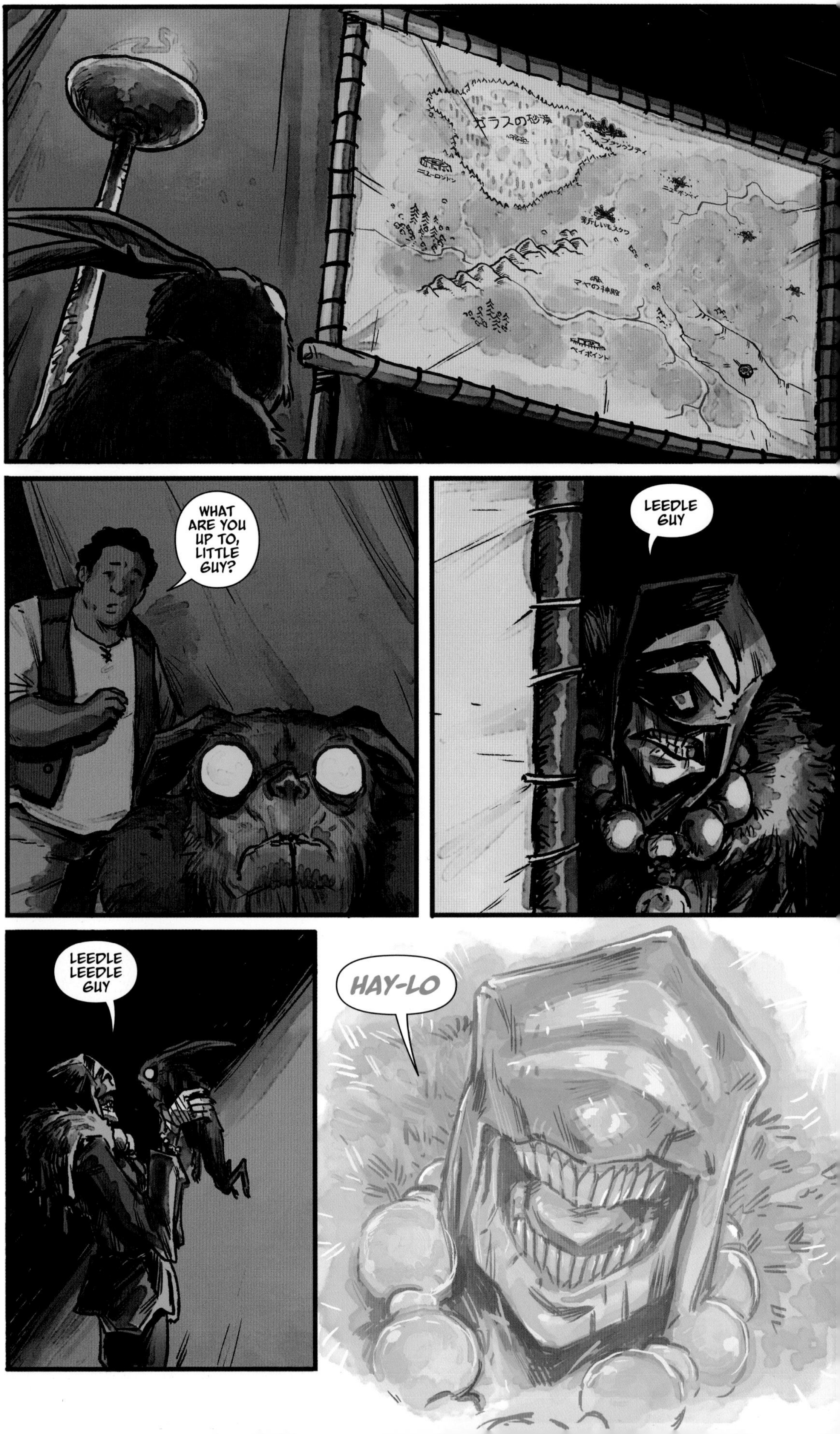
ガラスの砂漠
ニューロンドン
新しいモスクワ
マヤの神殿
ベイポイント
WHAT ARE YOU UP TO, LITTLE GUY?
LEEDLE GUY
LEEDLE LEEDLE GUY
HAY-LO

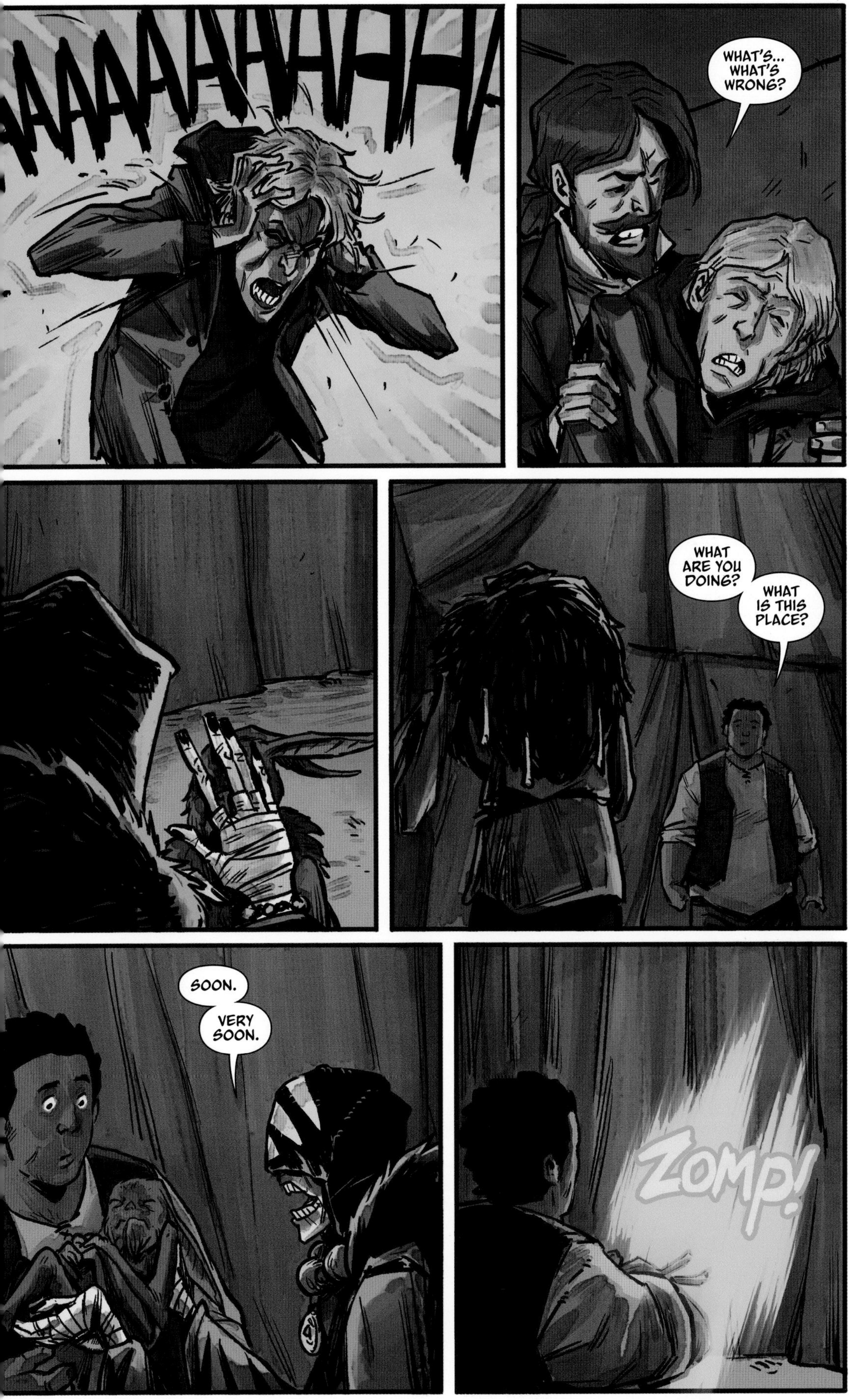
AAAAAAAAHHH
WHAT'S... WHAT'S WRONG?
WHAT ARE YOU DOING?
WHAT IS THIS PLACE?
SOON.
VERY SOON.
ZOMP!

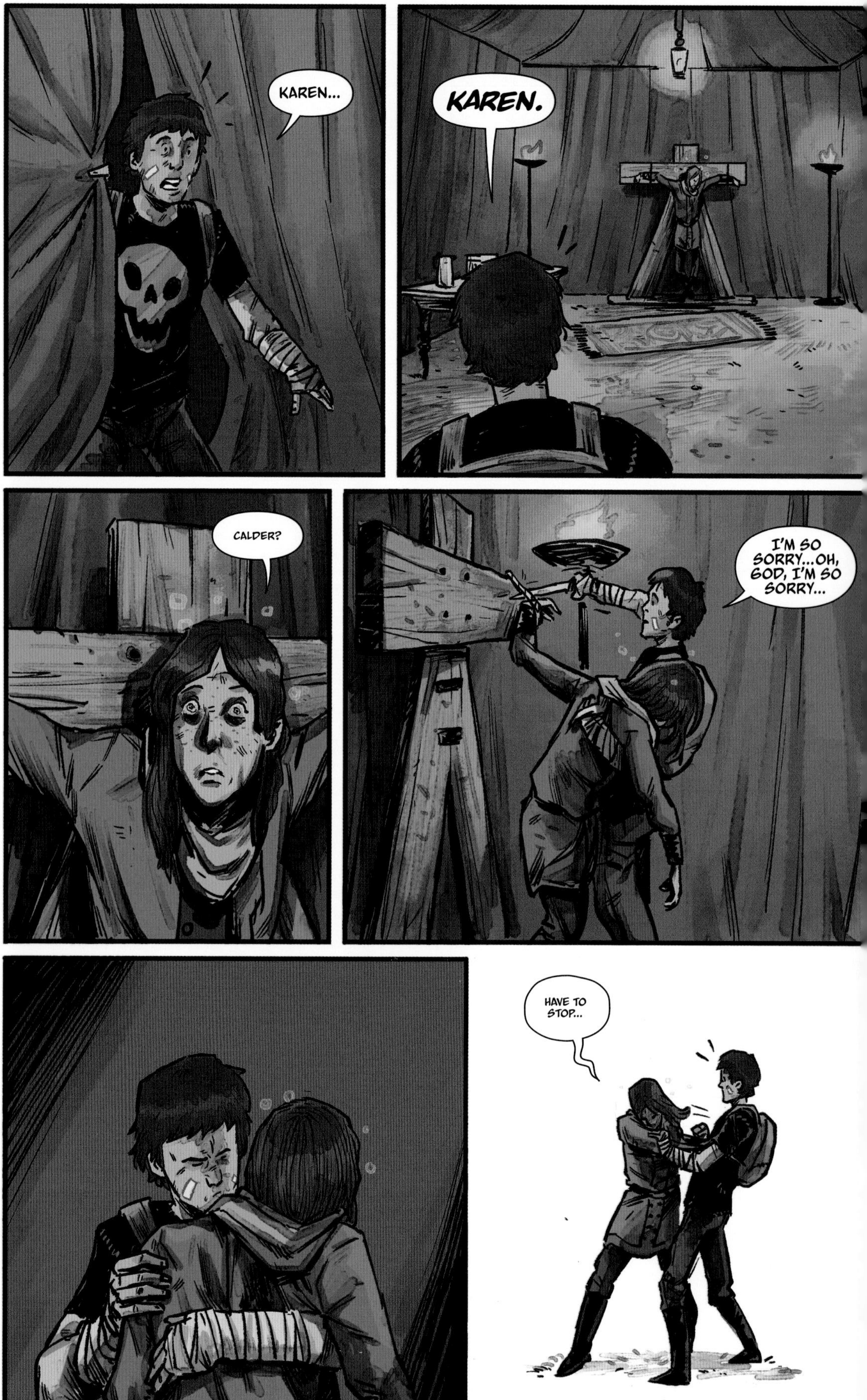
KAREN...
KAREN.
CALDER?
I'M SO SORRY...OH, GOD, I'M SO SORRY...
HAVE TO STOP...

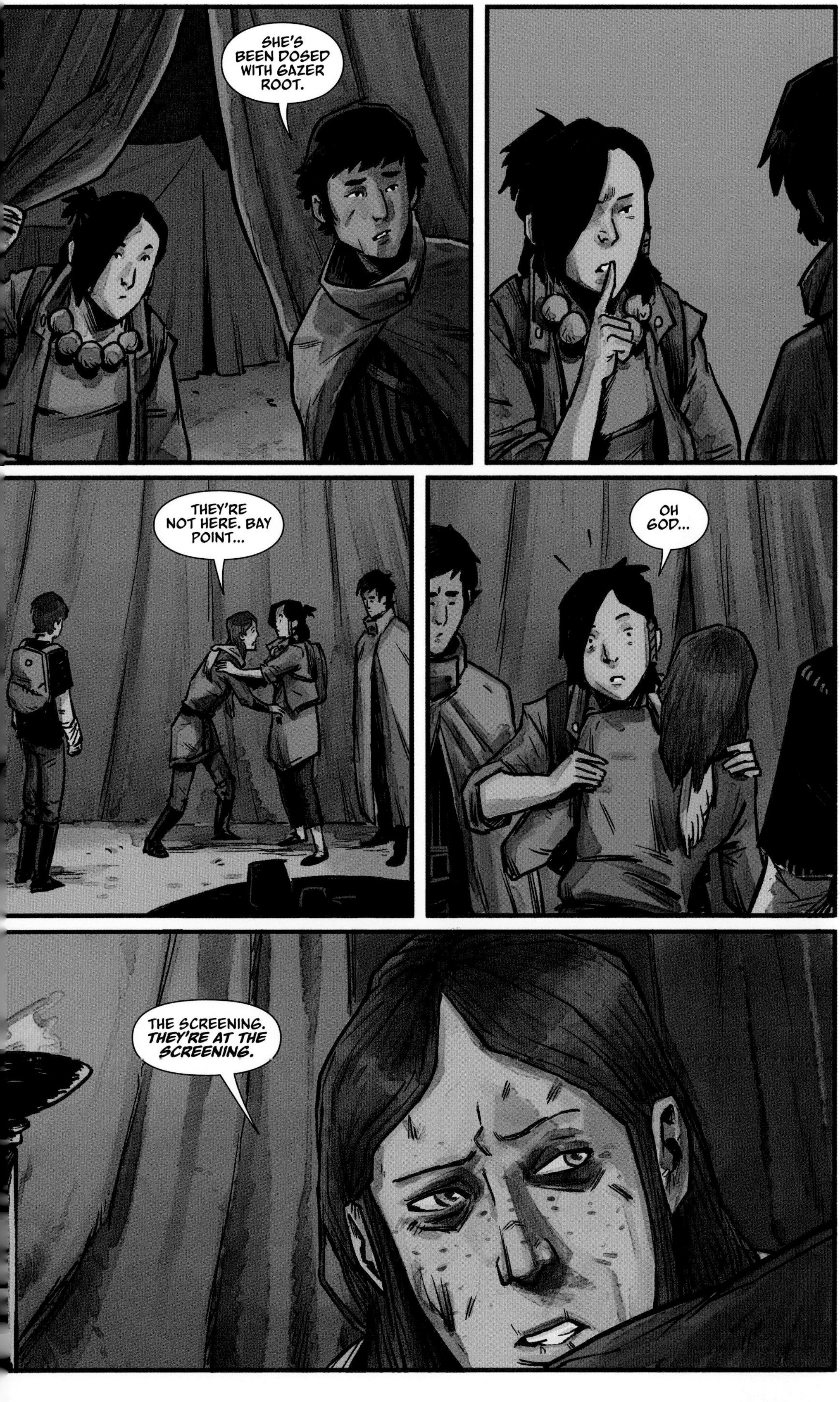
SHE'S BEEN DOSED WITH GAZER ROOT.
THEY'RE NOT HERE. BAY POINT...
OH GOD...
THE SCREENING. *THEY'RE AT THE SCREENING.*

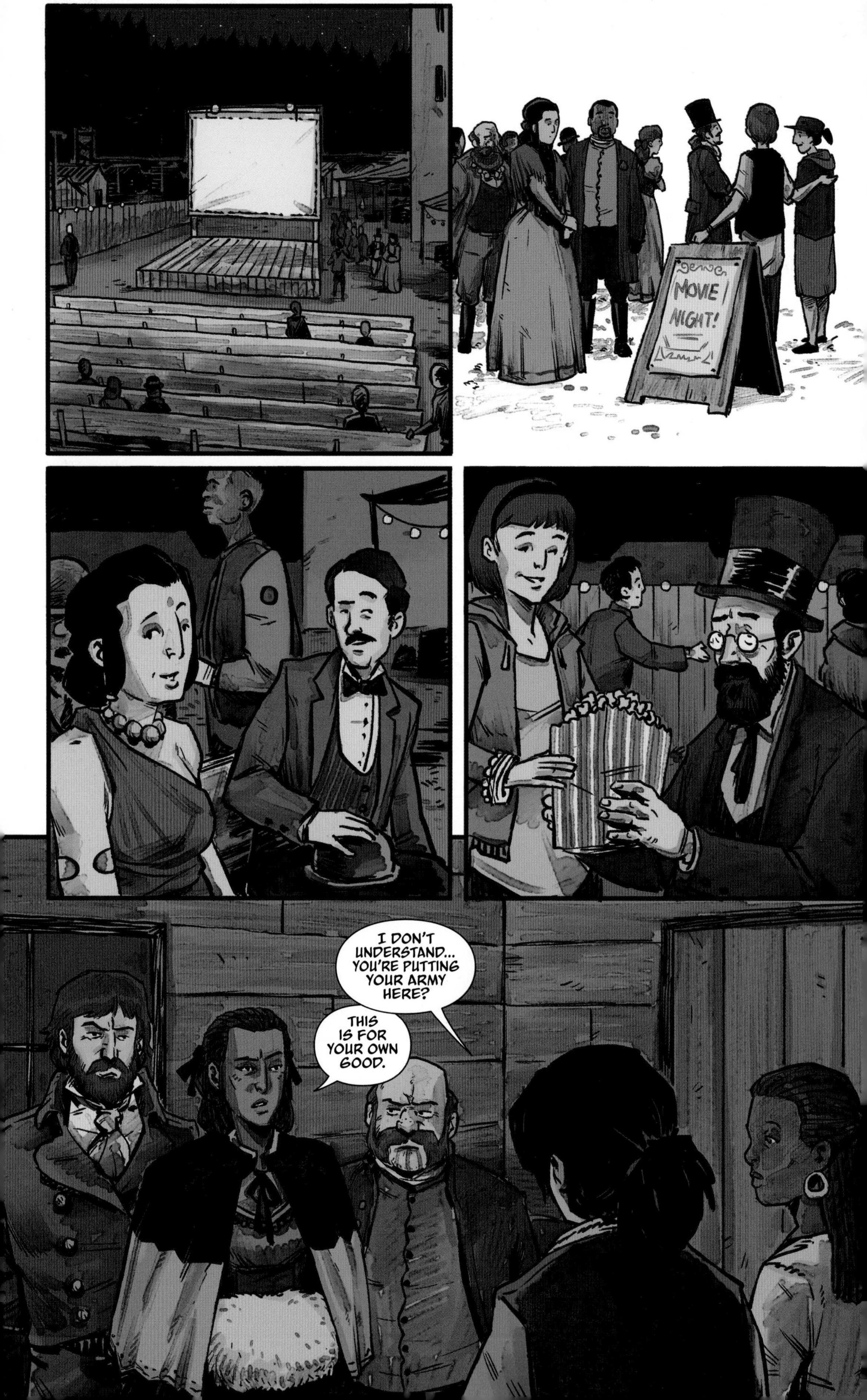
MOVIE NIGHT!
I DON'T UNDERSTAND... YOU'RE PUTTING YOUR ARMY HERE?
THIS IS FOR YOUR OWN GOOD.

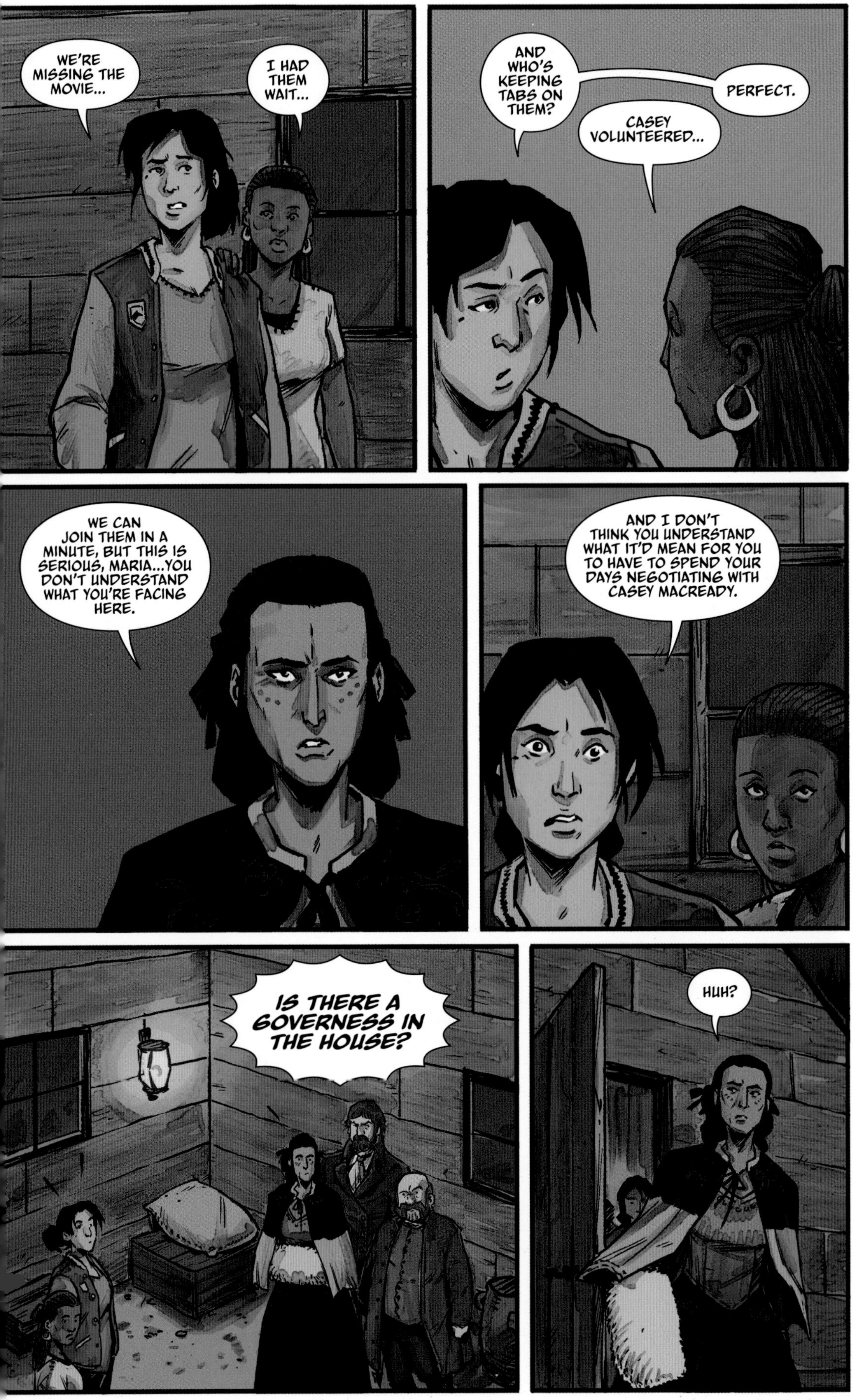
WE'RE MISSING THE MOVIE...
I HAD THEM WAIT...
AND WHO'S KEEPING TABS ON THEM?
CASEY VOLUNTEERED...
PERFECT.
WE CAN JOIN THEM IN A MINUTE, BUT THIS IS SERIOUS, MARIA...YOU DON'T UNDERSTAND WHAT YOU'RE FACING HERE.
AND I DON'T THINK YOU UNDERSTAND WHAT IT'D MEAN FOR YOU TO HAVE TO SPEND YOUR DAYS NEGOTIATING WITH CASEY MACREADY.
IS THERE A GOVERNESS IN THE HOUSE?
HUH?

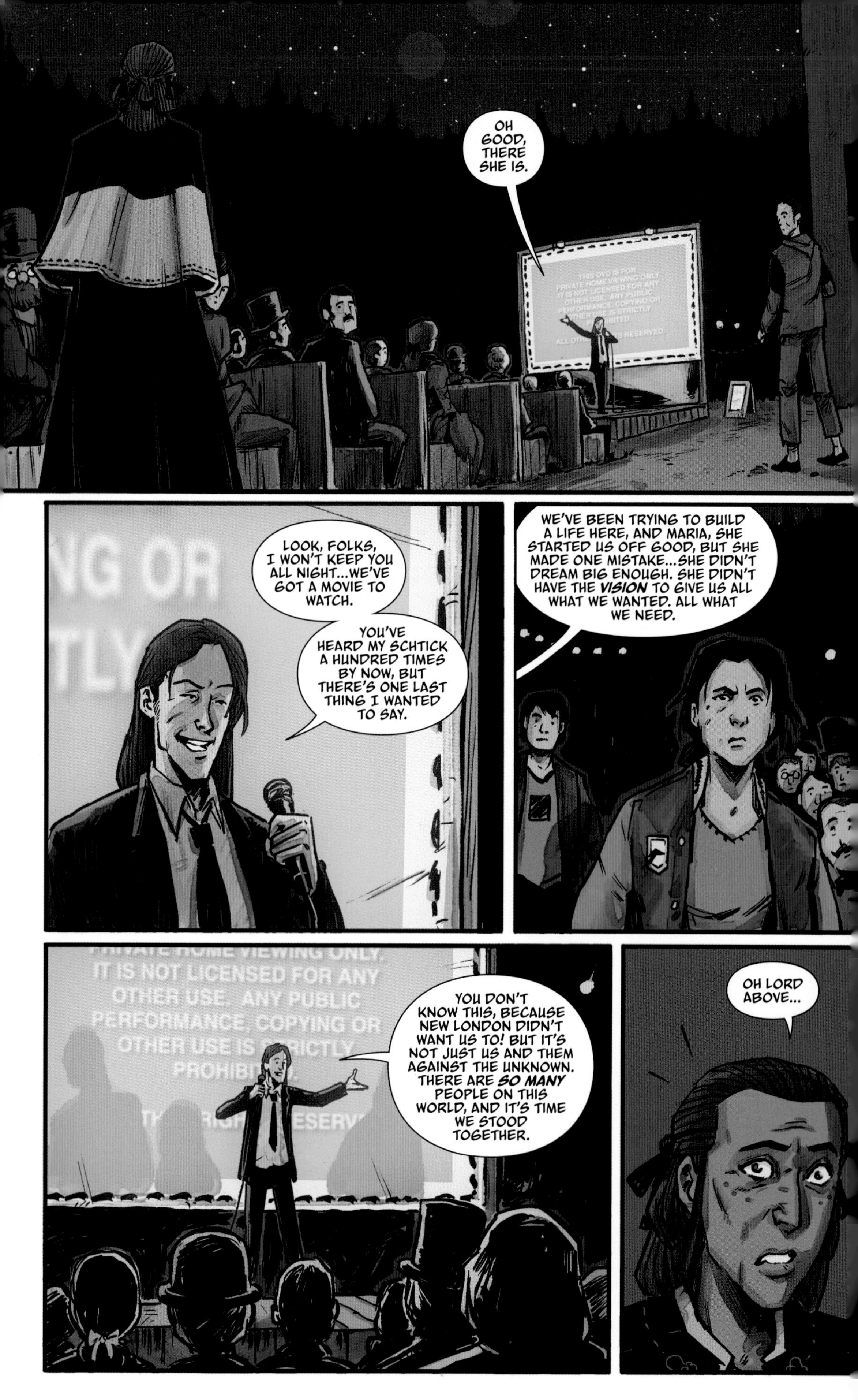
OH GOOD, THERE SHE IS.
LOOK, FOLKS, I WON'T KEEP YOU ALL NIGHT...WE'VE GOT A MOVIE TO WATCH.
YOU'VE HEARD MY SCHTICK A HUNDRED TIMES BY NOW, BUT THERE'S ONE LAST THING I WANTED TO SAY.
WE'VE BEEN TRYING TO BUILD A LIFE HERE, AND MARIA, SHE STARTED US OFF GOOD, BUT SHE MADE ONE MISTAKE...SHE DIDN'T DREAM BIG ENOUGH. SHE DIDN'T HAVE THE *VISION* TO GIVE US ALL WHAT WE WANTED. ALL WHAT WE NEED.
IT IS NOT LICENSED FOR ANY
OTHER USE. ANY PUBLIC
PERFORMANCE, COPYING OR
YOU DON'T KNOW THIS, BECAUSE NEW LONDON DIDN'T WANT US TO! BUT IT'S NOT JUST US AND THEM AGAINST THE UNKNOWN. THERE ARE *SO MANY* PEOPLE ON THIS WORLD, AND IT'S TIME WE STOOD TOGETHER.
OH LORD ABOVE...

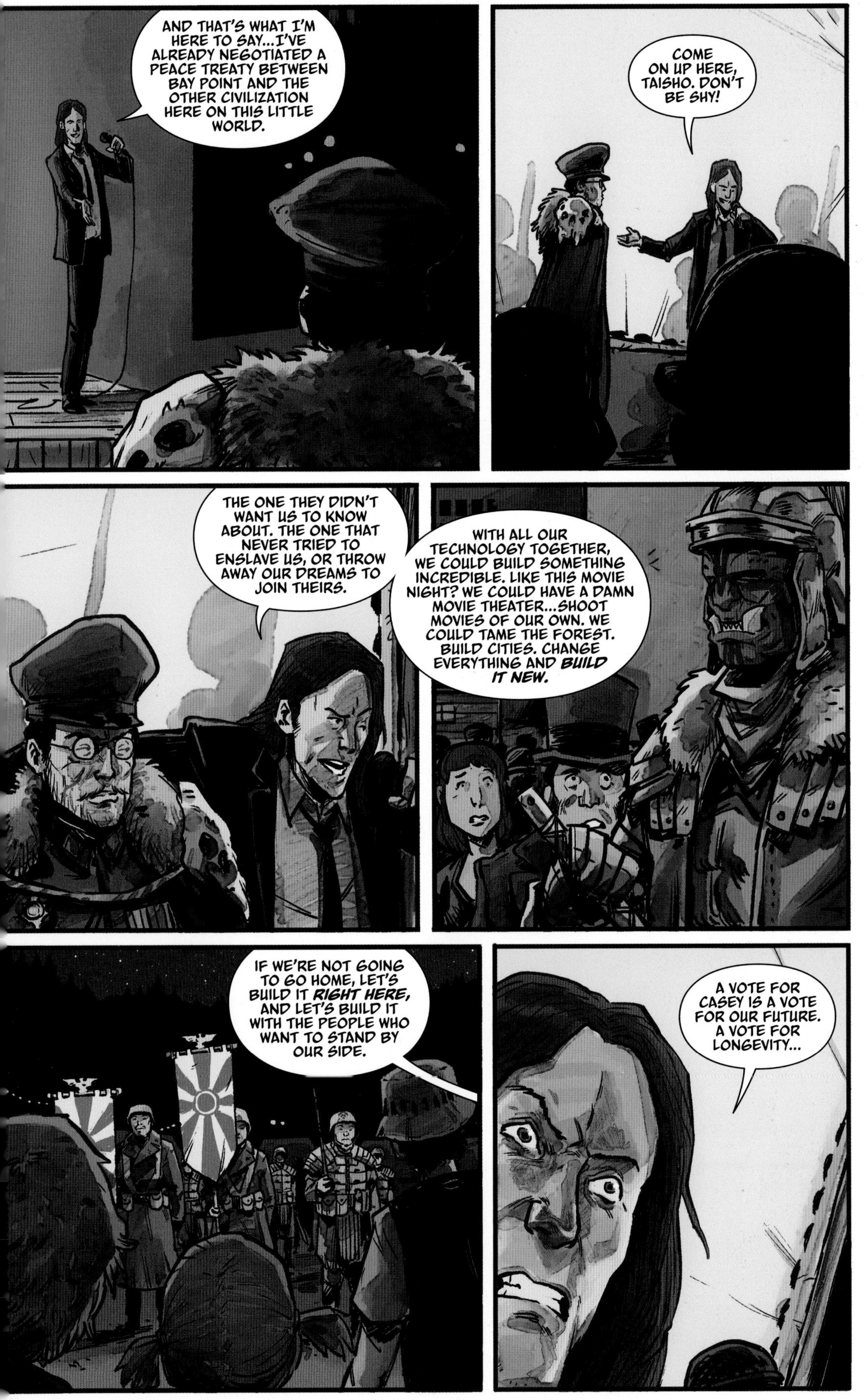
AND THAT'S WHAT I'M HERE TO SAY...I'VE ALREADY NEGOTIATED A PEACE TREATY BETWEEN BAY POINT AND THE OTHER CIVILIZATION HERE ON THIS LITTLE WORLD.
COME ON UP HERE, TAISHO. DON'T BE SHY!
THE ONE THEY DIDN'T WANT US TO KNOW ABOUT. THE ONE THAT NEVER TRIED TO ENSLAVE US, OR THROW AWAY OUR DREAMS TO JOIN THEIRS.
WITH ALL OUR TECHNOLOGY TOGETHER, WE COULD BUILD SOMETHING INCREDIBLE. LIKE THIS MOVIE NIGHT? WE COULD HAVE A DAMN MOVIE THEATER...SHOOT MOVIES OF OUR OWN. WE COULD TAME THE FOREST. BUILD CITIES. CHANGE EVERYTHING AND *BUILD IT NEW.*
IF WE'RE NOT GOING TO GO HOME, LET'S BUILD IT *RIGHT HERE,* AND LET'S BUILD IT WITH THE PEOPLE WHO WANT TO STAND BY OUR SIDE.
A VOTE FOR CASEY IS A VOTE FOR OUR FUTURE. A VOTE FOR LONGEVITY...

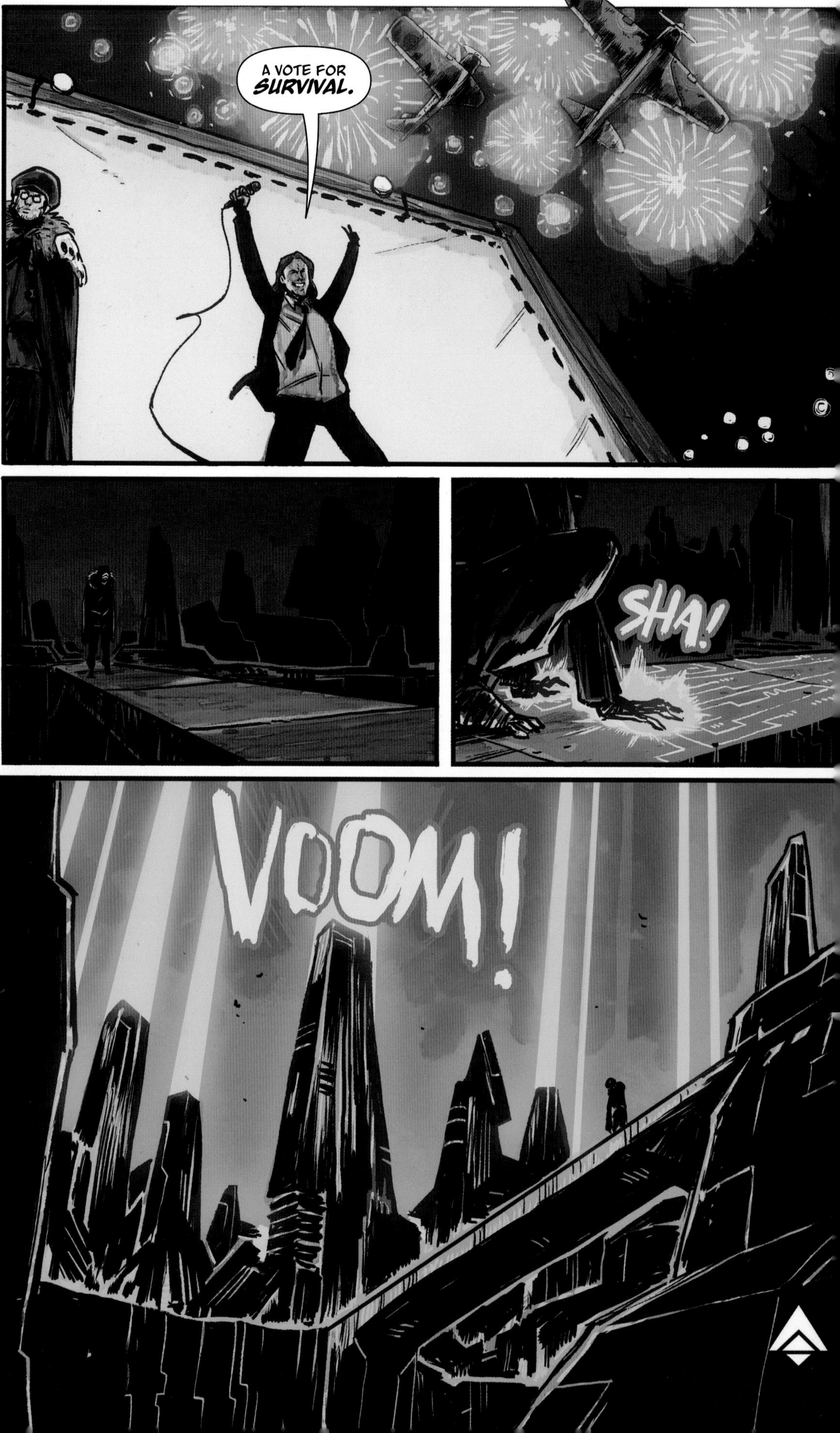
A VOTE FOR SURVIVAL.
SHA!
VOOM!

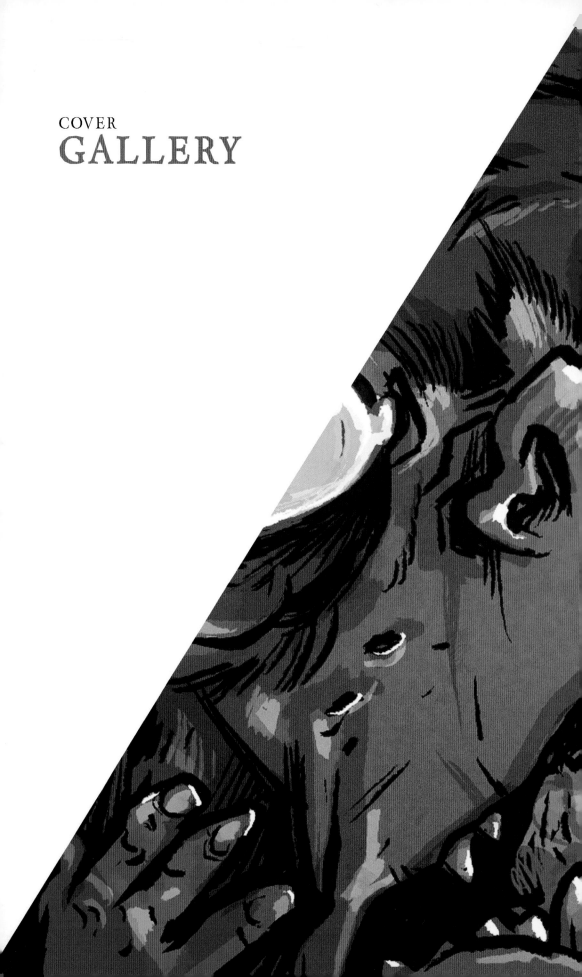

COVER
GALLERY

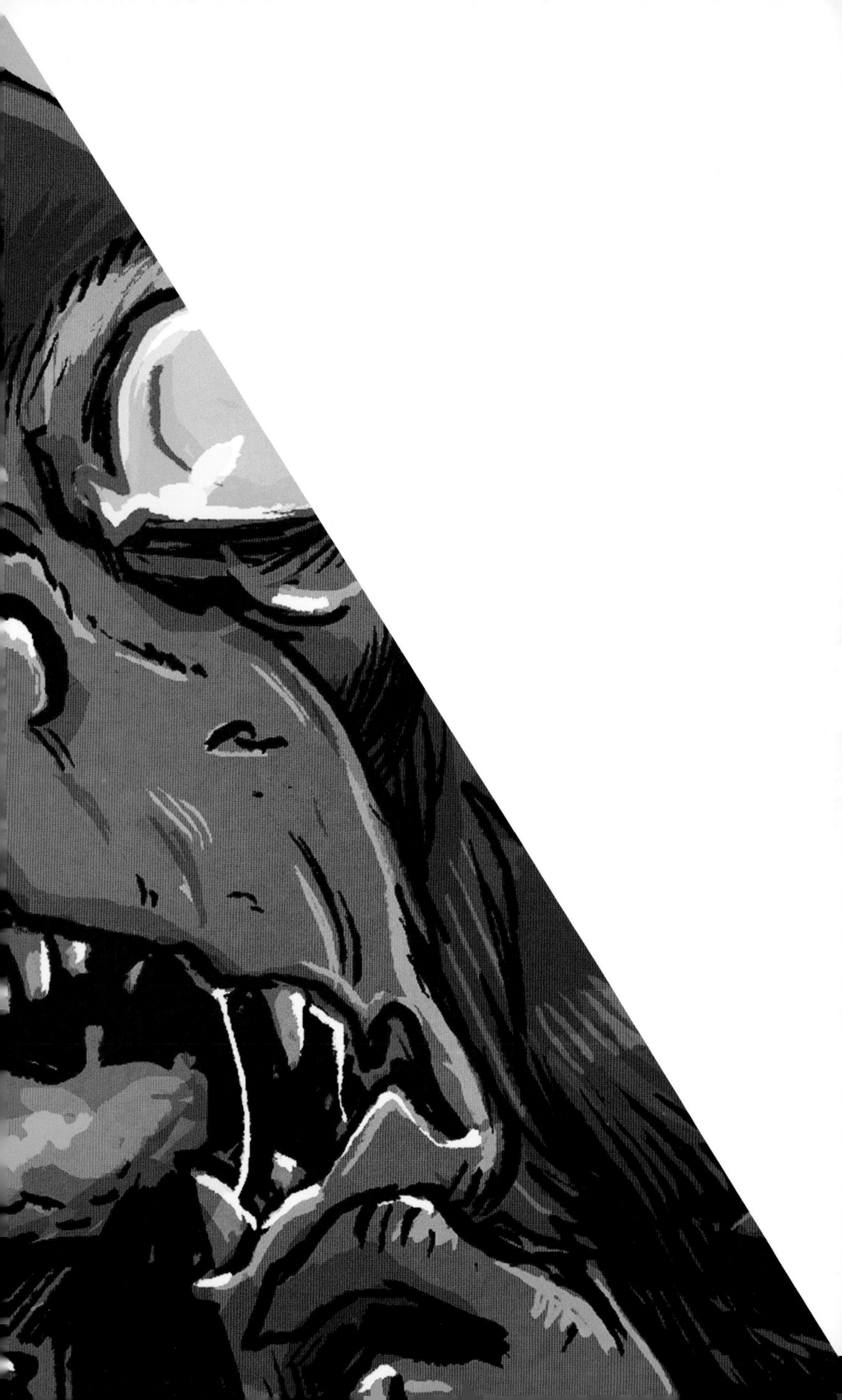

ISSUE THIRTEEN COVER **MICHAEL DIALYNAS**

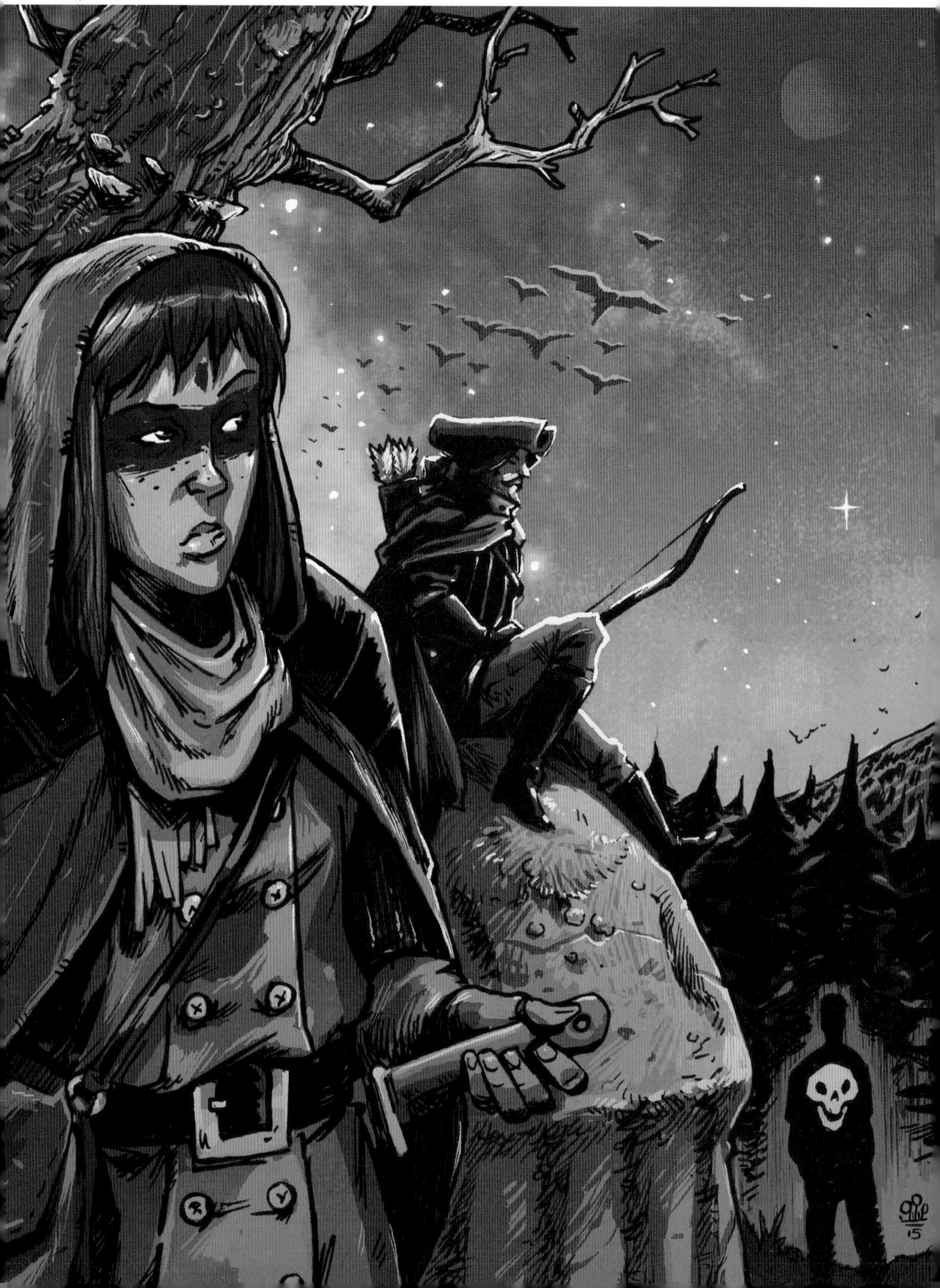

ISSUE THIRTEEN VARIANT COVER **BECKY CLOONAN**

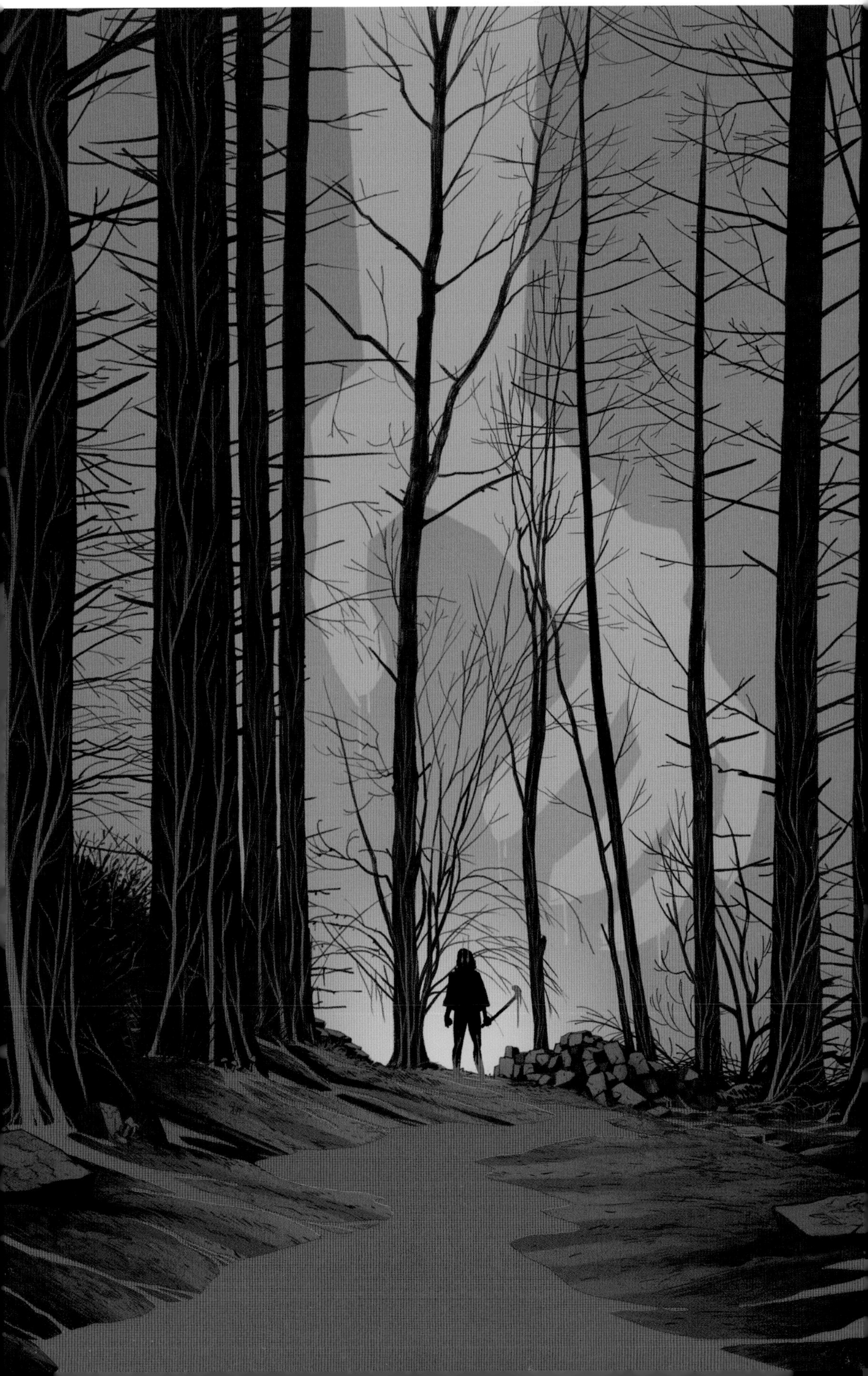

ISSUE FOURTEEN COVER **MICHAEL DIALYNAS**

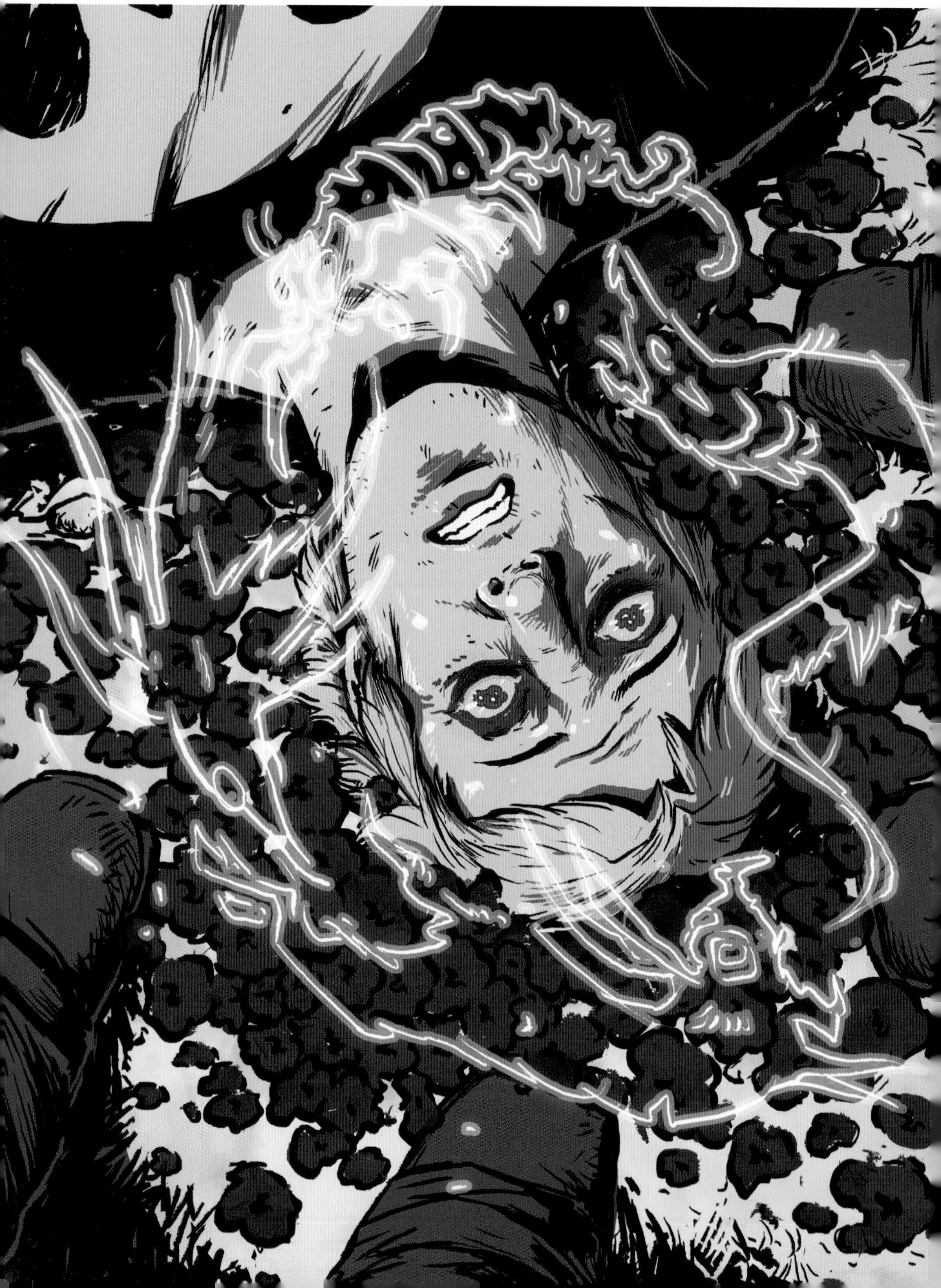

ISSUE FIFTEEN COVER **MICHAEL DIALYNAS**

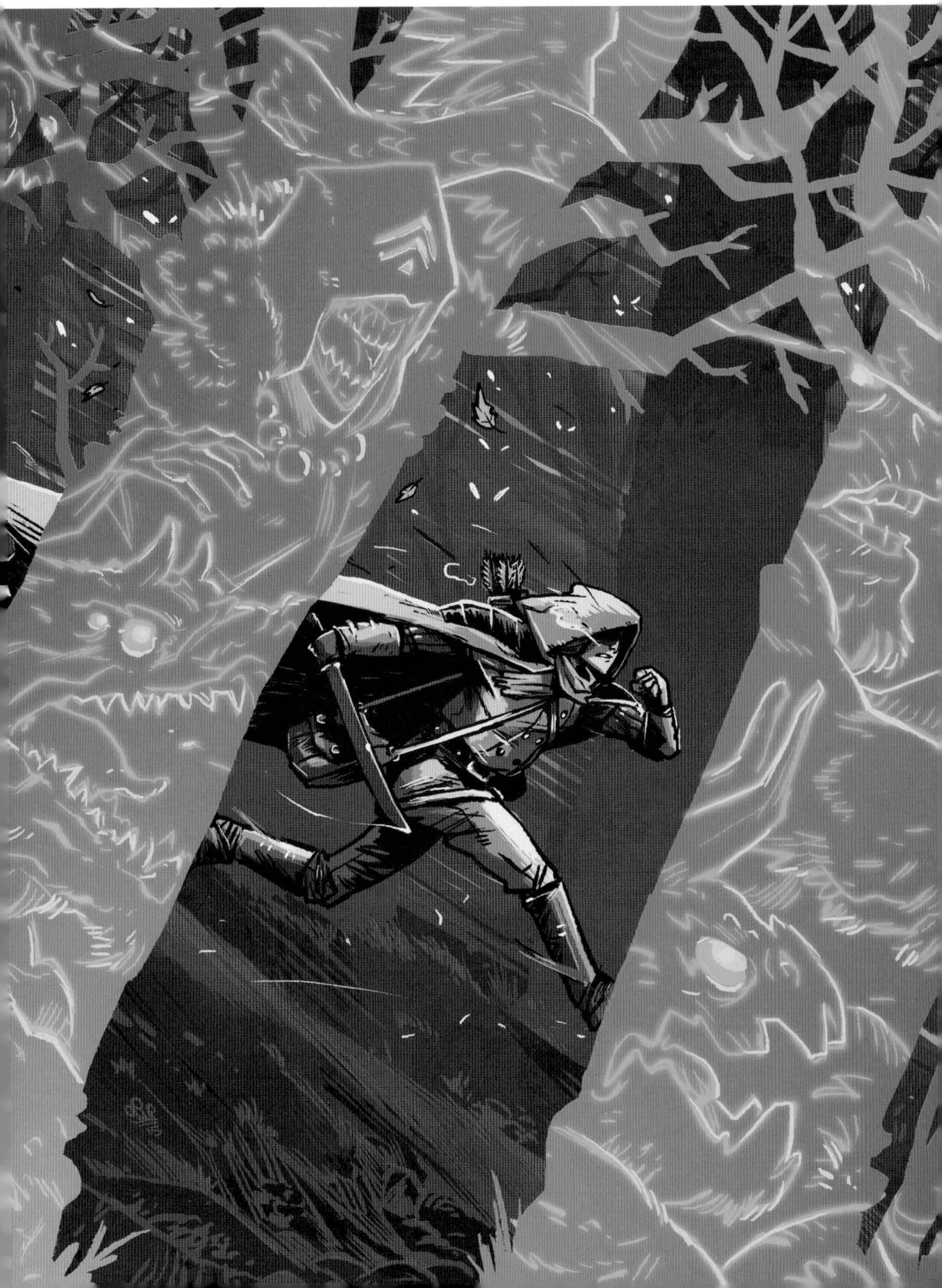

ISSUE SIXTEEN COVER **MICHAEL DIALYNAS**

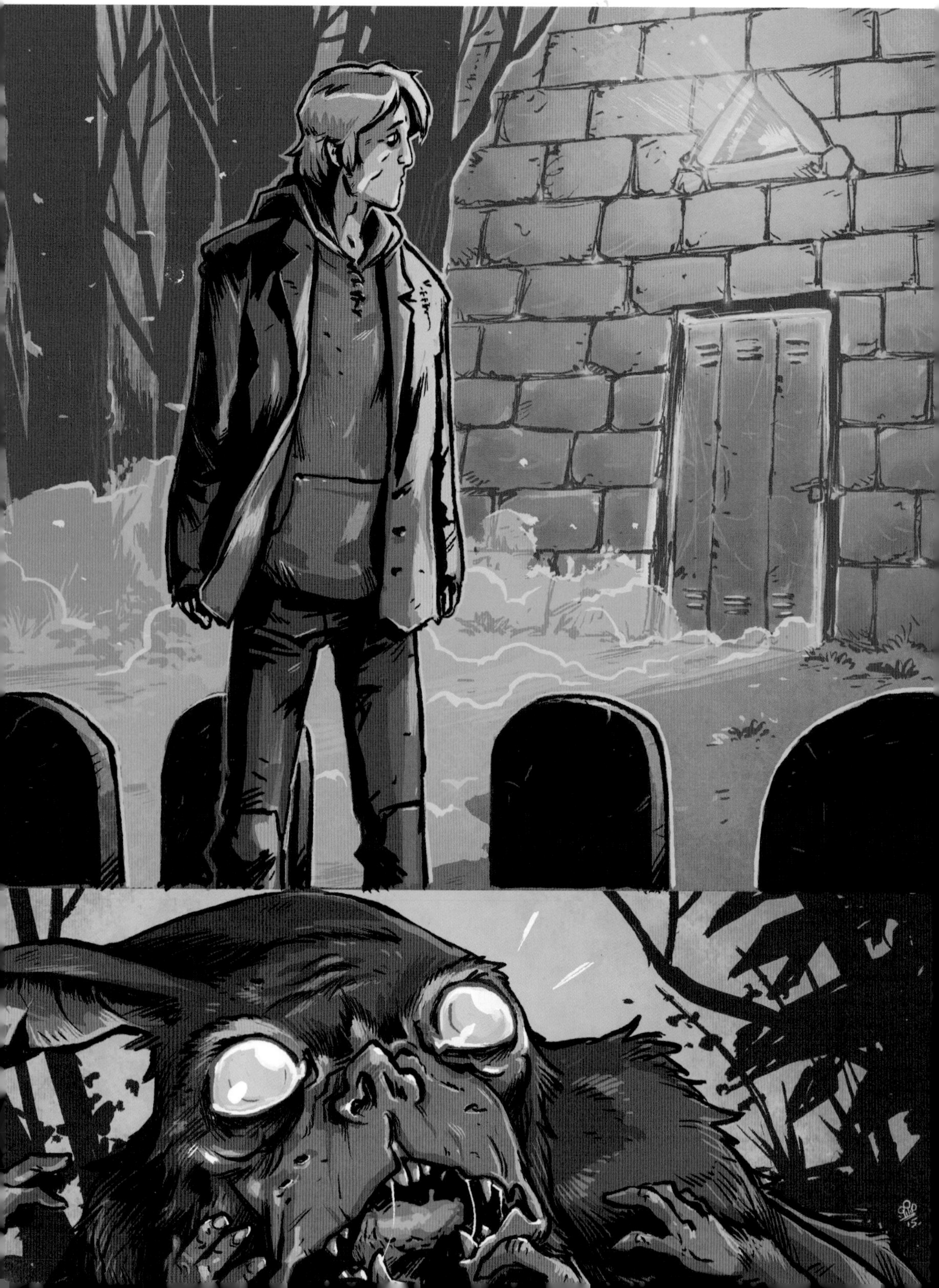

MICHAEL DIALYNAS
SKETCHBOOK

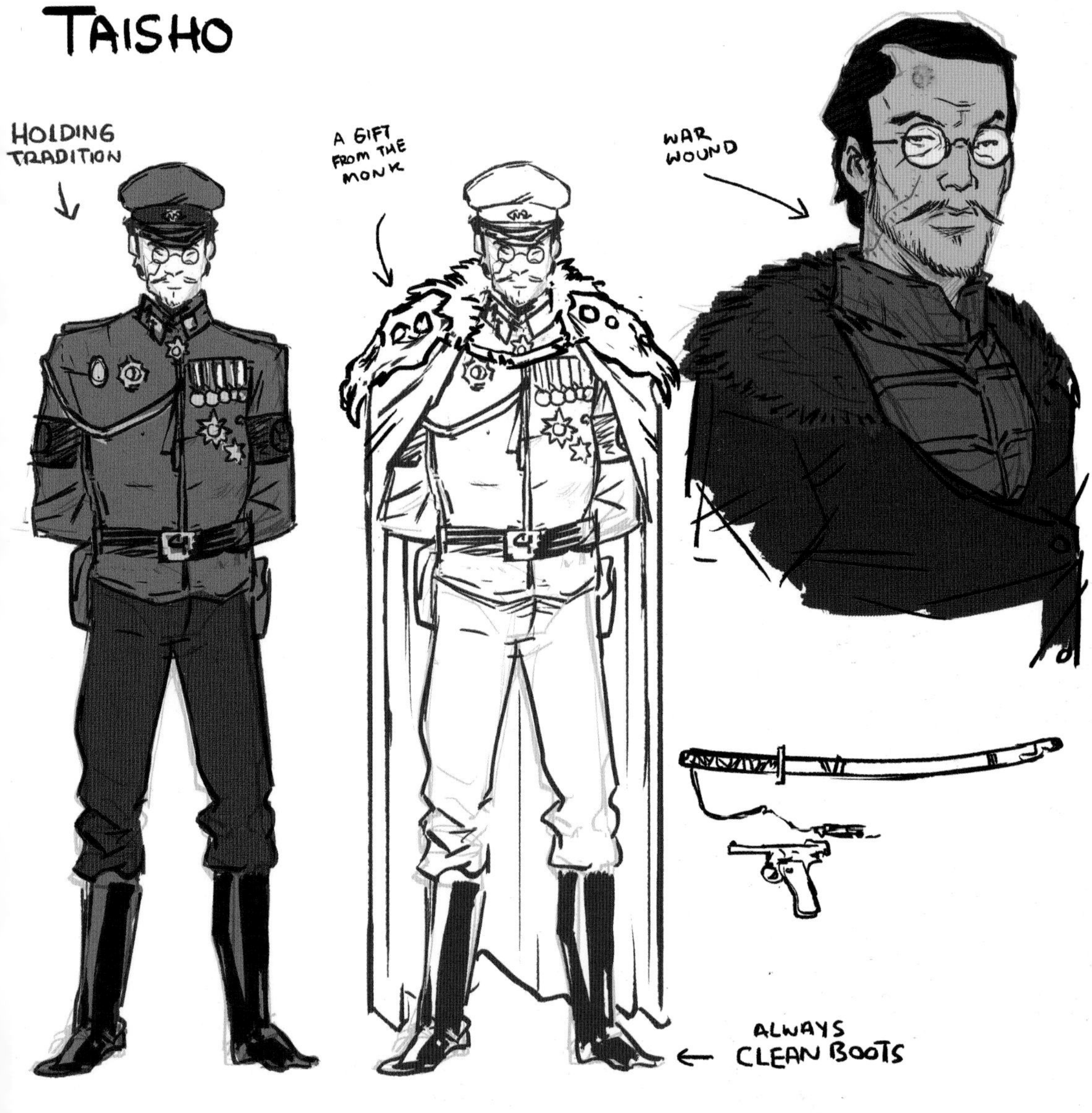
TAISHO
HOLDING TRADITION
A GIFT FROM THE MONK
WAR WOUND
ALWAYS CLEAN BOOTS

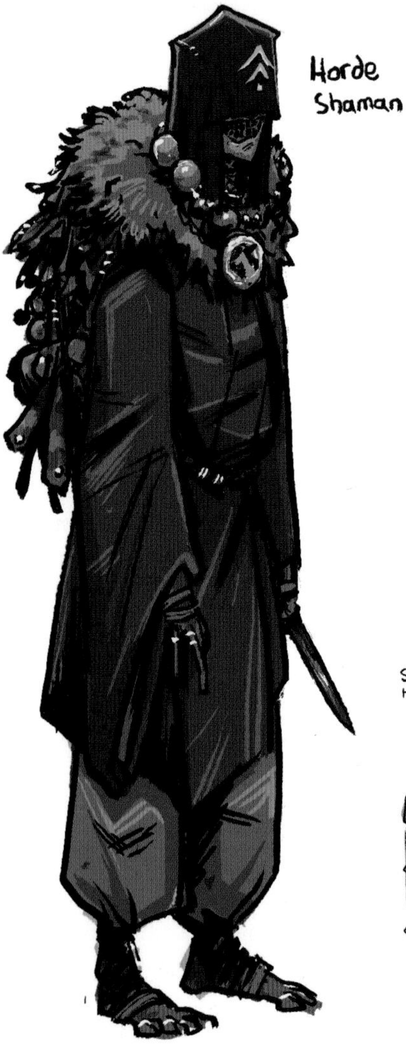
Horde
Shaman

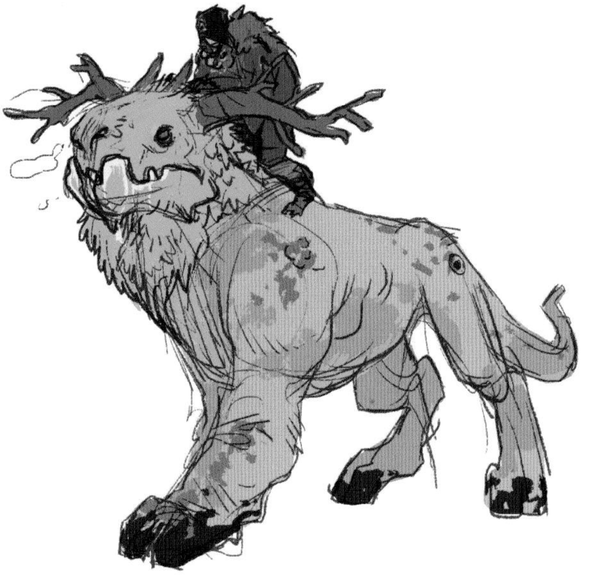

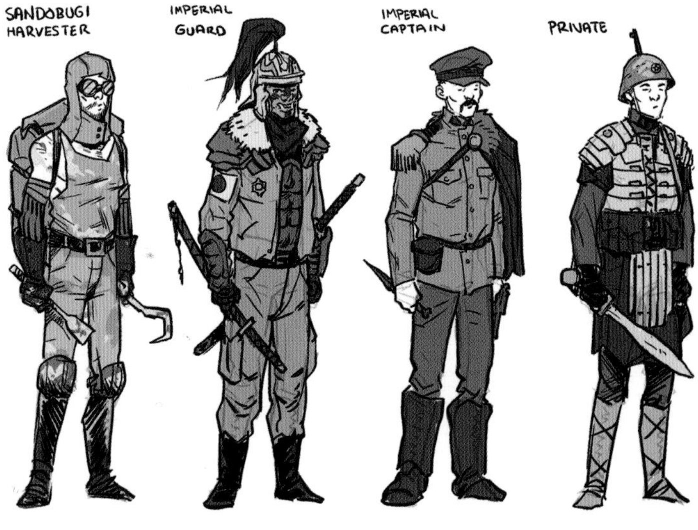
SANDOBUGI
HARVESTER
IMPERIAL
GUARD
IMPERIAL
CAPTAIN
PRIVATE

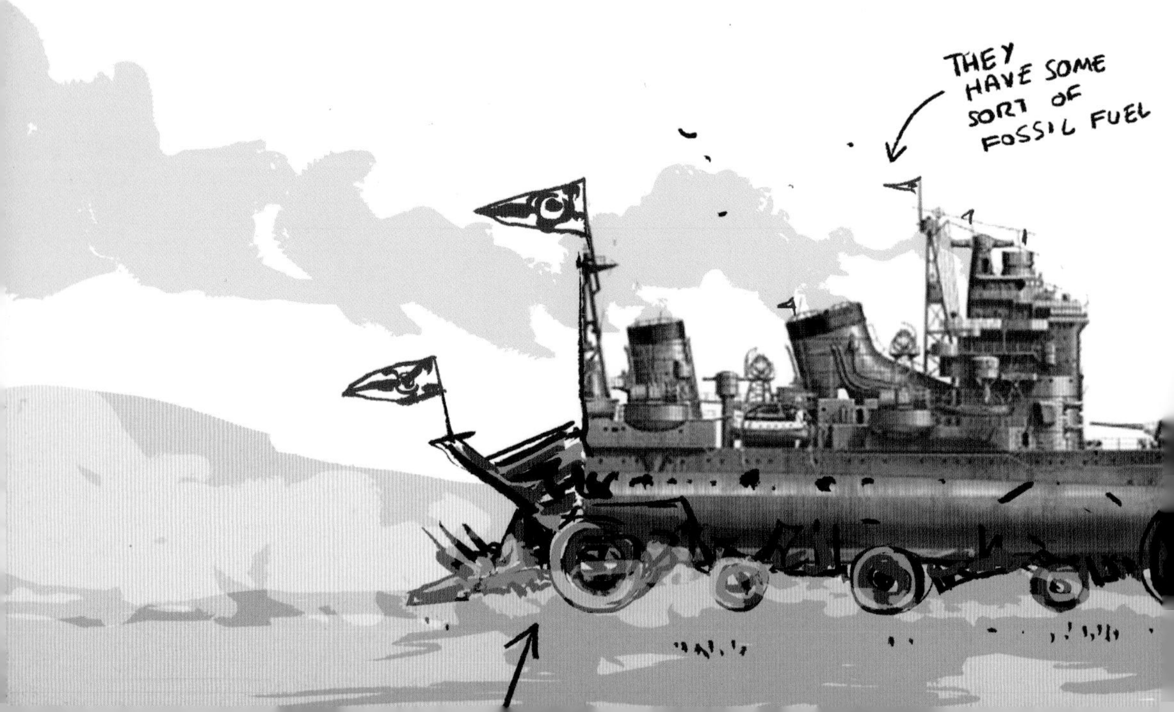
THEY
HAVE SOME
SORT OF
FOSSIL FUEL

1) SANDCRAB = SUNA NO KANI
2) SANDBUGGY = SANDOBAGI
3) SAND DUNE = SAKYUU

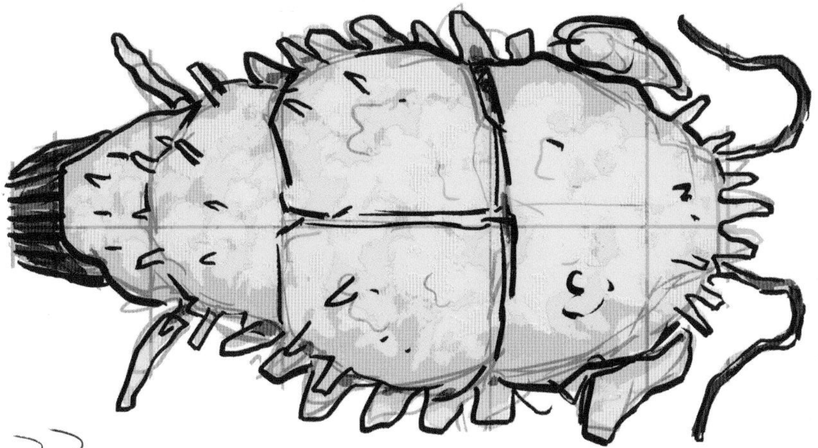

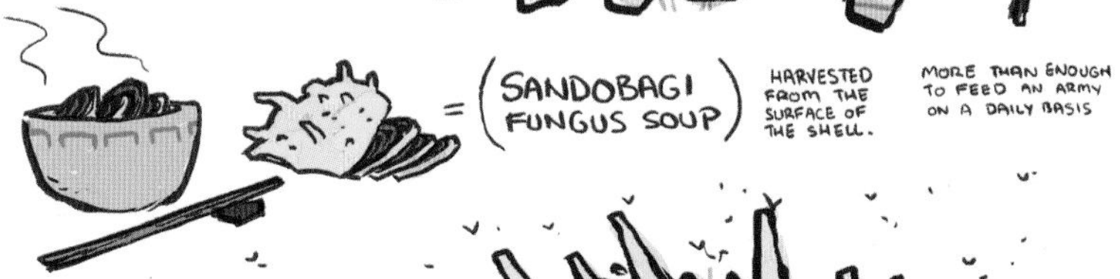
= (SANDOBAGI FUNGUS SOUP)
HARVESTED FROM THE SURFACE OF THE SHELL.
MORE THAN ENOUGH TO FEED AN ARMY ON A DAILY BASIS

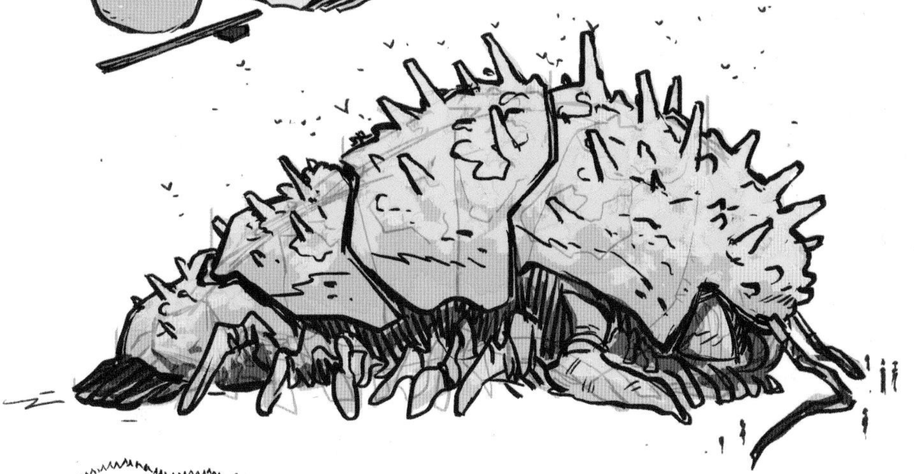

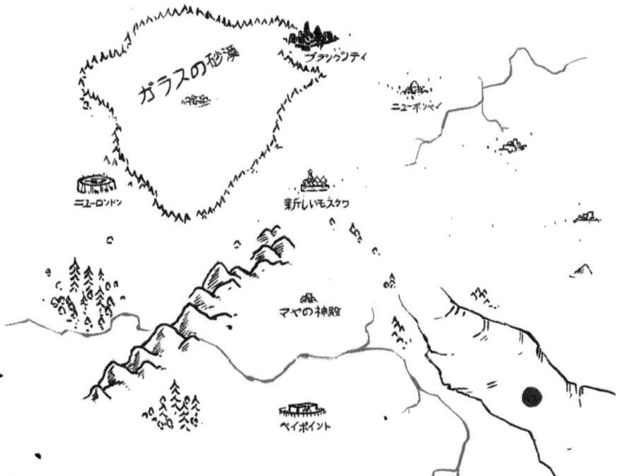
ガラスの砂漠
ブラックシティ
ニューポンペイ
ニューロンドン
新しいモスクワ
マヤの神殿
ベイポイント

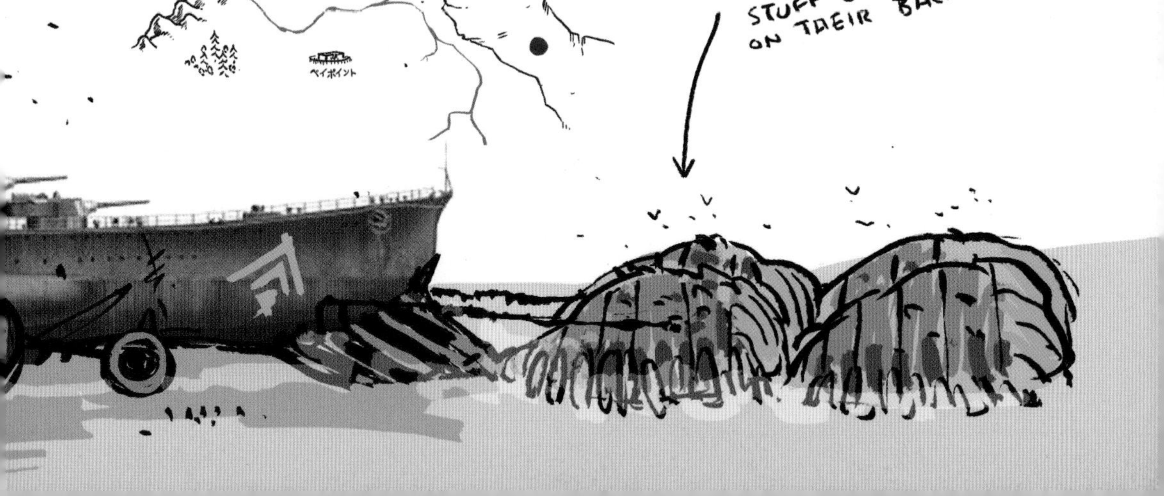
THE ARMY + BIRDS FEED OF THE STUFF GROWING ON THEIR BACKS